MINORITY REPORT

MINORITY
REPORT

Bernard DeVoto

Essay Index Reprint Series

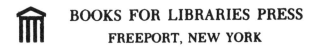

BOOKS FOR LIBRARIES PRESS
FREEPORT, NEW YORK

INTERNATIONAL STANDARD BOOK NUMBER:
0-8369-2105-4

LIBRARY OF CONGRESS CATALOG CARD NUMBER:
71-142619

PRINTED IN THE UNITED STATES OF AMERICA

TO

Robert F. Almy, Donald Born, AND *Garrett Mattingly*

In celebration of Fisk Hall, the lake front, coeds whose daughters
may be as pretty as they were but must learn wisdom from
instructors certainly duller than we were, a college that
indulged rather than liked us but was pleasant and amusing, walks to Winnetka and beyond, evenings above a
garage and within sound of the El, salaries fully half
as large as those paid the janitors who cleaned our
classrooms, and more geniality and intolerance
than any of us will ever feel again.

Preface

~~~~~~

Except for one passage, this book is made up of articles reprinted from *Harper's Magazine* and the *Saturday Review of Literature*. I am indebted to those magazines for permission to reprint the articles, and to Henry Reck for hard labor in preparing the typescript.

The book presents some of the work of a literary journalist during the years 1936–1939, and is published in the belief that some people are interested in reading or being able to refer to such journalism. A number of correspondents have asked me to reprint "English '37," "*Romans à Clef*," and several other editorials and Easy Chairs that deal with technical aspects of fiction. I do not do so because there is some expectation that I will some day write a book on the techniques of fiction. Similarly, I am not reprinting a number of pieces on military and Western history because I am working the same material in a book soon to be published.

This preface is continued on page 169.

BERNARD DEVOTO

Cambridge, Massachusetts
April 15, 1940

Contents

~~~~~~~~~~~~~~~~~~~~~~~~~~~~~~~~~~~~~

I

AN APOTHECARY'S SHOP

Passage to India

Monday 24th Decr. Some Snow this morning. we finished Setting pickets & arected a blacksmiths Shop. the afternoon pleasant. the Savages came as usal we fired our Swivels as tomorrow is cristmas day &. C.

THUS Sergeant John Ordway, sixteen hundred miles up the Missouri River, in 1804, with the expedition that President Jefferson had sent to traverse the lands purchased from France and discover a route to the Pacific. The pickets and the blacksmith shop meant the completion of a triangular, bullet-proof fort a mile or two below the Mandan villages, where Captains Lewis and Clark had halted their company for the winter some seven weeks before. The snow which fell that morning marked the end of a cold wave during which temperatures of thirty and forty below zero were common and the sentinel had to be changed every half hour. The river had long since frozen over and buffalo were crossing it in great herds. Captain Clark and eighteen men went hunting them, and had to spend a night on the snow with only the fresh hides for covering. Northern lights blazed almost to the zenith, many of the men had their hands and feet frostbitten, sunlight on snow produced a blindness which could only be treated by holding the face in the steam created by pouring water on heated stones. That was a Mandan remedy, but the Indians had already learned to prefer the expedition's medicine chest, which had cost the government $55, or rather less than the kit you would take on a vacation in the Orient. "A Womon brought a Child with an abcess on the lower part of the back, and offered as much Corn as she Could Carry for some Medison," Clark writes, and such entries had become common.

Those medicines, among which the favorite was Dr. Rush's famous pills, were one of the most valuable assets the expedition had, but a more valuable one had been added on November 4th, when Toussaint Charbonneau was hired as interpreter on the condition that one of his Indian wives should come with him. This was Sacajawea, "the Bird Woman," a Shoshone girl whom a Hidatsa war party had captured four years ago and brought east. Her husband was a bungler, a coward, and a bully, but Sacajawea at once became indispensable to the expedition. She had to be valiant to share the labor and privation of the journey, but she was more than valiant — she had an integrity and sweetness of personality unique among the women of her race whom history knows. Her services to the United States can hardly be overvalued; she saved the expedition at its crucial moment, and if, as the *Dictionary of American Biography* says, more memorials have been erected to her than to any other American woman, it is clear that she earned them.

The day before Ordway's note, Little Crow's wife had brought to the fort a present of corn and a "kittle of boiled Cimmins [summer squash], beens, Corn & Choke Cheries, which was palitable." On Christmas Eve, Sergeant Gass says,

"Flour, dried apples, pepper and other articles were distributed in the different messes to enable them to celebrate Christmas in a proper and social manner." Christmas morning was cloudy.

we fired the Swivels at day break [Ordway says], & each man fired one round. our officers Gave the party a drink of Taffee [Taffia, West Indian rum]. we had the best to eat that could be had, & continued firing dancing & frolicking dureing the whole day. the Savages did not Trouble us as we had requested them not to come as it was a Great medician day with us. we enjoyed a merry christmas dureing the day & evening untill nine oClock — all in peace and quietness.

Private Whitehouse complains that this festival was "all without the compy. of the female Seck, except three Squaws the Intreptirs wives and they took no part with us only to look on." The enlisted personnel had not lacked comfort, however, for the Mandans and most other tribes hospitably offered their wives and sisters, and when this fellowship was suspended the "squars" were both generous and cheaply purchasable. The black skin and kinky hair of York, Captain Clark's bodyservant, were attractive to women and had already given him a marked pre-eminence.

It was the *voyageur* Cruzatte, a mighty waterman, who played this irrecoverable Christmas music on a fiddle, while the fires blazed and the north wind moaned round the fort. Boating songs, probably, and minuets and carols that had crossed the Atlantic to New France and traveled the rivers for two centuries, to be sung never more incongruously than at the Mandan villages. He played them through the long winter and the men danced to them, and delighted Indians looked on — the chiefs swaggering in the laced and epauletted coats that had been formally presented to them, with dress-swords, feathers, and medals of the President, of domestic animals, or of farmers sowing grain, distributed according to their degree.

And Cruzatte's fiddle, like the loyalty of Sacajawea, had its part in making this the most successfully managed expedition in the history of exploration, as it was one of the most important.

That the company could spend Christmas "in peace and quietness" at the Mandan villages meant that Meriwether Lewis and William Clark had already proved their greatness as diplomats, no less than as commanders and explorers. The Osages frankly disbelieved that the Great White Father now dwelt in Washington rather than London or Paris, and this skepticism was shared by more important tribes — among whom traders adept in the management of savage minds had been nourishing the interests of Great Britain. As the keelboat and the pirogues moved up the river, rumors shaped in the interest of the crown ran ahead of them. To pacify the tribes while asserting American jurisdiction over them was one of Jefferson's prime objects, and a crisis of world policy turned on this handful of soldiers, a force so fragile that the slightest mismanagement must have wiped it out, would have given the Indian problem a wholly different shape, and might have changed the map of North America. Both the Aricaras and the Teton Sioux had listened to the double tongues, and Lewis magnificently served his nation by compelling the latter into respect and good behavior by a show of force. That episode was the last clash with the Indians until, on the journey home, Lewis was forced to shoot a Blackfoot and so created an implacable hostility which lasted for many years and made that tribe the greatest obstacle to the development of the interior West.

The conflict with the Sioux was behind them when they built their fort. So was the single fatality the expedition suffered, the death of Sergeant Floyd from "bilious fever." So were all infractions of discipline and all discord. The twenty-nine enlisted men, three sergeants, and two interpreters, who with Lewis and Clark and York and Sacajawea were to compose the final party, were welded into a superb, an unexcelled instrument for the exploration of the wilderness.

So they passed the winter among the Mandans, traditional friends of the whites, whose two villages stood where the Missouri turned southward, athwart a principal trade route of the tribes and fur companies. John Floyd, the blacksmith, mended tools for the Indians, and from the iron of a burnt-out camp stove forged tomahawks that enraptured them. The captains practised medicine, York widened his conquests, and chiefs from many tribes came to smoke with the agents of the White Father, to receive gifts from them, and to appraise their power. Traders of the North West Company came also and were ordered to abandon their propaganda on American soil, or charged with suaver messages for their headquarters. And always, from the Mandans, from the traders, from the visiting chiefs, the captains sought information about the country they must traverse. For a few miles still they would be on waters sometimes traveled by whites, but beyond the mouth of the Rochejaune even rumor would cease. So while the ice groaned and shuddered by night, they sat with blanketed braves before the great fires in the fort, and patiently drew from them all they had seen or heard about the Western waters.

One sees that firelight on intent faces as the Indians draw river courses on the puncheon floor, scrawling with bits of charcoal the known bends and rapids and the bearings of distant peaks, shaping a handful of ashes to show how a range loops down from the north, grunting and disputing, sending to the village for a brave whom chance may have led up some unknown creek. The captains listened, trying to check their informants by one another, never sure how much was guessed or rumored or perhaps merely invented about the uncharted waste, so many of whose rivers and summits they were to christen in the months ahead. The Mandans had never crossed the main range or journeyed to the Spanish lands. They had heard of the great westward-running river whose mouth the captains had been ordered to find, and of the big, stinking salt pond it emptied into, but how far away it was or by what route it might be reached not even Sacajawea, who had been born beyond the divide, could tell them.

On February 11th, Sacajawea's first child was born, "a fine boy," writes Lewis, who eased her labor by grinding a rattle-snake's rattle and administering a little of it dissolved in water. He was named John Baptist; before long Clark was calling him "Pomp" and offering to educate him among the whites; strapped on his mother's back, the infant was to cross the continent and come back in safety. . . . Already they were trying to get the boats out of the ice, but did not succeed until the 26th. Then the ice shivered and splintered, northing swans arrived, the larger flights followed them. They packed cases with animal and Indian mementoes for Mr. Jefferson, wrote a last report to him, and sent all off together in the keelboat with the discharged men under Corporal Warfington. About five in the afternoon of April 7th, 1805, in "six small canoes and two large periogues," they started upstream toward the un-known.

Stripped to the waist, they were in ice water most of the time, pulling the boats off the Missouri's fiendish sand bars. They had seen the country change many times and now it changed again, for they were in the high plains, the semi-arid region of the real West. They encountered the alkali for the first time; it made the water bitter and purgative, as thousands were to learn who followed after them. It also gave the whole party sore eyes, which the captains correctly treated with "a solution of two grains of white vitriol," and may have in part accounted for the boils that now became common. There was a new danger also in the "white bears," the grizzlies for whose ferocity the Indians had tried to prepare them. The first one they saw set out after Lewis after it had been shot, and chased him till killed by another hunter; a few days later, another one furiously pursued Private Bratton for over half a mile, though it had a bullet "through the center of the lungs"; three days later, two hunters had to dive into the river to escape one that had been shot seven times.

Peril, of course, was nothing new. A mere dot of sentient, vigilant skill, they had moved through an immensity of multiple and unintermitted danger. But now, in the untrodden country, the journey becomes something simple and immortal — a tableau of courage and endurance in clear light, one of the world's heroic stories that seem like myths. They toiled westward on the sun's path, toward the fourth house of the sky, fulfilling a dream which Meriwether Lewis had had in his boyhood, fulfilling an older, more complex dream of Thomas Jefferson's, and by strength and skill and valor they rolled the unknown back before them. The country ahead of them was an untraveled chaos, the boundary of man's knowledge moved with them, they passed and the map was made forever. The day's march lay between walls of the capricious and treacherous wilderness and walls of a capricious and malevolent race of savages; the day's march ended and the walls had been moved farther back.

Past the Little Missouri, past the Rochejaune which they were the first to call the Yellowstone, past the Big Muddy and the Milk River and the Musselshell. On the 26th of May, Lewis climbed the highest neighboring hill and looking westward saw lines lift and waver above the horizon and sun flash on distant snow — "the object of all our hopes and the reward of all our ambition," the Rocky Mountains. On June 2nd they reached a large river coming down from the north and faced a decision on which success or irrevocable failure hinged. For nothing in their data sufficed to tell them which fork was the true Missouri and would lead them to the continental divide. The north fork, which Lewis was to call Maria's, looked far likelier than the other, and even after both had been reconnoitered the whole party except the captains thought that it was the Missouri. The process by which they determined on the other one might serve as a model of scientific analysis and must be granted a high place in the history of thought. The decision made, Lewis hurried up the south fork to be sure, and was sure when he heard the thunder of the great falls, felt the spray borne by the wind for several miles to fall for the first time on white man's cheeks, and finally stood deafened and dazzled above the gorge.

They got the boats round the falls by a gigantic labor, and went on. A cloudburst nearly destroyed them and, not for the last time, Sacajawea owed her life and her child's to William Clark. Navigation would soon be impossible, game began to fail, the summer was shortening and ice formed in the buckets overnight. Whether they would do Thomas Jefferson's will or fail and probably perish on the continental crest depended on their finding the Shoshones at their accustomed hunting ground — on the Shoshones' being friendly — on their having horses to sell. Clark, the more skillful frontiersman, ranged ahead but did not meet them; then Lewis went and it was he who finally found them, unfriendly, suspicious, disposed to flight or murder. The Shoshones feared that this prodigy, the first white man they had ever seen, might be working some corrupt device of their enemies and might betray them into ambush. Failure of the great adventure now hung by a single thread above the commander's head, but, telling them about the party of white men to the eastward, of the woman of their nation who was with it, of the marvelous black-skinned man, Lewis managed to allay part of their distrust and they turned back with him. They might have killed him, as in fact he thought they would; they might have gone on to overwhelm the party that was toiling on with Clark — and, ominously, came later than Lewis had promised. But they did not. The arrival of Clark proved Lewis's tongue straight, and at once history soared into that purer ether where fiction dare not venture. For Lewis, desiring clearer speech with the chief Cameahwait, who had accompanied him, sent for Sacajawea to interpret. A moment later she threw her blanket round the chief and was weeping violently. Just below the continental divide, after five years of separation, she had met her own brother, from whose tent she had been ravished. "After some conversation between them she resumed her seat and attempted to interpret for us; but her new situation seemed to overpower her and she was frequently interrupted by her tears."

They now reached the limit of strain and exhaustion. There was no game to be found, all of their flour had been used up, and they had only a little corn. They had long since learned to like dog meat, which at first had nauseated them, but after they left the Shoshones there were no dogs to buy. Every day's travel among the peaks cost a fatigue of man and beast alike that amounted to collapse. They ranged widely for game but found none, ate the three colts they had, at last had to kill some of the horses for food. They killed a coyote, then another horse, and the remnants of this fed two of their hunters the next day, returning to the party without game — who "roasted the head of the horse, which even our appetites had spared, and supped on the ears, skin, and lips of the animal." At last, on westward-running waters, they found Indians who had dried salmon and berries and camas roots to sell. But hearty meals after weeks of privation sickened them, and the camas, besides, was both purgative and emetic when prepared badly. Various of the men, then Clark, and finally Lewis fell ill. They dosed themselves with Rush's pills and pressed on. The cold thin air of the mountains yielded to sweltering heat as they descended, and this too weakened them. "Today he [Lewis] could hardly sit on his horse, while others were obliged to be put on horseback, and some, from extreme weakness and pain, were forced to lie down alongside of the road [trail] for some time."

But in the mountains circumstance and the impersonal malice of the wilderness had done their utmost, and the expedition now reached navigable water again, the Kooskooskee River. They camped on its bank and while the sick recovered, the well made canoes for the last stage of the appointed labor. Reverting to a water route, they had no more to face than a daily, routine hazard of skill against destruction. Down the Kooskooskee to the Snake they went, and down the Snake till at last they reached the river for which they had set out. Two years and three months before, the Columbia had been just a dead reckoning in Thomas Jefferson's study, just a hole pricked in blank white paper with the point of his dividers. But now, forever, a known line was drawn in ink across that white paper from Jefferson's study in Washington to the great river of the West.

There were dangerous rapids still to pass, and the food failed sometimes, and wood for fires was scarce. The Indians too were different, treacherous, occasionally dangerous; they were greater thieves, having been more in contact with white men, whose pea jackets, hardware, and venereal diseases came up the Columbia along the immemorial trade route. They shot the last rapid of the Cascades and came on November 2nd to tidewater. The journey now added one climactic indignity: as they floated down the river a storm rose and, after crossing the continental divide and breaking a trail across the arid wilderness, they must be seasick. It was the rainy season, too, and they were hardly to be dry again till next spring. The river widened, high winds made the waves furious, at night their camp was nearly washed from under them. Almost at journey's end, they had to stop on November 10th, and for two days gales, thunder, and hailstorms buffeted them. There was a final precarious moment with some anonymous Indians and, on November 14th, Captain Lewis rounded a last point and saw the open sea.

They were too uncomfortable, too waterlogged, too weary, and much too seasoned to rejoice. The journal says, "Ocian in View! O! the joy," and says little more. A campsite must be found and preparations for the winter must be begun — better to think of such urgent things than of significances that hovered above that stormy promontory. But the continent had been crossed and was no longer unknown. The trail was blazed, the Americans had occupied their country, the Republic had reached its farthest frontier. An idea with which the restless mind of Thomas Jefferson had wrestled through many nights had been given flesh, Meriwether Lewis's dream had come true, and the thing was done. It was November 14, 1805, and the journey of Lewis and Clark to a foreseen but unknown end had reached that end on a rainy Pacific beach. Another, older, more dream-bound journey ended too. The passage to India was achieved, and three ships made harbor that had sailed from the port of Palos on Friday, the third of August, 1492, at about eight in the morning.

They were still looking for a campsite when one of the captains carved a legend on a large pine tree. "William Clark December 3d 1805. By Land from the U. States in 1804 & 5." One reads the legend, seeing that inked line move westward across blank paper. "By Land from the U. States." Yes.

They found their campsite, up Netul River from Meriwether Bay, where wood was plentiful and game abundant. They began building their fort, in the endless rain. It was not finished till after the new year and in fact was never satisfactory or even watertight, but within a few days it had a roof. They established an outpost on the beach, where salt would be made for the winter and the homeward journey — and whence word came that evoked the only selfish request Sacajawea is known to have made. A whale had stranded there, and she asked leave to go see it, to behold a marvel and take word of it back with her to her own people. About this time, too, she sacrificed a treasured gaud. The captains wanted, so that they might send it to Mr. Jefferson, a magnificent sea-otter coat that a visiting chief wore. But they could not buy it, for their stock had been depleted, in part lost, in part cached in the mountains, and they had no blue beads, which alone its owner valued. Sacajawea had a necklace of blue beads — and so Mr. Jefferson in due time was able to see for himself the principal article for which his merchants would contend with the Russians in these waters. Her generosity must have cost William Clark a pang. He had come to feel for her not only a complete respect but a tenderness compounded of shared hazards and proved trust. He called her "Janey," in full comradeship, and had named a great rock Pompey's Pillar after her infant son. And once, after the mountains were passed, she had secretly given him a small piece of bread which she had saved and carried heaven knows how long to feed the child.

So they came to their second Christmas, with no salt and the rain rapidly spoiling the meat they shot. "we would have spent this day the nativity of Christ in feasting," Clark says, "had we any thing either to raise our Sperits or even gratify our appetites, our Diner concisted of pore Elk, so much spoiled that we eate it through mear necessity, some Spoiled pounded fish and a fiew roots." Sergeant Ordway speaks:

Wednesday 25th Decr 1805. rainy & wet. disagreeable weather. we all moved in to our new Fort, which our officers name Fort Clatsop after the name of the Clatsop nation of Indians who live nearest to us. the party Saluted our officers by each man firing a gun at their quarters at day break this morning. they divided out the last of their tobacco among the men that used [it] and the rest they gave each a Silk handkerchief, as a Christmast gift, to keep us in remembrance of it as we have no ardent Spirits, but are all in good health which we all esteem more than all the ardent Spirits in the world.

They were of the world's great adventurers, they had come up the Missouri, over the mountains, and down to the Pacific, by ways no white man had ever taken before, and they had kept their health. They had the winter before them, and the back trail at its end — shirts and leggings and hundreds of pairs of moccasins to make, more than three months of wind and rain, of short rations, of salt making and wood gathering, of yarning and singing and dancing to Cruzatte's fiddle at night, within sound of the Pacific sea. No ardent spirits were left, there was only a pound or two of tobacco and a silk handkerchief apiece to symbolize Christmas for this crew of a greater Argo. But they had reason enough to be content.

And Captain Clark fared better:

I recved a pres[e]nt of Capt. Lewis of a fleece hosrie [hosiery] Shirt Draws and Socks, a pr. Mockersons of Whitehouse a small Indian basket of Gutherich [Goodrich], two Dozen white weazil tails of the Indian woman, & some black root of the Indians before their departure.

A hero's Christmas presents, on the edge of the Pacific, with the now traversed continent behind him and the dream achieved. They attest an immortal deed, the affection of his comrade, the respect of his men. And the warm heart of Sacajawea, whose ailments he had treated with niter and zinc sulphate and Rush's pills, whom he had delivered from her husband's blows, whose child also he had nursed and doctored, whom he had several times snatched from death, whom he had come to think of not as an Indian squaw but as a woman of extraordinary fineness and staunchness. And whose gratitude and loyalty were his. She had but inadequate words to give him on Christmas, the great medicine day of his race, but, accepting the custom she could not comprehend, knowing that he had been kind to her and that this was a day of kindness, she gave him what she had. History will remember William Clark as one of the greatest of its captains, and, remembering him, it will not forget the twenty-four white weasel tails that Janey gave him on Christmas Day.

Gettysburg

THE GOVERNMENT has done a good job at Gettysburg. The park area is neat and quiet, lawns and roads ameliorate the chaos of several hundred monuments and several thousand regimental markers, a decent unaggressiveness is enforced on the guides. Souvenir stands are held to the unavoidable minimum and there are no sideshows. The place is seemly; it has a gravity in keeping with the dignity of great events.

The National Cemetery seems a small place to hold so many hundred graves, but the shrubbery is ordered and discreet, the two monuments are severely simple, and an impressiveness that will not be quelled quietly lays hold of you. The wide stone arcs above the known dead, the small stones of unidentified graves, the markers that chart the battle lines in the burial place of those who fought on them evoke the deepest emotions. On other plaques by the side of the drive a quite bad poem acquires a sudden validity:

On Fame's eternal camping ground
    Their silent tents are spread
And Glory guards with solemn round
    The bivouac of the dead.

It is bad poetry but, in the presence of that bivouac, you realize that it is true. Its small, clean tinkle will have a meaning for you hereafter that it did not have before, but it is of course lost in the organ tones of the great poetry spoken at the dedication. You do not need to read the Address, which is carved on the monument, for it is an almost oppressive rhythm in your mind, among the evergreens that frame the spot where it was delivered. A paradox in logic, it was set in the paradox of war, but, nevertheless, the highest meaning of American life found expression in those words and has not found it a second time. The nation has not done ignobly by its setting and occasion, and part of the strange exaltation that one carries away from the Cemetery is a realization that republics do, after all, remember.

One must probe deep to explain the fascination that the battlefield has for the hundreds of thousands who visit it every year. At the surface is the fact that this battle, unlike most, was simple and can be clearly seen. From either of the two famous ridges, or from Culp's Hill or Round Top, you can reconstruct with startling clarity the decisive actions and most of the lesser ones of the three days' fighting. He would have a sluggish imagination indeed who could stand in the Peach Orchard, the Wheat Field, or Devil's Den, or on Little Round Top, or at the Angle without an overwhelming realization of the will, the agony, and the lives that were spent in trying to seize and to defend them. Here tilled land and pasturage and woodland were suddenly so precious that no amount of blood shed to purchase them was too high a price. The stupendous drama of war wakes round you, though the cannons are antiques now, though the grass is untrodden and no thunder rolls across the fields.

It is a drama greatly composed, for the battle develops as a fine artist might have imagined it, with the swift change and interchange of fortune, the arcs of achievement and frustration crossing and retracing each other, the will to take and the will to hold rising in a steady and all but intolerable equipoise, all at the extremity of human effort and all gathering centrally toward the last assault, the climax in which so much was lost and so much more won. It is all in sight here, from either ridge, so that the throat dries and the pulse pounds as if one could indeed see them coming on. And this drama, the spectator knows, is not fictitious, not actors running and shouting under a painted sky; when the curtain falls these dead men do not rise and walk offstage.

Yet if it were only drama, even the white-hot, actual drama of war, Gettysburg would not draw its hundreds of thousands. For those schooled in the history or the design of war there is more technical splendor in Chancellorsville, more irony in Shiloh, more obstinate incandescence in Chickamauga, more hypnotic horror in the Wilderness. Nor, even with seventy-four years between, could the visitor so soon lose his realization of the thousands dead or dying round him, the screams at night, the fetor of rotting flesh. The horror of the event is lost in its significance, and the last argument as well of republics as of kings here comes into justification. Whether the prophecy in Lincoln's words teaches it or whether the knowledge comes by inheritance or divination, the public knows, against the dogmas of historians, that Gettysburg was the decisive action of the war. And, no matter how dogma may dissent, stressing the two years that followed it, it was just that. From ridge to ridge, on the three July days, the issue of the Civil War was decided here, and so the future course of the American people, and so the pattern of Western civilization.

Here, compressing into three days of desire, struggle, and agony, are the sequence of events, the impacts of force and consequence, the calculus of cause following upon cause by which the undetermined was determined, the doubt resolved,

the scaffold of the future built. However obscured or unrecognized, there must be present in everyone who visits Gettysburg the wish to stand where the unprecipitated came out of
solution into crystallization and the egg was fertilized of
which the future was born, where all might have gone otherwise but what now exists was established instead, where what
we have come to be was shaped. In this way the battle rises
from drama to destiny. One sees chaos, flux, chance, and the
unknowable come into the discipline of the determined.

Yet to catch a glimpse in men and nations of the force that
shapes the embryo's bones and curves the bough of a tree in
the appointed balance is not the deepest desire stirring in the
visitor to Gettysburg. Even if you believe that, with this battle settled as it was, history acquired a better logic and that a
vast and crippling paradox at the nation's core was resolved
forever — even then you have not explored the full fascination. For if the battle compresses the process of destiny into
three days, it also focuses the searching spotlight of war on the
process by which men move toward a desired end. War is a
concentrated action of men, a social action in quintessence,
with men nerved to their maximum capability and many of
the accessory and inconsequent factors weakened or removed
altogether. The process shows clear; and at Gettysburg you
can see more of it than elsewhere.

With Lee in Pennsylvania, it was certain that the armies
would fight. Both were perfected instruments — as nearly perfected, that is, as the instruments of human action ever are.
They were composed of veteran troops, hardened by cam-
paigning, picked over and selected, forged in the habit and
experience of combat — as good armies as war has ever seen.
But the Army of Northern Virginia, Lee's army, had been
recently reorganized, so that its staff work was not facile and
many of its organizations must fight under commanders un-
used to their individualities; and the Army of the Potomac,
Meade's, had suffered the shock of a change in the high command while it was actually marching to the foreseen but un-

known battle. In war, as in politics or business or the management of social dreams, it was also impossible to annul the
friction and attrition of personality in the subordinate commanders. Longstreet's understanding of the campaign was different from Lee's and his understanding of the battle was to
be different; Ewell was what he had grown to be and not what
logic required him to be; Lee's mathematics assigned to Stuart
a function which Stuart's mind and heart prevented him from
serving. And Meade's understanding of his instrument and the
work it was to be employed in was such that some of his sub-
ordinates rode toward the battle in a conviction of defeat.

The armies felt toward each other, tentatively, fumblingly,
the general directions known but the specific objective not
only unknown but nonexistent. That they must fight was certain but when or where was not, and in fact they met before
either of the commanders meant them to and fought on ground
that neither of them would have chosen. Time and place were
determined by the development of events, could not have been
anticipated by any forecast or calculation, and, though implicit in the actions under way, were beyond plan or control.

In war, as in politics or banking, strategy consists of gener-
alizing the theoretically desirable thing. But when strategy
ends and tactics begin war passes from the speculative and
theoretical to a body of knowledge more exact and of principles more solidly grounded in experience than anything with
which either government or commerce can work. It approaches the conditions of a craft, even a science. From a corporal to a general, from a squad to an army, what to do in
battle, why to do it, and how to do it are clearly known — always within the conditions set by what is possible, by the
morale and capacity of the troops, the terrain, and the dictation of the circumstances immediately at hand. A battle is a
planned action toward a clearly stated goal, by means of specialized instruments, in accordance with an established technique.

Well, strategy passed into tactics when the armies met at the incalculable place for the premeditated but unpredictable battle. They fought it expertly according to opportunity, experience, knowledge, and the dictation of facts. And this is a basic part of the fascination the field has for those who visit it. The last argument of republics and their destiny come out of the impalpable into the moment of determination. For three days, at the extreme of their power and capability, fired not only by the imminence of death but by their deepest desire and belief, men try to do the thing envisioned by means of the instruments prepared. The thing must be done now, by known means; the means are tried, and the thing is done. In those three days the abstract symbols in the complex formula are translated into known values. Men do what they can, and by what they do are the lines laid down. The lines are laid down forever, and on the way to them are the details of skill and awkwardness, of courage and faltering, of knowledge and guess, of strength and weakness, of planning, of management, of personality, of time, of chance — with the battle and all that hangs on it hanging also on every move and on the components, human and inert, of every move. The visitor's breath shortens because he sees the outcome in the steps leading to it, and perceives in each step the forces of human effort as components and as a sum. Thus, not otherwise, things came about. Thus, not otherwise, things happen when men act together.

So the battle was fought. Rather more clearly than most battles, it was won and lost. And something fundamental may be observed about how men think of social actions in the fact that Lee's best biographer, Mr. Freeman, thinks of it seventy years later as lost, not won. He thinks of it, that is, as a logical plan miscarrying because of what was hardly more than sabotage, a reasoned procedure toward the envisioned end that could and should have worked out successfully but was frustrated by irrelevance and mere chance. Mr. Freeman writes a long chapter analyzing the reasons why Gettysburg was lost, but he does not mention among them the important fact that the Union army was on the field. What decided the outcome was not the presence of another force but only omissions or misunderstandings within the ideal plan. But in all social actions there is always an opposing force on the field, as there was here. Events cannot be made logically inescapable within their solution merely by perfecting a plan; they crystallize out of a solution in which the opposing force is a primary condition. An irrevocable error is to think of results rather than of resultants.

It seems probable that, at Gettysburg, Lee's thinking was tinctured somewhat with the mistake that his biographer makes. Certainly if the battle was lost rather than won, as most battles are, then it was lost primarily because Lee's plan of battle was too close to the ideal, and it is the nature of ideal plans to be impossible. The ideal plan called for simultaneous action on both flanks by converging attacks from the exterior line — but throughout the history of society it has proved impossible to adjust the minds or the actions of men to a time schedule, even in the simplified social conditions of battle. The ideal plan called for the perfect subordination of other intelligences to the will of the commander, so that Longstreet's doubts are charged with the defeat — but subordination without margin for the tangential view is impossible in Congress or the Supreme Court or a sit-down strike. (In the history of sentiment Longstreet has indeed lost Gettysburg, but in the history of afterthoughts he is one of the few social prophets vindicated by events; for the realist was right.) The ideal plan assumed that the manpower of the Army of Northern Virginia was invincible, whereas the plain lesson of the last preceding year was that not manpower but mechanical power, the power of massed fire, was invincible. The ideal plan called for Stuart to act contrary to the laws of his nature and to forgo a magnificent exhibition of skill and gallantry in order to perform the unspectacular duty of providing information. And that shows how ideal plans miscarry: they assume that men can be re-made, that a great cause and a shining goal will transform men from what they are to what they ought to be, that at the crisis on which everything depends men will be something other than what we know they are. If Lee lost Gettysburg, he lost it through idealism — through softening facts and subordinating them to his vision of the end and the means.

Yet it is not clear that Gettysburg was lost. Rather, it was won. It was won not by Meade but by rule of thumb. What the Army of the Potomac did was to meet successive events by doing the immediately expedient thing, in relation to the events themselves, not in relation to a plan or a time schedule. If there is such a thing as the tyranny of events, it is their power to compel action in terms of immediacy or opportunism rather than in terms of to-morrow's good, and the Union army adapted its moves to that compulsion. There could be no plan for the defense of Cemetery Ridge, Culp's Hill, and the Round Tops. The need was to hold on to them — to repel attacks as attacks might be made. To do the next thing by means at hand. That was all that could be done and all that needed to be. It was done, and the Army of Northern Virginia was broken at its moment of climax and slipped back into the hills and turned southward. With it went something that had not existed before, something that had crystallized out of solution in a pattern established by the lines of force: the certainty that the Confederacy would lose the war. There had been no mold for the future in America, but now there was one — and for the Western world as well.

Page from a Primer

I T IS the morning of November 6, 1860. As you make your way through crowded and excited streets you know that the national destiny walks invisibly at your side. The way to this day has lain through such passion and dissension as the Republic has never seen before. Now it is here: all that reason, persuasion, threat, and panic can do has been done, and, albeit imperfectly as all the issues of men's intent must be shaped, these issues are now shaped finally and you must answer to them. You are on your way to cast a vote for President in what you know is the most momentous and is likely to be the most dangerous election since the Constitution was adopted by which the United States was formed. A tag line wakes out of your school days, from an old book about other civil strife, and you feel that when your vote is cast the die will be cast too.

Looking back on that moment with whatever wisdom may be read in time's primer, when all the unknowns have been solved by the painstaking calculus of the events themselves, looking back seventy-seven years, which ballot would you have cast? There were four principal tickets to choose from: the Republican, Abraham Lincoln and Hannibal Hamlin; the Democratic, Stephen A. Douglas and Herschel V. Johnson; the Southern Democratic, John C. Breckinridge and Joseph Lane; and the Constitutional Union, John Bell and Edward Everett. Whom, in 1937, would you have voted for in 1860?

Do not answer too hastily or too forthrightly, for though haste and forthrightness were the essence of the question then, it may be that the primer overbids them. . . . Already in November, 1860, the crisis had developed to the edge of catastrophe. Either the development could be stopped short of that edge or it must go on. No one, in 1937, would want it to go on if it could satisfactorily be stopped short.

One group of voters in 1860 felt that the supreme need was to arrest the crisis, no matter how. True, the crisis came straight from an unresolved question at the very core of the American political system and an unsolved problem at the very core of the social system — but urgent as it was to solve them, it was more urgent still to gain time to solve them in. There might be within the existing structure means for compromise and such orderly revision and adaptation as would appease the two sections from whose conflict the catastrophe would arise. It was a sectional conflict, a sectional crisis, and there must be some way of solving it nationally, of reconciling the opposed interests in the greater interest of the nation. What was most necessary was time — time to devise a new compromise, to make another trial at the old muddle, to reduce the pressure of emotion, to find implements for reason. Sacrifice everything, that need be, to gain more time!

So thought a considerable number of people — among them the majority of those who lived nearest the line of sectional cleavage. The primer says, in 1937, that there was much in what they said. Much of the Republican ardor came from the decision of the Supreme Court that Congress had no power to prohibit slavery in the territories. If opposition to that decision had been abandoned much of the Southern Democratic ardor would have abated. Moreover, the Supreme Court has been known to reverse itself in time, and it has been packed too, more peacefully than is currently proposed. The whole political point about slavery in the territories could have been abandoned, leaving the entire political and constitutional position in the hands of the most fanatical Southerners — and with slavery sanctioned in the territories as far as Puget Sound, climate and economics would have made free soil of them as States. So point by point, compromised or ceded, all the demands of the inflamed South could have been granted and still, the primer says, time would have made an end to slavery as it had already set a limit. And economic development and the spread of population would have established the other thesis which we say the war established: the thesis that in a democracy the majority shall control the government.

You might have decided, therefore, that time and the preservation of the established way of political control were the first necessity — that whatever the cost of preserving that control, the price would be cheap compared to the cost of overthrowing it and starting anew. You would then have voted for the party of compromise, for Bell and Everett.

That ticket finished third.

More likely you would have cast your vote for Breckinridge or for Lincoln, and though you would have had quite as persuasive arguments to support it, you would actually have cast it in obedience to a sentiment which did not differ much, North and South — a sentiment which held that the time for compromise had passed and the inevitable decision was better made now than postponed once more, peacefully if peace did not involve further yielding, by force if it should come to force. Along with the tag line from Caesar you might well have remembered one from another crisis in the American state:

"Don't fire unless fired upon, but if they mean to have a war, let it begin here."

The votes for Breckinridge stemmed from the simplest and most nearly unified sentiments. For the most part they were votes in the belief that the North had progressively usurped "Southern rights" and must be stopped. Actually the only right threatened was the uncodified one which the South had exercised for two generations, that of minority control of the government. Slavery in the territories was guaranteed by the Supreme Court, property in slaves was guaranteed by the Constitution and by Congress, slavery in the States was in no danger and no threat to it existed but in the rapt visions of fanatics. The tariff, a great shibboleth with Southern orators, was sustained by Southern votes, and there was nowhere any overt or even threatened invasion of the legal or social authority within its own borders that the South possessed. Nevertheless, the rationalization "Southern Rights" covered an awareness too sharp to be borne or even phrased. The logic of an expanding nation was now unmistakable, the minority section in fact must soon become the minority section in power, and understanding that, the South divined, or thought it divined, that when its control passed its safety must pass too.

A vote for Lincoln is not to be so unanimously rationalized. It might have been a vaguely humanitarian vote or specifically an abolition vote, but it might also have been a vote for a manufacturing and financial combination that betrayed the Middle West into an alliance not clearly in its interest. It might have been a vote for immigration, for a Pacific railroad, for free homesteads, for skillfully contrived new opportunities for exploitation. But in the largest part it was a vote for majority rule. Not for majority aggression against slavery but, specifically, for free soil in the territories and, generally, for maintenance of democratic logic by support of democratic forms.

Well, the votes were cast and civil war began at once. And

it at once began to demonstrate that civil war is like all wars: that it is never what it seems to be, never does what it seems to be meant to do, and never comes out at the end the same war it was at the beginning.

For the Confederacy it was to be, in its ideal end, a war in defense of a nation grounded on certain ideas of government and polity and dedicated to a certain way of life. But at once the government so grounded showed itself almost as inconceivable in logic as it was impossible in fact; step by step it had to violate its conception, abandon its first principles, and make itself into the exact opposite of what it had undertaken to be. And war proved that way of life altogether implausible in the modern world — proved that the society it expressed was, not decadent, as has sometimes been said, for a decadent society cannot organize such a nation and fight such a war as the Confederacy did, but what is more final, an anachronism. The league of sovereign States had to become a centralized national government more absolute than the one it had left, and was defeated, in part, because it could not become one soon enough. The agricultural economy was broken on the steel edge of the industrial order, and the economic determination of the future was proved a mirage when cotton did not rule diplomacy, finance, the seas, or even friendship. The society turned its back on the entire tradition of American life which it shared the moment it sought to ally itself with English mills and the British government. It had refuted its own assumptions and mocked its whole vision, by the end of the war, with the approaching measures to free and arm the slaves. And it had overturned for all time the one axiom that went still more deeply into its ideal vision, that two nations could occupy the place where there had been but one.

For the North it was, in its ideal end, a war to preserve the Union. Or, if the paradox is not intolerable, to maintain the processes of democratic government by supporting the majority with force. Yet the Union must not be saved too quickly.

One by one the democratic processes faded out, a good many of them never to return, and they were replaced by an autocratic bureaucracy never imagined by anyone up to then, which in great part was to remain. And presently the war which was to preserve the Union swerved in its orbit and became a war to free the slaves. A war also to occupy in subtler ways than by military action the great Western empire and to make sure that the instruments for exploiting it came into the hands of men skillful at using them. A war to facilitate the emergence and secure the power of a new kind of governing class, one that was not too happy an omen for the Republic. And finally a war neither to save the Union nor to free the slaves but, as it ended and went into a phase not quite so deadly but rather more destructive, quite simply a war to maintain the Republican Party in control of the government. Saving the Union and freeing the slaves oddly turned out to be securing the use and usufructs of government, the power and the patronage, the profits and the graft, to a political faction — no matter what happened to the nation. When you voted for Lincoln on that morning of November 6, 1860, your noble dream nowhere mentioned Reconstruction.

For whoever lost the war — and nearly everyone did, especially the American Republic — the winners were the Republican Party and an industrial order that might otherwise have been in part directed and in part restrained. The abolitionists had laws freeing the slaves and making them citizens, which satisfied all that their ideal vision had asked, and they also had a universal peonage, of which the worst was that many whites would come to share it too. The Middle West had an alliance that drained a large part of its wealth for decades, and drains it fairly effectively still. The West had a practical subjugation and the South had an actual one. The nation had the Solid South and the Negro Problem and the Bloody Shirt, hundreds of thousands of dead, millions of blasted lives, a harvest of treason and corruption and chicanery and hatred of which the end is not yet, hundreds of public leaders whose depravity could not be matched this side of hell, and millions to follow them for two generations. It had too a structure and an organization it had not had before, had not desired, above all, had not intended. It was not thus that the humanitarians, the pure in heart, the idealists, and the dreamers had planned.

So maybe the craven thing in 1860 would have turned out to be the best thing by 1937. Maybe the section caught between the sections, the class caught between the classes, had the best idea. Maybe the hope to have held by, the course to have taken, was the time-serving and even cowardly one for which Bell and Everett stood. Maybe the thing to have done was to hold on somehow, to give here and take there, to compromise when possible and yield when compromise failed, to do the next thing next no matter how little of the long view or the austere vision it had — but to insist on the established forms, maintain the accustomed mechanism, allay as much passion as might be and reduce as much friction, give the thing space to writhe in, and above all gain time. To let the structure heave and strain but keep it together in spite of hell — knowing that hell would be upon you if you did not, as it soon was. This was hardly a counsel of honor, of noble dedication to justice and the right. But there were two justices, two idealisms, two rights, two noble visions, two dedications to the highest law and the highest good — and the war came, hundreds of thousands died, the nation was changed altogether, what happened was different from what had been nobly planned, and nothing that had gone into the great dream came out in the finished thing.

Be of good cheer. Nothing now visible above the horizon shows signs of developing the pattern that led to 1860. The only class caught between classes, for instance, is infinitely bigger than those on its flanks, and so powerful that they are not likely to test its tensile strength. No line of cleavage anywhere is so distinct as the one along which the sections parted. This has never been a mild nation and the violence now pock-marking it is, to a historian, no more than its normal complement of force. It does not, by any omen our history has seen, presage a general violence.

But the voice of the dreamer is heard in the land and those who readily uncover God's purposes in their own desires are active in making His commandments known. It may be that we have too many noble souls, too much altruistic vision. It would be well to keep a cold and hostile eye on those who, from any quarter or in the name of any ideal, talk too much about right, justice, or the ideal end. North and South, they were the ones who whipped the battle up last time. Probably they are most perfectly to be seen under glass by looking at the South, where right, justice, the ideal end, and the great vision burned with the fiercest light. They talked well, they had a passionate vision, and they planned nobly — far more than could be borne. Their plan blew away like dust before the wind they finally raised, their right and justice are in the tomb they themselves dug. That much is clear. Is it clear that the ideal vision of the North came, in the end, to any other fulfillment?

Seed Corn and Mistletoe

No one can approach through winter darkness a house from whose windows light shines out on the snow without feeling quieted and heartened. Psychic subtleties may be active in such a response, but there is no need to invoke them; for the obvious facts provide all the explanation we require. A house means warmth and shelter, light means human society. Snow and the dark have simplified the detail of the picture and deadened sound — they suggest tranquillity, which may mean much at the end of the day, and food or drink for restoration, and the talk of friends or family. The human mind is addicted to symbolism, and here is an image of ease, comfort, and reassurance that speaks directly to us in early childhood and from then on. . . . It is likely that very few people seeing a light on snow and quickening to the thought of warmth within pause to inquire whether the warmth comes from a gas furnace controlled by a thermostat or from the hickory logs burning on a spacious hearth to which a poetic sense would more properly attribute it. The light shining on the snow is quite as beautiful and quite as heartening when power to furnish it has been carried along a hundred miles of copper wire and stepped down through a transformer as when it comes from a candle dipped by hand.

Somewhere here is a text for a sermon, and sermons are appropriate to Christmas time, though with the clergy currently talking about a planned economy which will plow them under altogether, they may have to be preached by laymen. And everything about Christmas fares badly among the cerebral, who deplore its clearly reactionary nature, mutter about its vulgarization by trade and commerce, protest against its evil effects on children, and complain that it isn't what it used to be anyway and never can be again. Let us deal with these indignations first; for though the cerebral are always running a slight temperature on logical grounds, if the winter festival does indeed constitute a menace to society even a lay pulpit should take notice of it.

About the children. There are no statistical tables to tell us how many of them are still being deceived with an old and probably capitalistic myth called Santa Claus. Probably millions of them, for the mass of mankind has a gratifying disregard of theory, and parents continue, in spite of the heroic labors of educational psychologists, to deceive their children because they themselves were deceived a generation ago, remember liking it, and observe that their children like it too. The myth offends both a moral theory which holds that it is wrong to lie to children about anything and a highly scientific one which holds that you must not confuse a child's sense of reality by adding to his difficulty in dealing with real things the further difficulty of dealing with the altogether fictitious. Yet everyone knows that a child's sense of reality is quite incommensurable with an adult's and that children will make up phantasies of their own to supply the lack of any that may not be given them by others. The people who object to lying to children about Santa Claus must perforce lie to them about all the daily phenomena of existence, if indeed it is possible to say what a lie to a child is. And the very people who object to Santa Claus as a myth are prone to instruct them in such conceptions as human brotherhood, justice, and the classless society.

Both objections are on the level of the nostalgia which feels that the festival was all right for children when they themselves strung popcorn and cranberries to make decorations for the tree instead of the machine-made tinsel of to-day (but if that was Group Participation, was it not also Child Labor?), and that colored electric lights are tawdry whereas little candles once had a simple purity — it apparently being all right to burn the house up on Christmas Day so long as you keep the festival simple and pure. This is on the same level with that other sentiment of the thoughtful which sets out to make wars impossible, along with racketeering and unfair competition, by keeping toy guns, cannon, and lead soldiers out of the hands of children. Beat the toy sword into a toy steamshovel, the notion goes, and you will turn the child forever to the ways of peace, at whatever cost of overproduction in the heavy industries. But if you do not permit the normal warlike phantasies of the child a normal expression at the right time you head straight for trouble. Either you will render him unfit for normal aggression later on, thus making him an easy prey for the combative, or you will insure such phantasies getting an abnormal and delayed expression, thus making war inevitable.

The unregarding behavior of untheoretical people is certainly sounder. They act on an assumption that the important thing is to make children happy. If you can give a child an experience of authentic awe and wonder and anticipation by telling him that a mythical fat man with a kind heart brings presents to children, why, the thing that counts is giving him the experience. If children like to play with toy guns, who is harmed? And if a child catches his breath in ecstasy because here in the living room stands an evergreen that has blossomed with colored lights, why that is everything in itself. You have given the child an experience of ecstasy, which needs neither justification nor analysis on logical principles.

One is constrained to be equally skeptical of the indignation that sees Christmas as a conspiracy against the public peace and interest by people who have Christmas presents to sell. Like so many other causes of the cerebral, this presents itself as a benevolent championship of the exploited, whereas it is really a contempt of the common man. It is the old, old cry of Utopians: the people are fools. The people, that is, are weak, gullible, infatuated, unstable, venal, too foolish to follow after righteousness — give us machine guns and we will make them virtuous. A cerebral dictatorship, ever so kindly but quite firm, would safeguard them from exploitation by the hucksters, defend them from the seductions of advertising, deliver them from the pumped-up hysteria of crowds. How pitiful that they should give one another presents because the department store tells them to, how intolerable that the System should make money from a sentiment that the people only think they feel! See how mechanically the common man jerks about on his wire and how slavishly he does what he is told to do by conspirators in the service of commerce. Therefore let us save him from himself, teach him that his emotions are not his own, and deliver him into self-knowledge and emancipation — at the point of a bayonet. . . . A lay pulpit must denounce all this fervor as propaganda — fascist or communist, whichever epithet will most affront the kindly theorist. It is an ancient despair uttering an ancient cry, the lust of the fretted to save the people by force. The people should ignore it altogether.

As of course they do. They go on giving one another presents at Christmas time no matter how the profits of the hucksters may pile up. They spend as much as they can afford to, and usually a good deal more. If trade prospers and the banks can express Christmas in the form of graphs, the public is not appalled. Nor is its feeling degraded. The cathedrals of the age of faith, which the theories treat with the greatest respect, were fenced round by the booths of traders, and an earlier Christianity managed to combine a good deal of commerce with its devotion — and the roads to the American camp-meeting were thronged with peddlers whom the devout patronized without in the least diminishing their pious exercises. Not the trading booths but the devotion was the important thing about the cathedrals, and the important thing about Christmas is not that the people are sold presents but that they give them to one another. The most diverse and even the most irrelevant motives may enter in, many of them doubtless a good deal less than ideal; but the principal one, the one without which none of the others could possibly operate, is the human warmth of friends and relatives seeking expression and finding it. Christmas may be commercialized till it has become indispensable to the business system and vulgarized till a sensitive theory shudders when dealing with it, but people go on making gifts to those who are dear to them. The custom has the natural force of a stream flowing and takes its curve as a stream does, from its own nature. It is the popular fulfillment of human need and desire. The people behave that way, and you can do nothing whatever about them.

That is the firstly of a lay sermon. The secondly goes on to point out how, though in the American Christmas are recognizable many elements taken from many places, the whole is something altogether in its own terms. Our Christmas Eve is English and our Christmas morning looks very German. The carols sung in our churches and streets (and, to advertise soap or engine oil, in our broadcasting studios, a native touch probably loathsome to the sensitive) come from all over Europe but are French to a functional anthropologist, and medieval French at that. A good many of the conventional symbols are Asiatic, and the firecrackers which children set off in San Francisco and New Orleans exorcise demons and propitiate gods that are clearly Chinese. The mistletoe is Norse, and a vigilant suspicion, observing the holly and the eggnog, can detect compulsions bubbling in the blood of pagans far older than the rise of that star in the East which they are used to commemorate. Yes, a hodgepodge of rituals and symbols and of beliefs gathered at random, but it has taken a shape of its own which no one who has experienced it can ever possibly confuse with any other Christmas. One who has known the American Christmas as a child, a lover, or a parent knows a festival which has shaped his thought and patterns of emotion lying far deeper than thought, in a way uniquely its own. In whatever corner of the earth he may find himself on Christmas Eve, the rhythms pulsing in his nerves and the images translating them will have reference to the common and unique experience of Americans. That remembered, remembering child seeing the filled stocking and the lighted tree, hearing a Catholic carol so illogically sung in a Congregational meetinghouse, hurrying to deliver a holly wreath to a friend of his parents in order to try his skates the sooner on the ice of country pond or city sidewalk — is set off from all foreign children in things remembered and things experienced. An American tradition, different from all other traditions, has created its own symbols.

There are a good many like them, and a lay preacher would call them into remembrance at Christmas, a time dedicated from its origin to remembering the justifications of hopefulness and disregarding the foundations of despair. Autumn comes and the President of the United States summons the nation to render formal thanks for its harvest, and lesser magistrates repeat his proclamation. Meanwhile at half the farm doorways in New England pumpkins stand on the stoop, a splash of color against the dulling landscape, though no one can explain the custom. In rural places across the continent boys nail on the barn door the tails of woodchucks and chipmunks and red squirrels they have shot; beside them, and on the walls of garages in the towns, their fathers add last year's automobile-license plates to the column of those that have gone before. Seed corn hangs in bunches on the wall that gets the sun, and the corn is shocked. The corn is shocked to dry, and so is the wheat, and the form and structure of the shocking are peculiar to the United States. We shock our corn differently, and the image also calls up associations unique to Americans; for it is part of an intricate organization of skills and customs and emotions, of social beliefs and relationships, of a way of living with and in society that is our own way and no one else's. A live symbol to Americans, and one whose meaning is beyond the instinct and out of the comprehension of all other people.

A symbol of an American way of life. Let it be remembered at Christmas time, and with it a great company of its kind, since Christmas is a time for symbols. Light shining on snow through winter dark is as universal as the star going before the Wise Men on their way, but also to all who have lived in America it has a special reference, being as well the light from a cabin in the clearing with the forest beyond them stretching toward the unknown West. Few Americans now have ever lived in a cabin or ever seen a clearing in the forest, yet the words mean something to them that they mean to no one else on earth. Fewer still have ever ridden in a stagecoach climbing toward Cumberland Gap, or plodded beside a canvas-covered wagon toward the land where the streams sink out of sight, with Indians possibly crouching behind the next rise. It is a long time since a mythical Indian princess interceded for a probably lying Captain John Smith; none of us has driven the *Sovereign of the Seas* round the Horn to beat the clipper fleet; none of us has ridden down the Natchez Trace or forced a plow for the first time through matted grass roots to prairie soil; Andrew Jackson and Abe Lincoln and Buffalo Bill and Daniel Boone are dead; Huck Finn is only someone in a book, and Paul Bunyan is not even that but only talk sleepy at best and now no longer uttered. But though none of us ever saw the Wise Men coming from the East, we still make gifts to our friends and children on Christmas Day. And the cabin in the clearing, the clipper fleet, the departed heroes, and the corn standing in shocks are systolic in us, part of the rhythm of our breath and of our desire — and part too of our fate. They stand for our own way of life, they are our living tradition; and we understand them, being shaped by them and being inescapably obedient to them, and no one else understands them. That is the way our corn is shocked.

That may as well be remembered at Christmas time, at Christmas time especially in a period of tribulation. The cerebral — people characterized primarily by fear and by contempt of the unconsidered multitudes and by a lust for absolutes and for absolute power — tell us that America must choose between two ways of life, both European, both essentially the same, both intolerable. Let there be read to them the prayer appointed to be read in churches on Christmas Day: they are fools and liars and the truth is not in them. That is not our choice but an alien one, and our choice is foreordained for us by our own tradition; our native way of life formed by our own systole and diastole. Our corn is maize, and Europe had no maize.

On *Moving* to New York

THE ST. NICHOLAS and the Metropolitan, the poet Mackay once noted, have dwarfed the Astor House in size and eclipsed it in splendor. Making up from five hundred to seven hundred beds, the St. Nicholas shows the magnificent scale on which the New Yorkers do business, as well as the more than Parisian publicity in which families eat and drink and pass the day. You can hardly get to the door, so crowded is Broadway, and by night the throng increases, gaping at the illuminated front. By night also you will see the fire companies parading, and between them battalions of torches carried by the hosts of democracy on the march. But when the lights break out along Broadway, turn from the fire companies and tour the oyster bars, savoring the fries, the stews, the roasts, the oysters *à l'anglaise* — treasure of Shrewsbury, Oyster Bay, Rock Bay, Virginia Bay, and Spuyten Duyvil. Do not linger long but at least glance at the great bars which the palatial St. Nicholas, the Clarendon, the St. Denis, the Laffarge House have set up — rather vulgarly, since you cannot imagine the

Reform Club at home, or the Carlton, permitting a bar on the premises. You may frugally taste the native drinks, the gin-sling, brandy-smash, whisky-skin, streak of lightning, cock-tail, and rum-salad.

But understand that family life suffers in New York and nothing is more deplorable than the lack of homes. The young bride disdains housekeeping, demanding to be maintained in the false luxury of a boarding house, where sloth and vain-glory beset her and the sacred sentiments of matrimony come to be endangered. Her character is undermined, the seducer prowls abroad, and motherhood becomes a target of smart satire. Let us also deplore the city children. They become prematurely old for want of fresh air and exercise, and over-knowing from the experiences they acquire and the acquaint-ances they contract. New York, that great city, is hell on the sentiments, on the finer feelings, and on family life.

City, too, of cynically celebrated crime. The daily journals teem with accounts of murder, robbery, and outrage. Ladies are stopped and robbed in the broad light of day. Murderous affrays take place with practical impunity to the perpetrators, within reach of the public offices and under the very eye of the chief magistrate. Decent people go about their daily business armed, as if an enemy lurked in every lane and gateway of the streets. But, nevertheless, a gay city, a city of colorful pleasures, a city infinitely various in its amusements. There is Niblo's, there is Pastor's. *Mem.*: After I have seen the great shops, notably that of Mr. Stewart which begot the career of Mark the Matchboy, be sure to visit the new cyclorama of the stars. And since I follow letters, I must not ignore Bohemia's seacoast, I must visit Pfaff's. The young Mr. William Winter is to be seen there, and Mr. Arnold and Mr. Wood, those famous literary folk, and Mr. Whitman, the poet, who lives dangerously, wearing no scarf. Mr. Clapp also, and the chief dignity of Pfaff's, Mr. O'Brien, who writes in the daring new mode. Sometimes Mr. Leland shows himself at Pfaff's, though he does not care to pose as a vagabond; lately, in the most generous way, he suggested and sketched out the memoirs of the exhibitor of waxworks which are making such a name for young Mr. Browne in *Vanity Fair*. The great city contains many who have quite as much generosity as Mr. Leland and are quite as willing to acknowledge it. All, all are there, *savants*, *littérateurs*, the bards of Mannahatta whom Mr. Whitman praises. It will be a privilege to get to know the literary.

So the Boston chapter ends. No Nevinson has bothered to bid Boston farewell in tinted prose. It has no steam-wrapped towers to catch the trained reporter's eye; it has no towers at all. And Henry Mencken, praising Mannahatta's lordly site between its rivers, comes to Boston only to be jailed and finds no beauty there. No one finds beauty there: the town has long been disdained by *savants* and *littérateurs*. Something or other disastrously happened there long ago, they understand — it was repression or Puritanism or the town's eccentric unwillingness to publicize its adulteries, or just the passing of Dr. Holmes, maybe — and the literary, who have little aesthetics and no eyes at all, who have only derivative perceptions, perceive nothing lovely in Boston. . . . Then, Mr. Nevinson supplying the idiom, good-by, most beautiful of cities! Good-by, clean air and the high skies of Boston; good-by, blue dusk on Beacon Hill, gulls going to the harbor on the west wind, the homeward-making lights of cars across the Basin where rain strikes at nightfall, the long curve of the Esplanade, the lift of roofs upward to the Bulfinch dome, winter sunset closing over the Charles, spring noons when forsythia breaks out across the town, the Old South Meeting House against a twilight storm. Good-by, city of autumn, city of dusk and morning, city of lavender and gray and mauve, city of cornices and fanlights — most intimate and least known of cities, friendliest and most aloof, most full-bodied, most passionate, most beautiful. Good-by, Boston: I'm moving to New York.

Good-by to the cleanest of streets and the most terrifying of traffic, to crowds walking down the middle of Washington Street, to the tulips and tortured granite of the Public Garden, to the Frog Pond and the swan boats, to Cornhill and Scollay Square, to brown leaves blowing down Chestnut Street and the smell of roasting coffee along Atlantic Avenue, to library windows above the Charles and to little hidden gardens of hydrangea and ailanthus. Good-by to hot bread at Durgin-Park's, to crabmeat and steak at the Parker House, to venison and lobster Savannah at Locke's — will the St. Nicholas have food a man can eat? Good-by to the Pops, to the worst newspapers and the best libraries in America, to twisting alleys and soft voices, to bad manners full of kindness, to a formalized ineptitude that thinks itself courtliness, to Adam paneling and Phyfe tables in the offices of executives. Good-by to unhurried walkers, to women in Queen Mary hats and men without gloves, to bombazine skirts and alpaca jackets and steel pens, to grimy wallpaper and windowpanes on Beacon Street mended with adhesive tape, to pegged shoes and hot-air furnaces and mid-nineteenth-century bathrooms. Good-by to privacy, to suburbs of wide lawns and tall hedges twenty minutes from Park Street, to family dinners and the last homes in the East. Good-by to the Athenaeum's calf-bound eighteenth-century books and the hidebound eighteenth-century people who read them. Good-by to all that is left of the eighteenth century, its last shimmer above the horizon of thought, its last habit and color maintaining the village still in the midst of the city. Good-by to simple dignity and simple quiet — good-by, Boston, I'm moving to New York.

A vigorous culture quite without art, a tradition believed in but not defended, a past praised but not honored. The Bostonians are a people of paradox, cruelly roweled by conflict within. They have lost the courage of race but have strangely preserved the responsibility of position. They have no faith; but what faith should do for them, the will does quite as well, and very possibly better. They have let their government sink to a vileness hardly to be comprehended, and yet have advanced it beyond any other in the service of its citizens. They believe in nothing, and especially in nothing that calls itself humanitarian or progressive or altruistic (who admits himself an idealist tells them he is a fool); yet the uneasy will proliferates their State so widely that cautious trustees will not buy its bonds. They are the immortal Cotton Whigs, and yet they have reared the invisible city of the intelligence that takes the stranger in when his job is respected, provides unstressed help for it, gives it the only dignity it is likely to get in America. . . . So good-by to individuality, to eccentricity, to the ancestral memory of salt water and the present, saving touch of granite, good-by to awkward goodwill and honest respect for decent endeavor — good-by, Boston, I'm moving to New York.

And good-by to Harvard. To L.J. and Hans, to Ted and George, to Kenneth and Perry, to Arthur and Fred, to the college that conscripts your energy and writes you doubtful letters, to the republic that no one knows except those who have held its citizenship, to the dedication admitted only with a jeer but never betrayed, to the fellowship of fatigue and brain-fag and to the fraternity who know how to carry them lightly. To the lifetime job for which no lifetime can be enough, to the unwritten book toward which a man labors with his full strength, to midnight coming up in laboratory and library with to-day's job unfinished and to-morrow's crowding near, to the satisfaction of the work that cannot be finished and the hard going, to the extremity of effort whose delight no one acknowledges except with a grin. . . . September, 1915, and the east wind bringing the sun-dazzle over the South Station; September, 1936, and tourists in the Yard and someone nods to me and when I see Harvard again I shall have no privilege there. Twenty-one years. No one, not President nor Dean nor department head, says, "Thanks, sorry you're going, you did a pretty good job." Why should they? They are Bostonians and don't know how. They are Harvard and take good jobs for granted. It was a long way, in 1915, from Utah to Harvard Square, but it's a longer one, in 1936, from Harvard Square to New York.

I'm going to a city where offal stays in the gutters till it rots away, where you have to climb forty stories high to lose the stench of the streets, where the applied ingenuity of mankind has striven to outdo the hideousness of the rat hole and has succeeded. Mr. Nevinson's city of steam-wrapped towers, Mr. Mencken's city of lordly waters, city which Mr. Nevinson fled from and Mr. Mencken never lived in. Mannahatta! City of discordant voices and tortured faces, city not of brain-fag but of nerve-fag. Warehouse, bazaar, auction block and clip joint of the world, where everyone buys and sells but no one works. No one, at least, in my trade. These twenty years I have never surprised an editor or a publisher at his desk nor so much as a stock girl busy in any of their offices. The books come out on schedule and journals are sacked on mailing day, but the job is done by no known human beings, is done by subterranean gnomes who come up to the pigsty streets at daybreak when the editors sleep at last. Creatures of the hour when ash cans crash, beings of nightmare's green-flecked froth, bubbles of tortured sleep, their orderly battalions defile with the precision of trained lice, work in obsession's manic intensity, then hive up on the under side of girders when the editors wake some hours after a half-day's work has been finished in Boston.

Mr. Whitman's Mannahatta. It drew Mr. Whitman from Jersey though he got away at last to Paumanok. He wrote in the daring new mode and set the mold for thousands following him, hastening from Idaho and West Virginia to novelty and the brave flush of conversation and publicity's darling glare. They too crowding in at noon from Westport and Croton, from Bronxville and Nyack, on the same trains with publishers who are amateurs of music and editors whose career is badminton. Obviously the manuscripts they bring in bales under their arms have been written, and obviously they write them in Nyack and Croton — but just when? When do they work? I carry no other curiosity from Boston to New York.

I suppose I can learn to live in Mr. Whitman's Mannahatta. I learned once to live in Chicago, which gives me confidence. The principal difference is that Chicago has conduits to America and one needs no passport when crossing the frontier. Odd that the most vivid realization on leaving Boston for New York is the knowledge that I am leaving behind the lines of communication with continental United States. It was Mr. Mencken's vision that a buffer State might be erected in Mannahatta, a free port that would serve as a barrier between America and the world outside. He thought that an invading army might do the job, but he could have spared the outlanders the trouble. For the job was done, and without recourse to arms, long before Mr. Mencken took thought of it. It was done by the bazaars and the clip joints, but most of all by the literary. *Mem.:* Always agree with the refrain of native Iowans on Fifty-second Street — New York is not America. The literary at least know that. The literary are annoyed by the Americans, a vigorous people, and terrified by their country.

Mem.: Keep the wires open beyond the Hudson, and retain the habit of work as long as possible. And get about the city — see the show. Have lunch at least once at the St. Nicholas, visit the oyster bars, stand at the curb and watch the fire companies go by. Go to the cyclorama of the stars and from the highest roof on Murray Hill see the gas lights come out. See the show. It is as a show that they celebrate the city, natives, residents, and tourists, as the nation's liveliest fire sale and its costliest spectacle. The barkers bark, the shills shower down, and the come-ons, the rubes, and the apple-knockers storm the grifter's booth. The main tent is doing so well, Mr. Mackay, that they are building an annex with crystal palace, streets of all nations, tribes doing the quaintest native dances, and the Florentine glassblowers at work before your eyes.

And, therefore, be sure to examine one exhibit and to study its proprietor exhaustively. Observe the Cataract of Niagara with real water, the Feejee Mermaid, the automaton speaker, the chromatrope and the physioscope, the golden pigeons from California, the albino family, the negro growing white, the fat boy, the living skeleton, the giants, and especially the three personages who get the best press, Lavinia Warren, Commodore Nutt, and General Tom Thumb. Observe them and, in the night watches, meditate on them. Meditate on the marvels that endlessly draw the New Yorkers to the American Museum and endlessly gratify them and absorb their admiration. And on the owner of this show, who gave the moral drama to New York and to Artemus Ward. "The one end aimed at," he says, "was to make men and women think and talk and wonder, and, as a practical result, go to the Museum." His wares were novelty and humbug and his art was advertising. He fed the town rumor and newsprint, stunts in the creation of conversation, and the town returned him glory. He ran a show and let it be known. Master of spectacle, master of publicity, and so master of New York — the man who knew the soul of the city, its first citizen, Mr. Phineas Taylor Barnum, time without end, amen.

On Moving from New York

THE LAW: Curb your dog. The sign is everywhere in
the city but commonest near the habitations of the comfortably
placed middle class, a few blocks each way from the Park.
Blustering, euphemistic, proved futile at every third step you
take, the phrase lodges in your mind and comes to stand
symbol of something frenetic, nightmarish, at the core of the
city's life. When I came to New York two years ago the
readers of the *Times* were discussing the condition it tries to
cope with, and an editor told me that the topic had evoked
more letters than any other broached in the correspondence
column during recent years. There were reasons enough that
autumn for anger and accusation: war in two hemispheres,
violence and starvation in the very streets this placard tries to
safeguard, the world and the nation wabbling in their orbits.
But the New Yorker, writing to the *Times* about the starving
or the murdered or the betrayed, could sustain a civilized
patience, the dispassionate liberality of the seeker after truth.
What brought him flaming out of his calm, what goaded him

to a desperate, last-ditch defense of justice, was a threat against the right of dogs to sewage facilities.

Whatever other freedom might be attainted in New York, dogs must be free to follow nature. If the sidewalks were therefore contaminated, if doormats and mud scrapers found a use not contemplated for them elsewhere, why, the New Yorker would pick his way with care and not complain, a citizen willingly suffering inconvenience on behalf of the common good and the life of the spirit. While he paused to give his dog ease, three blocks nearer the East River the children of the slums were urinating in the gutters because, no crusade having been raised for them, they had no place else to use. That problem, however, if debated at all, could be debated in tranquillity, the mind resuming its liberal calm. And it is diagnostic of New York that, in the manic and compulsive terms that life must adapt to here, the citizen was right. He can postpone the children of the slums, but his dog is central in the tenuous net of illusion and substitution that holds his life together and cannot be endangered without threatening his survival.

The sojourner finds an early pity for the New York dog. Mongrel or bench champion, pulling at the end of a lead along sidewalks that crack and ulcerate his pads, a strap round his jaw, constrained and disarmed, he has lost animality, he is phantasmal. He is a chimera, a creature proper to the visions of sick sleep. It is not only that he would promptly die if left unattended in this environment, from starvation if he escaped the traffic that long: a more monstrous distortion is inflicted on him in that he has been superbly bred for use and then denied it.

These two Borzois pacing down Fifth Avenue on a double lead are grotesque, as bizarre and fabulous as the belling of a beagle over Central Park. I have heard that music above the taxi horns; I have seen an English sheep dog peering through his fringe across that thin, scrofulous grass, and he seemed a paradox beyond the invention of the comic or the tragic imagination. Innumerable generations of his kind had been sifted in selection of intelligence and of the intricate, magnificently synchronized reflexes and instincts required to do a special job perfectly. So here he was, an autonomous and specialized organism, doubtless a better dog for the job intended than any of his ancestors, searching for a flock that the Park has not got, a flock that would be herded by attendants in uniform if there were one and folded by a photoelectric cell — here he was, and in his blood and nerves coursed God knows what impulses born of Devon and Salisbury but nurtured in New York, and never, in his whole life, to have a moment of function. And as counterpoint, as a poetic complement, once a year the biggest bench show brings in a flock of sheep to nibble tanbark in the Garden, and some of this dog's poor relations, and some authentic, perhaps hallmarked shepherds, to go through a counterfeit and heartbreaking parody of the act for which he was bred.

I have seen Labradors in the Park too, whose otter-tails were meant for rudders in the backwash of waves crackling with ice, waves against which the thick black coats would be a sure protection. And when the winds across Central Park turn chill, the cutest blankets are buckled over the black coats, and if a dog made a heretical, atavistic leap toward the lake there would be a mobilization of the police force to pull him out. But I will remember longest a magnificent Samoyed who had snapped his leash in the Park and broken free momentarily with no muzzle on his nose. In his stance and movement one could see his ancestors, who had herded reindeer on the tundras, beaten off wolves, and dragged sledges through blizzards over frozen snow — never with jaws so strong or teeth so sharp and clean as his, forelegs so straight, chests so deep, haunches so powerful. When he loped about the Park one could see and almost share his ecstasy, and he carried in his mouth an object which he would drop and back away from — then, crouching, he would leap at it as at a gray wolf's throat. I watched him till a feeling of indecency oppressed me and I had to turn away, leaving him, this watchdog with nothing to guard, this hunter with nothing to hunt, this workman with nothing to work at — flinging himself about the resinous grass of Central Park, growling and snorting in his counterfeit ferocity, and worrying his rubber rat.

There are rubber rats for these metropolitan dogs to chew, and composition bones; there are even treadmills for them to run on and so get a prophylactic exercise in the living room, safely away from drafts. There are veterinaries to treat the maladies that attack them, and probably psychiatric clinics where the neuroses begotten in them may be repaired. You pay, if you are the dog's owner and can afford to indulge his asthenias, a stiff price for such services, and you may have his meals served by a caterer. And, equally, if you are a poor man you must feed and protect and nurse your dog, for he can do nothing for himself. And if you own no dogs, you see the pitiful beasts, sniffing the stenches of the streets, cringing when the trucks backfire, promenading with a nurse, docilely awaiting the chemically formulated food that is compounded on behalf of their bones, their teeth, and the proper cell-counts of their blood.

Coming to New York, you work up a really powerful pity for the dogs, splendid and damned, bred perfectly to functions never exercised, living like Dr. Carrel's fragment of a chicken tissue in a solution sealed in a test tube. They are overspecialized beyond adaptation, and their splendid points ominously remind you of the textbook specimens of doom — say the beautiful spiral tusks of the Columbia mammoth. They are parasites, and you remember the degenerations that produced the tapeworm and similar creatures — the organs of locomotion drop away and the organism develops structures for attachment or adhesion, and simplifies its other organs and structures to fit a life cycle distorted and debased. "Hermaphroditism frequently characterizes the parasite," the textbook says, "and in some instances self-impregnation seems to occur. Parasitic plants lose many organs but never the blossoms, which are often of wondrous beauty, as for instance, the orchids." And great stress is laid on alimentation . . . and there are always rubber rats.

But you soon forget the dogs — perhaps first when you happen to glance at the crowds in front of pet-store windows. I have seen them there as late as three-thirty in the morning, peering compulsively at a cat stretched out asleep or a canary with its head tucked under its wing. Or the crowds at the windows of railroad and steamship companies and travel agencies, which sell passage to — anywhere else. Most of all, the windows I have passed twice a day for two years, never without seeing a crowd pressed against them. This week they will be full of paraphernalia for games to be played on lawns, idiotic, futile games — but the citizen's eye lightens and for a moment life breaks free. Next week the windows will be packed with salt-sea objects, all the absurd vestments and gadgets of yachtsmen, fishermen, swimmers, sunbathers — and all day long the citizens pause to hear the sound of water, taste spray on the lips, and see a wide and empty place. It is a drop of digitalis to steady the dragging heart, a grain of barbital to soothe the tortured nerves — for to-day. And to-morrow the windows will have camp axes in them, pocket compasses, sleeping bags, canoe paddles, fowling pieces, and a hundred other things to allay frustration and help the thinly held sac of living senses survive another day.

New York's most dependable wish-fulfillment for males, a friend of mine called those windows. If they were only that there would be nothing ominous in them. But what one reads in those faces pressed to glass is not a mere phantasy gratified by a moment's peering — it is something fixed and terrible. There is here discharged an energy, a libido, a love, that has been displaced. Life has been dammed off from its function, and it must dig such frustrate channels to flow in. . . . Shop windows are but one item of an immense symptomatology. At every hand one encounters the same deflection and conversion of life's essential energies from true function to substitutes which are most terrible in that they are accepted with delight. Theology tells us that sin sunk to acceptance is depravity, and psychiatry tells us that even a psychosis is an adaptation, a way of staying alive, and four million people are adapted to living with the aorta tied off. . . . But I no longer have to live under that ligature — I'm moving away.

They live, the New Yorkers, in the most splendid respirator, the most praiseworthy glassed-in, air-conditioned, violet-ray-irradiated sickroom. They have been magnificently bred, they have powerful haunches and straight forelegs and jaws evolved for gripping and teeth stronger and sharper and whiter than their ancestors, who used theirs, ever had. And they lope across the greasy grass of Central Park in a counterfeit delight that from a furlong off looks like the real thing, and they hurl themselves at a rubber rat and worry it and shake it as if they were killing a real rat. Use without function. They like it — but I don't. I'm getting out.

I've heard all the assurances, these last few weeks, and I admit them all. But isn't it a beautiful, a spectacular city, and isn't the skyline breath-taking? Why, yes, here and there, though the Grand Teton is still more so and this town's beauty would go better if it didn't smell so bad. But aren't there gorgeous colors at sunset and in winter dusk, and don't you love it when the lights come on? Yes, lovely colors when you can contrive to see them, and if you have forgotten what the desert looks like, if you can remember no countryside and no other skies, if you are willing to put up with milk for blood and ginger ale for water. And the orchids specialize in blossoms. But aren't the signs above Broadway like fairyland? They would be still better if I didn't know how to read. But where else will you find so many really excellent restaurants, from a corner sea-food bar to the Chambord, from Childs to anything you will? Yes, excellent food, and yes, I like to eat it, though preferably in my own house and not to the point of perversity, and isn't this stress on oral gratifications a trifle alarming, and do you remember how some parasites become just an alimentary canal? But the marvelous police force and the fire protection and the street cleaning and all the services of government — the theaters, the concerts, the libraries, the museums, the hospitals, the free helps and free shows and all the aids in time of trouble — where else does government give so much, where can one get so much amusement so expert and, if necessary, so cheap — where else are so many graces and diversions available to everyone? Yes, boys, they've built a fine ward for you: you've heard the stories about the lifers who are afraid to leave their cells. It is an opulent life here for those who can afford to pay for it, and surprisingly helpful to those who can't afford to pay, and the attendants or keepers are the most expert in the world, and the shows and assistances the most numerous. And you like it that way, boys, it has come to seem to you more desirable, more natural even, than the way life runs of its own momentum in its own ducts. You like it, and that is why your splendid dogs no longer seem pitiful to me — they can't when I see you chewing your own rubber rats. When you have come to mistake rubber for living fur, sawdust for blood, celluloid for bone — I know the word for it. And no thanks.

So long, boys, I'll be seeing you. I really will, after I've gone, for it is easier to travel five hours on the New Haven than twenty minutes on the subway or in a taxi. I saw you oftener before I came here, as the saying is, to live, than I did afterward. One doesn't see one's friends in New York. One only means to.

So long, Archie. We did have dinner once. That was sixteen months ago, and a good dinner too, as the local ritual and small talk require, and we phoned each other now and then, saying we'd do it again, and meaning to, but we never did. The grapevine says you're moving away too, and that has more sense in it than most things the literary sections print. So long, Lee, Elmer, Gene. We did meet occasionally, we did sit for a few minutes talking together, at long intervals, there was some sense of liking and mutual respect continuing across the city blocks that are really few, when you count them, but add up to more than we contrived to bridge. So long, Jim, George, Ernest, Howard, Simeon. Send me a postcard of the Empire State, say, or the grass in Central Park, or the Reservoir that people are said to walk round for nature's or sweet hygiene's sake. I'll send you one — of the Frog Pond. I'm getting out. I'm going back to America, to civilization. Civilization is a place where a man can, and does, sit sometimes talking with his friends.

And you may bury my rubber rat. No, you can't bury it for there is no ground to dig a grave in: incinerate it, or run it through one of those gadgets that make a pulp of everything but tin cans. I had my rubber rat: I came here to write about other men's books, and that gives the measure of this maniac town. In this air it seems sensible, it has the town's logic — and it is quite functional as any dog stretching his legs on a treadmill in a steam-heated room. I'm going away: I'm going to write my own books, and let someone here write about them.

So long, boys; good-by, proud towers. It's a swell place to visit. Especially the Museum of Natural History, which has those fine, white, spiral tusks of the extinct mammoth, those tapeworms with structures for grappling and adhesion.

Distempers of the Press

~~~~~~

TOWARD the end of 1936 American journalism offered the bystander several instructive exercises. Two were especially edifying, and of these the more woeful was the ordeal by dilemma forced on the liberal weeklies by an unpleasantness at the University of Wisconsin. A low-comedy mind bent on pinching idealism in sensitive places could hardly have invented a more painful situation than the one which the regents of that University provided. It was the mirror image of a situation that has caused much fever in the past, and one knew from the beginning that, no matter how it ended, idealism must come out with a tail feather or two missing.

Like the liberal editors, the Easy Chair does not know whether or not Mr. Frank is incompetent at his job, as the regents assert. When a similar assertion has been made about the supposed victims of other college tyrannies, idealism has always answered that professional competence is irrelevant to the issue of academic freedom. But this was a mirror image and now the accusation came from the children of light, from the side of progressive thought and what the *Nation* calls "a truly liberal and democratic party." It was accompanied by the usual secrecy, with the usual explanation that those who moved in secret were benevolently protecting the accused from publicity. The other side retorted, as usual, that the regents' charges against Mr. Frank were a mere smoke-screen, that the real reason for his dismissal was the fact that he held political and economic ideas offensive to those in power. Sticking closely to type, the victim's oppressors then alleged that the political issue had been raised to divert attention from his incompetence and to bring to his support the powerful sentiment which demands freedom of thought for educators, a principle which, we would please understand, was not involved in any way. And so on. The bystander was privileged to observe the familiar routine of charges and countercharges, of red herrings and white (or black) banners, of student demonstrations and polls conducted by inquiring reporters, of attacks on the probity and disinterestedness of everyone involved, especially the newspapers, of the propagation of rumor as fact and the repudiation of alleged fact as rumor. Only this time the victim smelled of reaction (although, alas, some years back our editors certified him as a progressive) and the villain had always up to now been cast in the hero's role.

It was all most uncomfortable — and most salutary. Whether or not the La Follette machine has tried to influence the conduct of a great university, our editors have been forced to face the possibility that such pressure might be applied by "a truly liberal and democratic party." That is an instructive and even hygienic experience, and a still healthier realization has been forced on them. The *New Republic* has been driven to a disquieting admission "that absolutely clear cases [of the violation of academic freedom] almost never arise, that universities have duties to their students and the public other than maintaining freedom of expression, and that decisions must rest on the careful weighing of a number of factors." It would be ungenerous to inquire whether Yale, for instance, has other duties to its students and the public, and whether other factors should be weighed in, say, the case of Jerome Davis. But let us remember the *New Republic's* decree, for with it the mother-of-pearl simplicity of idealistic journalism has been grievously tarnished with contingency and relativity. It is now established that a number of forces and a number of issues may conceivably be present in the kind of case that has hitherto been treated as single, simple, and crying unto God. The sky grows dark and strange and liberalism gets thrown for a ten-yard loss, but a very welcome realism has entered the discussion.

But that is only a ten-yard loss and in midfield at that, whereas in the *Nation* reaction intercepts a pass and scores a touchdown. Mr. Villard does indeed stand by his belief, declaring that if political pressure has been brought to bear on the university by the forces of enlightenment, then the forces of enlightenment must be denounced, trampled down, and plowed under. His editors, however, will stand for no such frivolity in time of crisis and militantly set Mr. Villard right. Mr. Ward refutes the charges of political pressure by converting them to the service of the other side (in the Martyr's Gambit this pawn is refused), and both Mr. Ward and the unsigned editorial end with the staggering conclusion that the only issue of any consequence is whether Mr. Frank is competent for his job. Please observe, it is not an organ of social fascism that decides, "If the regents wish at this date to correct an original error, that is their privilege."

The distant tinkling that you hear is the collapse of the platform on which idealism has been accustomed to take its heroic stand. Original errors in the employment of educators may now be corrected without reference to the political ideas of those educators, and the governing bodies of universities are privileged to govern in accordance with their own best judgment. Even a political radical may be discharged because he is a poor scholar or an ineffective teacher. A professor who would have been fired for incompetence long ago if his employers had not been reluctant to provoke the publicity which sentimental journalism has been happy to provide may now be fired for incompetence even if he is a Marxian — and the *Nation* will abide by the judgment of the regents.

Or rather, it won't. This curtailment of the intuition of journalism will last no longer than the present embarrassment at Wisconsin. To the liberal editors, the freedom of college teachers is exactly like other liberties: Something used to keep the opposing team perpetually offside. Can you recall an occasion when the *New Republic* protested against a Senate committee's seizing the mail or telegrams of an electric power company without process of law? No; and see what happens when the committee gets round to the mail of a labor union. Six months from now some dreadful bore who voted for Landon and never had an unorthodox economic idea till his job was imperiled will finally use up the margin of tolerance and forbearance that has kept him on the faculty of Princeton or Iowa. He will then discover overnight that he dislikes Kuhn, Loeb & Company, and our organs of pure thought will go crusading once more for single, simple, unalloyed justice. But meanwhile the Wisconsin case has been valuable for the colleges. It has dramatized the possibility that outside pressure may come from other directions than the right and on behalf of other interests than financial ones — and that may help in the unending defense of the charter. And it has illuminated the important fact that, in these cases, the issue is never single and simple and the administration seldom so subversive as the pleadings on behalf of the victim make out. Illumination should now move on to facts much more cynical. There are ways of bringing pressure to bear on the colleges and there are forces which sometimes try to influence opinion in them. But these forces are seldom so crude as to discharge a man, and in fact work so suavely that the best tentative assumption is that a man who has actually been discharged either is incompetent or else has made himself personally intolerable to his colleagues. The occasional person whose economic or political notions offend the administration is handled in ways that avoid discharge. But it cannot be too emphatically asserted that interference with economic opinion is far less common than cases in which it is alleged. Many college professors hold and freely teach heterodox opinions about economics, finance, and politics, though of course it is a conservative profession as a whole. More common and more powerful than political dictation is religious and moral dictation, and while we are naming the forces of unrighteousness, let us remember that professional jealousy is the commonest of all. But you do not hear about these in the believing press.

The other object lesson in journalism has a greater social importance. It is hard to be solemn about a superb joke, but someone must point out that the most distinguished public service of American journalism in 1936 was performed by Mr. Wolcott Gibbs and the editors of the *New Yorker* with their burlesque of *Time*. One read it with tears of ecstasy rolling down one's cheeks; but underneath that mirth was a realization that a classic tradition of American literature was being invoked on behalf of the decencies of democracy.

On its merits, *Time* has made itself indispensable. Everyone reads it, everyone relies on it for part of his information about the modern scene, everyone derives instruction and amusement from it. Its coverage is amazing, its accuracy good, its editorializing stimulating and frequently fair. Its weekly reviews have valuably served science, the arts, and the learned professions. If its flip style soon grew banal, at least it has shown that freshness in the writing of news is possible, a lesson which journalism needed. If it has frequently been brash, it has also frequently been courageous, treating subjects tabooed by many newspapers and sometimes risking offense to its public in the interest of truth. All of these elements have been present in the formula of its startling success. But also present in that formula have been less lovely elements. No one may say how great a part they played in that success, but anyone can see that they are dangerous.

A necessary implication of democracy is that it must permit the utilization of its own mechanisms for attacks on itself. Thus the United States must permit the organization and propaganda of Nazi, Communist, and Fascist groups, and must allow them, under the protection it guarantees thought and expression, to agitate for forms of government which repudiate freedom of thought and expression. Similarly freedom of the press, the public service performed by newspapers, and the necessity for complete objectivity in getting and presenting news serve to protect the sensational press in abusing the sanctions these principles imply. And part of *Time's* successful formula has been a willingness to abuse those sanctions in ways against which no defense can be made. We should all be humble about this, for we have all enjoyed the appeal to our own particular pleasures and prejudices, and such methods could not prosper unless we responded to them. But we should realize that such methods are a corruption of democracy and a debauch of public decency.

Objectivity? *Time* has shown that it is possible to be objective by presenting all the facts while coloring them on behalf of any emotion whatever with the droll epithets you apply to the participants in them. It is a suave and bombproof objectivity, for there can be no appeal, by protest or rebuttal, to an adjective. But the apparent jocosity of the presentation has done the work, pointing the story in the direction of any prejudice or any whim of its writer, or in the direction of the greatest box-office appeal. Objectivity can thus become a function of circulation, and public service may be performed on behalf of the most ambiguous caprice.

But more important, as well as more subtle and indefensible, is the power *Time* shares with any yellow newspaper, to violate the privacy of individuals. This power springs from the interest of the public in getting all the news there is and having it written as it is. The yellow press invariably defends its corruption of democracy by appealing to that principle, by alleging that it is serving the public interest when it is really pandering to public curiosity and public cruelty. In fact, the yellow press frequently serves the public by publishing mere rumor only distantly related to the news, irresponsible allegation and gossip, innocent-appearing juxtapositions that say nothing but imply much, and even maliciously generated but profitable inventions. Against this protected activity the individual is absolutely defenseless. His helplessness in the hands of powerful news organizations is one of the greatest indecencies of modern life, and one of the greatest perils. Any newspaper may, inadvertently or deliberately, ruin the life of any individual who happens to have the remotest connection with any news story, or who may, even, merely happen to have some eccentricity, deformity, or momentarily interesting attribute that can be given box-office value.

And he has no redress. A paper may damage him irreparably without even misrepresenting him — for no reason except that it makes circulation by holding him up to the public gaze. If it does misrepresent him it is quite willing to run his letter of protest — after the damage has been done beyond recall and has gone out over the wire services. Or he may sue. Even if he can afford the long appeal to the courts he will probably lose in the end, for in America libel is almost impossible to prove — and he is certain to bring down on himself more publicity of the same kind, this time with no holds barred and the rest of the guild chiming in, once more motivated by an affecting solicitude for the public good. It is even rumored that the most public-spirited yellow sheets have slush funds with which to compromise the suits they may invite through too great earnestness in the service of their readers. And in the end, writing to the paper, being paid out of a slush fund, or even winning damages, the individual will have an enduring public notoriety and a permanently blasted reputation.

Time has not hesitated to condemn these practices of its competitors, denouncing the familiar formula, "Mr. Smith denies that he spent last night in a downtown hotel with a chorus girl," Mr. Smith having issued the denial from a hospital bed where he has spent the last month with a broken leg. Yet a part of *Time's* success has come from the skill with which it pursues personalities into the area where news and curiosity meet — and over the line into the domain of sheer curiosity. It has developed great power and prestige, and part of them has come from its ability to protect with the sanctions of the free press the tangential ridicule and even contempt it can direct on individuals who are absolutely without defense or appeal. Something of the arrogance that this power has produced may be seen from *Time's* covert boast that it drove Edward VIII from the throne. Well, the press always has great power, and the only security the public has is a sense of responsibility in those who own and operate the press.

That sense of responsibility was recommended to the owners and editors of *Time* in the only effective way when the *New Yorker* used *Time's* own methods to direct an uproarious and highly unscrupulous burlesque at them. The *New Yorker* has shown them that they too may come within the scope of those methods. The lesson will probably not go deep nor last long after the first shock of lese majesty has passed. But the nation-wide yell of delight that greeted the burlesque may point a more durable lesson. The virtue of a successful parody is that the thing parodied is never again, in the mind of the reading public, quite the same. Everyone who read this parody will have echoes of it ringing in his mind when hereafter he sees *Time* doing one of its jobs. The sheet has been magnificently laughed at, and in a democracy ridicule is more effective than censorship.

The Liberation of Spring City

~~~~~~

THE DATE of its beginning cannot be determined. Social movements, like forest fires, burn deep below the surface of old leaves and pine needles and sometimes spread across an entire nation before the first smoke shows and the right breeze brings them to the upper air. It is enough that a time comes when the people, the leadership, the cause, and the opportunity come into the right conjunction in the summer of 1937. No doubt some will decide that the social upheavals of that momentous summer had some correlation with those other convulsions that passed across the surface of the sun. But others will take the surer ground that not astronomers but mythologists can best explain what happened. This, they will say, was the year when the myth sought release in flesh, and from woods and templed hills the Americans rose answering. This was the year of the apotheosis of Mr. Henry Jones.

In May, George Johnson (in common with many millions) had never heard of Henry Jones. But the tale tells how, that night, the queue at the box office of a midtown theater moved sluggishly till George Johnson was about twentieth from the window. At that moment a woman bosomed like a Greek goddess and thewed like a mother in a Norse saga swept up the lobby to the window and thrust a mighty shoulder between it and the man who was buying tickets. George Johnson saw the expression on her face and decided that it was what Victorian novelists meant by "bridling": women bridled when they performed acts of safe and conspicuous public injustice. He sighed and came near retching; such moments always made his soul sick with awareness of the futility of human life but the man who was sixth from the window stepped out of line, took from the woman's hand the tickets she had bought, handed them to the man she had displaced, and then, grabbing her by the hair, dragged her out of the lobby to the sidewalk. George Johnson heard him say courteously, "My name is Henry Jones," and heard another sound on which historians will expend much meditation and analysis. The queue was cheering. With those cheers the fire may have begun to rise from the pine needles to the underbrush.

On a Sunday afternoon in July George Johnson was driving down a curving, high-crowned country road when he had to stop in a line that was waiting for a freight train to pass. The line lengthened behind him and a horn began to blow — continuously, someone resting an elbow on the button. Looking round, George Johnson saw a bright-green car full of merrymakers, driven by a man in shirtsleeves and eyeshade who was smoking a cigar and laughing loudly at such moments as he was not swearing at the cars ahead. The line began to move and, horn still blowing, the green car shot by at the left, weaving in and out, taking the blind curves blind, grazing fenders, giving off profanity and jokes. George Johnson shuddered and when, a few miles farther on, he saw the green car at a filling station, he was tempted to draw up and wait till it had gone on. Sure enough, it came up behind him doing at least eighty-five, cut round him and the car ahead, held its place for a moment, cut round the next car, wove in, and cut to the left once more. A car coming down the other lane swerved off the road, two other cars stopped, the green car flashed through a diminishing slot, and the horn blew.

But the scene was not played out. The second car ahead accelerated and, weaving, caught the green car square in the middle and bowled it off the road. My oldest dream comes true, George Johnson thought, awed, and he too pulled off the road and went forward to shake a hero's hand. The hero, climbing out of the wreckage, said, "My name is Henry Jones. Perhaps you will help me. Half-drowning, I think." George Johnson had not noticed that there was a pond but, helping Henry Jones hold the driver of the green car under its surface, he knew with a mystical certainty that there would always be ponds where Henry Jones could make use of them.

"Believers in a planned society can never have driven an automobile on Sunday afternoon," Henry Jones said. "He is unconscious now — let him go. I don't think we should kill them in the first stage. It will come to sacrificial murder and general massacre before we're done, but in revolution, as in great things, let us move slowly. You don't mind driving me to the next town?" Hope warmed his commonplace, unforgettable face, and his voice was a prayer. "Perhaps the insurance company will try to cancel my policy. Or maybe the garage will want to charge me fifteen dollars for towing me."

But what happened in the next town was that a woman driving a jalopy came up a one-way street against the traffic, swung in a circle before a "No U turn" sign, screamed, stopped square across the intersection, glared, and began to berate the traffic cop. Henry Jones's eye gleamed. "In Utopia," he said, "stout, middle-aged women with nose glasses will not drive cars."

He went up to the car and George Johnson could not hear what he said but he knew, as in a dream, that one life had been blasted forever and society had been enormously improved.

The day had a lovelier sunlight and Henry Jones was coming back through it, but he stopped to drop a penny in a slot machine. A moment later, when he was kicking it off its pillar, George Johnson saw that he was shod with steel.

"The hour has struck and the heart of man is ready! Let the dream fulfill itself," Henry Jones said when they were seated in a restaurant and had ordered sandwiches and beer. "First we will form locals, nuclei round which volunteers may rally. In the first stage we will deal with officials, with those in places of authority, with public servants, with those who make and those who break regulations, with corporations and stores and service agencies and civic bodies and representatives of government. When they have been shattered we will move on to those who alarm and scold and castigate and interpret the public, with the intellectuals, the parsons, the columnists, the professors. By then the dream will be magnificently on the march and we can turn to . . . Excuse me, is your beer arctic? Has it been iced?"

Henry Jones flung his beer into the waiter's face. At that moment George Johnson found that the filling of his sandwich was canned chicken. A buoyant energy he had never felt before flowed along his nerves. Plate and sandwich splashed against the wall, and when the girl at the desk shortchanged him George Johnson shoved the cash register through the glass walls of her coop. There was song in his soul and a mighty purpose in his heart. . . . Thus George Johnson met Henry Jones and life was changed for him forever.

And so the dream woke all over America that summer. At night Spring City would be only a drowsy and despairing town, sunk with the weight of man's docility. Then, with the morning, men would find the breeze bringing some fragrance from the hills, and at once there would be a committee of public decency, complete with staff, intelligence service, specialists, and corps of demolition. By evening all would be quiet except where a derailed trolley car burned in the street or glass tinkled falling from the window of a gutted store. When night fell the very taxi drivers were saying "Sir."

As St. Christopher, Henry Jones had much to do with taxi drivers and with motorists in general. Incessantly moving from town to town, he liked to travel by automobile. "You have only to act on your dream," he would tell the farmer in whose meadow some itinerants had picnicked. "Here is their litter and here is their car — yonder your pigpen. A bucket of swill in the back seat for a pile of cans and paper napkins. They stripped your cherry trees? Their spare tire would be useful to your children, and a headlight would make a pretty souvenir. A cigarette started that blaze in the west pasture? Try dropping a cigarette on the upholstery or, for a prettier blaze, in the gas tank." Fires marked his passing. He dispatched loud-mouthed traffic cops to them, he lighted them under cars doing twenty miles an hour on arterial highways, he made them the hazards of impromptu steeplechases for ten-ton trucks found traveling by back roads. To the St. Christopher phase must also be attributed a mysterious malady among subway guards, and the bodies of hostesses heaved from parlor cars, busses, and airplanes, presumably slaughtered for introducing people who did not want to meet but preferred to sit alone and think great thoughts. Yet this was but an incidental phase, an interlude to the hero's travels, a pause in the greater business of asphyxiating the entrance clerks of hospitals who made the expectant mother wait while her husband filled out a blank and wrote a check. Motorists were small game while there were laundries which starched the collars of his soft shirts and bank cashiers who would not be convinced of his identity.

Henry Jones was the soul's need finding its answer. In Spring City a housewife bent on buying lamb chops and broccoli would discover that the chain store had sold her to-day's combination special of six cakes of soap, two rolls of toilet paper, a box of oat nifties, and two and a half pounds of floor cleanser. A calm and commonplace man at her elbow would say, "My name is Henry Jones. I am everyman and I come from everywhere. What does your heart whisper about the combination special?" Desire the more vertiginous because she suddenly knew it could be gratified would run along her nerves, and Henry Jones would say, "You have only to act on your dream." At ten feet, hurling the combination special without a windup, she never missed the pyramid of eggs.

That moment always marked the formation of the Women's Auxiliary in Spring City. Dream-bound, the woman would whisper, "The Duchess!" Henry Jones would say, "In Schmidt's Department Store?" and when she nodded, "There is always Schmidt's and always Schmidt's has a Duchess. Let us go." So presently on the fifth floor of Schmidt's the woman — her name was Carrie Stone — would be waiting while a goddess in henna and sun tan polished her scarlet fingernails and finished the saga of love and deception she was sharing with a wood nymph in blondine. After a long time the Duchess would come cloud-borne, tapering hand on swaying hip, lip curled, nostril retracted, and Carrie Stone would say, "I want a simple house dress for about eight dollars." Time flapped loosely in a void till at last the Duchess would come back again bearing a creation which, long experience told Carrie Stone, was marked thirty-eight-ninety-five. The bloody work would soon be finished and Carrie Stone would turn away murmuring, "The milkman who leaves the cream in the sun, the hairdresser who knows how I ought to do my hair — but first there is a girl here in the corset department . . ."

Here the tale divides. One congeries is the battle saga and tells the story of a nation's deeds. Scholars still debate it, some saying that every lamppost with a corpse dangling from it was a historical scaffold whereon the folk hanged an oppressor when they rose at last, others declaring that the lamppost is a symbol only and that the chants which the risen people sang were enough of themselves. We need not argue with the scholars. It is enough that the folk found a continent adequately equipped with telephone poles and lampposts and the beams of elevated structures and other crossarms that would support weight at a rope's end, and came to understand how they might be made to serve the dignity of the human spirit. Ballad lovers will find many cycles in this saga: the Hanging of the Credit Manager, the Death of the Information Clerk, the Mangled Floor Walker, the Telephone Operator Who Went Too Far, the Fatal Ticket or the Policeman's Dance Racket, the Poppy Salesman or Death by Trampling. Cycles of party givers and party guests, of inspectors, of show-offs, of custodians of morality, of fountain pens that leak, of questionnaires, of garments shrunk at the dry cleaner's. Violent and triumphant ballads, dripping with blood, resonant with vindication, the poetry of a people's soul.

The other congeries is the culture saga, where the gigantic figure of Henry Jones rises against the blood-red sky. A figure of midnight and chain lightning, a figure of granite that cannot be moved aside, of mist that cannot be shut out, of fire running onward that can be neither halted nor quenched. He is with you in your most need. There are always bricks for those who will throw them, he says, and it is craven not to throw them when some little tyrant relies on your embarrassment to keep you meek. A dream denied poisons the soul, he says, and just why should you permit a clerk or a traffic cop or the gas company's collector to bawl you out? You have only to reach for a crowbar or a shotgun, he says, and in the name of enfranchised humanity women will cease giggling in the theater and there will be no more gawkers when a truck driver all but runs you down; in fact, there will be no more truck drivers. My name is Henry Jones, he says, and yours is too, and for too long you have let shame and self-consciousness keep you humble when strident folk and the agents of corporations and the officials of government usurped your rights. You have only to act on your dream, he says — you have only to let the dream go free when the enemy confronts you, and you will find a piece of paving stone in your hand, of the right size for throwing.

Thus it was that, one day late in the fall of 1937, a citizen entered the post office of Spring City and went up to the window. He cleared his throat and said diffidently, "I am Elmer Smith and I live at the corner of Murchison Place. When I got home I found that you had given me two-cent stamps when I asked for threes and that you had shortchanged me twenty-one cents. Moreover, though the weekly magazine to which I subscribe reaches Spring City on Thursday, the carrier leaves it in a lock box till he gets a lighter load, which is never before Monday and is more frequently Wednesday or next Thursday."

The clerk flushed red and his wattles quivered. The bystanders held their breath. But quite suddenly anger left that postal clerk's face. "Ah, yes, Mr. Smith," he said. "Please understand me, Mr. Smith, when I say that in a fallible world there must sometimes be mistakes. Here, Mr. Smith, are your three-cent stamps, and here are your twenty-one cents, and I am sorrier than I can tell. Moreover, Mr. Smith," he said, speaking in an all but obsolete idiom, "hereafter you will get your magazine on the first Thursday, and I think, Mr. Smith, — in fact I am sure, — that there will now be another carrier for Murchison Place."

Henry Jones smiled happily in his mists above the world, and the Americans were at last a free people.

The Terror

"AUGUST," the Easy Chair's favorite commonplace book says, "August, the eighth month; named after Augustus; formerly Sextilis, the sixth month. This is the month when you may have a good time if you can have a good time." The misgiving coiled inside that rhetoric can be fully appreciated, probably, only by the correspondents of Mr. Wilson Follett and by the Easy Chair's chief, the editor of *Harper's Magazine*, who annually decrees that in August his subscribers may read fiction if they can read fiction. August, the eighth month, named after a dictator. Until the confusion caused by the Uprising of August, 1939, it was known as the month when the Americans went on vacation. It was a time of adjournment and postponement, of the relaxed mind, of undutiful pleasure. And the newspapers used to call it the silly season.

The Americans used to take vacations in August whether or not they could afford to. You used to see them running about tennis courts, striding down golf courses, eating peanuts in bleachers, sprawling on beaches, halting for breath on mountain trails, propelling various kinds of boats. You found them drinking beer under electric fans, picnicking along streams, or lunching at sidewalk tables, sliding down roller coasters, kissing their girls in the tunnels of the Old Mill. August was the month when the blue-plate special consisted of cold cuts and when road commissioners blocked off the main highway so that they could detour millions of pleasure cars through the swamp.

It used to be the month for which summer clothes were designed. Large women wore play suits and tall women wore shorts and both were convinced, because the garments came only halfway down their thighs, that they dressed more intelligently than men. (But if trousers are a hot garment, few men wear corsets under them.) Men took off their neckties, rolled up their sleeves, and disregarded waistlines it would have been seemlier to keep concealed. (And, on bathing beaches, abstained from the use of depilatories.) In this month a mass delusion of both sexes reached maximum: that leathery skin is attractive. And millions of skins oiled for the tanning process had also to be treated with poison-ivy lotions.

All this was before the Uprising.

Walter Pitkin, Vilfredo Pareto, Thurman Arnold, Sigmund Freud, and other thinkers have shown that irrational sentiments are necessary to the health of individuals and of society. It follows that any attack on the sacred rituals of the American vacation is against the public interest, and the Easy Chair finds disturbing Mr. Ben Ames Williams's recent, probably Moscow-inspired jeers at the superstitions of fishermen. Catching fish, Mr. Williams said, is simpler and easier than anglers believe; most of the theories and practices associated with it are irrational; much of the expensive tackle believed to be indispensable is really useless; if you want to catch fish go where they are and offer them what they want, without regard to precedent or ceremony. The Easy Chair gave up the art years ago and has since gratified its ego in other ways than in endeavoring to outwit and subdue a pound and a half of fish. There were of course the minnows and suckers and mud carp of boyhood and, up to the age of seventeen or thereabout, an occasional mountain trout taken in the orthodox way with a fly (wet) on the headwaters of the Ogden River. And also there was, now and then, a rattlefin — which is why the Easy Chair brings fishing into this August calm. For word comes that, like the beaver, the rattlefin is on the increase again, that it has begun to come down out of the back country and once more lurks at the river crossings, and if that is true, then all who have had experience with it must put away their private interests for the public good. The rattlefin has a direct bearing on the crisis of August, 1939, and those who are not with us are against us.

Few men are left alive who have seen the rattlefin (*Crotalmo atrox*) and fewer still who have taken it. Once it was so plentiful in the Western rivers that the outriders of emigrant trains had to gallop ahead to the fords and beat the water with long whips before the wagons could cross in safety — and the history of the West records many tragedies that this technique did not prevent. When rain filled the buffalo wallows the monsters' flight toward them made the prairie air vibrate, and though Indian and white hunters killed their millions, the extinction of the buffalo was really due to the rattlefin. When travelers saw the partially devoured carcass of a grizzly bear floating down the Platte, the Musselshell, or the Yellowstone they knew that another of nature's most savage battles had ended in the usual way. But the advancing frontier dealt courageously with its greatest peril and, like the grizzly and the buffalo, the rattlefin lost out. It withdrew to the most inaccessible fastnesses of the Rocky Mountains and pursuing it became not a social process but a sport. Its habitat could be reached only by pack train; only the most skillful and persistent hunters could locate its hiding places. One packed into the wilderness and then, some night, was waked by one's horses breaking their hobbles and stampeding: they had caught the scent and ancestral terrors were bubbling in their blood. Or the night quivered with the characteristic, unmistakable scream as a rattlefin broke from its pool when a great owl had swooped too low, and the rattling of its dorsal fin halted one's pulse, and one heard a hissing as of gigantic air-brakes when the terrible fangs went home. The next morning one got out the double-bitted axes, the rods reinforced with rawhide, the long gaffs; one buckled on hip boots of flexible stovepipe and, remembering the pioneers, took up the chase. . . . If the rattlefin is truly increasing, the old pioneer spirit must be invoked again.

These words were written at the end of May, 1939, partly in the calm of Cambridge, Massachusetts, partly in the greater calm of the Harvard Club of New York. Ten weeks later the Uprising came. There was a scream by night and the hiss of escaping steam and a storming party of communists, who had been disguised as scoutmasters, seized the Watertown Arsenal, two miles up the Charles River, and marched out to take over the power houses, the water systems, the trolley lines, and the subways of Greater Boston. That was how Cambridge learned that the zero hour had come—and all over America similar bands, who had been disguised as Good Humor salesmen, were simultaneously striking at the nerve centers of our urban civilization. Wayfarers going homeward in the lonely hours saw battalions mustering beneath the hammer and sickle in Altoona and Alameda, in Houston and Hartford, in Madison and Macon, in Passaic and Peoria, in Topeka and Tulsa, in Yonkers and Youngstown. In every town arms had been concealed at a rallying point where a short-wave station had been set up, and the shock troops reported there, throwing off the innocent-appearing garments that had concealed the uniforms of the Spanish Loyalist army. (They had been imported under diplomatic privilege and stored in the Russian building at the World of Tomorrow.) A switch had been thrown in an exclusive New York club and the long wait was over: the revolution was made.

Early reports got the name of that club wrong: the Easy Chair can now show that it was the Union League. International bankers had been meeting there, conspiring with the Third International to destroy private wealth. Many details of the conspiracy have been made public, the most saddening of them the fact that a hundred and fifty thousand soldiers trained in Spain were considered sufficient to control the United States. The nation has grown soft with time. It required at least that many Masons (or Catholics) to subdue us when there were only twenty-four States and hardly twenty-four million Americans. Ninety years ago the uprising of the slaves that horrified the Senate whenever a Southern orator hit his stride enlisted recruits by the half million. Even thirty-five years ago, in Theodore Roosevelt's time, it took three hundred thousand armed Japanese, disguised as truck gardeners, to capture the single State of California. The Army must have been chagrined when it heard that General George Van Horn Moseley was going to need it to quell the Uprising. Some generals on active duty, and more top sergeants, must have remembered an occasion not so long ago when a terrified Texas mayor wired for the Rangers to suppress a riot that was taking his town apart. Word came from headquarters that help was on the way, and the mayor sneaked down back alleys to meet the three-fifteen — from which a single Ranger got off. Dazed, the mayor asked if the commandant thought one man enough to restore tranquillity. "Why?" the Ranger asked. "You got more than one riot?" They must have remembered that at Army posts when they read the testimony before the Dies Committee.

The Easy Chair has got hold of some details of the conspiracy that the Dies Committee missed. Mr. William Allen White's name figured in the testimony, a suspicious man because he had approved certain acts of the Roosevelt Administration and because his ancestry is strewn with Obadiahs, Jerushas, and other Old Testament names. But the Committee did not learn that his newspaper, the *Emporia Gazette*, had long served the conspiracy; its headlines communicated secret information by cipher to other newspapers (there were a few) favorable to the New Deal. Worse, apparently safe papers were really manipulated by the conspiracy to screen danger spots and lull the citizenry asleep. Thus the *Herald-Tribune* was staffed by fellow travelers, and at zero hour the *Chicago Tribune* was to throw off its mask and reveal that for years it had been secretly edited by Mr. Oswald Garrison Villard. Carelessness had permitted the disclosure of Miss Shirley Temple's function in another program of revolt, and a new leader had to be found. Mr. Boris Karloff was finally passed over in favor of Miss Zasu Pitts. Long ago the colleges had been incorporated in the red network; without exception they were all making the revolution and conspiracy needed only to perform a few symbolic acts, such as transferring Professor Phelps's chair at Yale to Mr. Heywood Broun. But the secondary schools, which are much more important, remained unincorporated and presented a serious emergency situation. It was to be solved by organizing them under the control of Teachers College, where revolution of all kinds has been going on for years, and calling President Hutchins from Chicago to work in double harness with that other veteran revolutionist, Nicholas Murray Butler.

There is no space here for further details of the Terror that was precipitated in that red dawn while the nation slept. You know, however, that the Uprising was suppressed. Approved history books tell us that Providence looks after the Americans, and Providence had not only stationed a patriotic waiter at the Union League Club but, in an ecstasy of creative imagination, had provided General Moseley. The nation might sleep, fattened by seven years of communist pampering, but General Moseley did not sleep. He heard a hideous scream as the monster broke from its mountain pool, the buzz of its angry fin, the steampipe horror of its fangs going home. General Moseley buckled on his stovepipe leggings and got to work. He was also interested in the manufacture of patent medicines.

"In August," the commonplace book continues, "the iridescent loops of the sea serpent will be sighted off Provincetown; Sunday editors may obtain line cuts from the agencies. Moreover, it is the mating season of the whiffenpoof, which occurs but once in every hundred years, and next we have the goldangit emerging from the woods at twilight to fly backward over the cooling fields. Mickey, move the screen! For we're going to the Hamburg Show, and eggs with two yolks prophesying the winner in 1940 may be come upon in most henhouses. The stomach of a shark caught at Montauk Point contains three gold watches, the engine of a 1934 Chevrolet, two cans of tomato-juice cocktail, and a signed photograph of Bea Lillie. A German submarine rises to the surface in Lake Superior, and the cuckoo clock that has never ticked since that August afternoon forty-seven years ago when Uncle Frederick died bursts into song. The attendance at Billy Rose's Aquacade quadruples, eleven weeks after disappearing from Pasadena a footsore fox terrier turns up at its old home in Baltimore, and salmon making out to sea snarl peevishly at Ben Ames Williams."

A curious defect of the military mind was responsible for General Moseley's whiff of grape. The sound of marching feet which he heard in the August dawn came from a far more formidable army than the pitiful hundred and fifty thousand armed reds to whom he ascribed it. It was the Woodmen of the World mustering for their annual field day at Belair Park. It was the Young Democrats of Ward Twenty going to the boat that would take them down the bay to beer, speeches, baseball, and a clambake. It was the joint celebration of Protestant Sunday Schools, the Neighborhood Bird Watchers, the F:2 Camera Club, the Model Plane Makers, the Railroad Enthusiasts, the Bridle Path Society, the Oar and Paddle, and several hundred other organizations getting an early start on a fair day.

General Moseley's horrors could have interested them only if he had molded the Uprising in wax and charged a dime admission. One of the General's collaborators built a retreat for himself in the mountains of Kentucky (though the hoarded gold at Fort Knox might be expected to bring the conspirators to that vicinity on the run), just as in August, 1896, rich men were fortifying their estates against the armed hordes of William Jennings Bryan. But the public was not alarmed; it was thinking about sunburn and the cost of a new tire. The General's panic erupted on the front pages of the nation's press, which was so much velvet for the Dies Committee, but day by day it moved backward toward the classified ads. . . . This was the wrong season for conspiracy. The Americans bought gardening tools, studied road maps, decided that last year's bathing suit simply would not last through the summer, and tried to find money enough for another full day at the Fair. The conspirators had made a stupid blunder and any Sunday editor could have allayed the General's fears. The revolution will not be made in America during August: the bird watchers, the canoeists, and the softball players are too preoccupied, they are having too good a time. Intelligent conspirators will select a day when the national mood is more subversive. How about March 15th?

Meditation in Fading Sunlight

〜〜〜〜〜〜〜〜〜〜〜〜〜〜〜〜〜〜〜〜〜〜〜〜〜〜

THE WIND turned, coolness came into the air, and the light changed. There was the sound of surf and of children laughing as they ran and, more distantly, of a band playing — playing not some swung lamentation of the moment but "*Wein, Weib, und Gesang.*" People sat drinking and talking at tables in the shade and in the dulling sunlight. In a midsummer of drought and emptiness and the omens of war, one had happened without warning on a good time, and on the spectacle that becomes more poignant as one grows older, of people enjoying themselves. One sipped cool beer, watched a cloud begin to color with sunset, listened as much to the unhurried rustle of voices as to the faint music, and there was no pressure, no necessity, no Europe, no war. A boy came down the avenue between tables, selling papers, incongruous in this peace and, because habits are fixed, one bought the tallest headlines. But it wasn't the tall headlines that one saw; it was two inches of print under a single-column head: "Havelock Ellis Dead." So this moment of leisure filled with the drift of half a century, with the spate waters of thought, with the world's change and Havelock Ellis's part in change. Havelock Ellis dead! It was as though Mount Everest had died.

One thought: he did something, he got something changed, when he blotted the last page he signed his name on a difference that would last. And: he had a happy life, there was bravery and serenity in him, his mind was like the peace of remembering triumph long afterward, hopefulness and belief were in his breathing. And, looking round one at the tables where people chatted: no man or woman here would be just what he is if Ellis had not lived. Then, immediately: and there is no man or woman here who has not had to struggle with more than Ellis ever took into account.

One cannot undertake hopefully to determine what a great man has done. What he thinks it was is likely to be wrong and what is generally accepted about it is almost certain to be wrong. The title of Ellis's great work was a misnomer. He called it *Studies in the Psychology of Sex*, but it wasn't that. It was studies in the anthropology of sex, it was the world's first scientific encyclopedia of sexual information — and it was of course, incidentally to its purpose, the first charter of sexual inquiry and a vindication of the mind's decencies. He went out to determine what the facts were, the tabooed facts, the facts forbidden recognition by church and state and by resistances much stronger than either, the "real natural facts of sex apart from all would-be moralistic or sentimental notions." It is an astonishing thing that no such effort, on a useful scale, had ever been made in all the world's history before Ellis undertook it toward the beginning of the last decade of the nineteenth century. He carried it through to the end he had envisioned, opposed as savagely as any enemy of an established religion, attacked as unscrupulously as any enemy of an established government, vilified in a grotesque and obscene furor that was diagnostic of the conditions he wanted to clear up. And the book that embodied his findings is a great book, a monument in the advance of thought, of science, of (if the word may still be spoken with grave lips) civilization. It is great not only in what it revealed but in what it accomplished. A book that has altered the substance of things and produced a probably permanent effect on mankind.

But it is not a psychology of sex. Ellis's illimitable energy was expended almost altogether in determining facts of behavior and had little concern with relating them to motive or necessity. He had few theorems, few hypotheses, and such as he had were superficial and optimistic and tended to be mystical. Follow him only a little way beyond what the Ubangi do and what the church fathers said and how such people or such others behave on such occasions — and you get either into an anarchy abhorrent to science where no law operates, not even probability, or into a dewy vision colored with the century's most illusory hope, where things happen as if by the flowers' will and where a freer, finer, godlike race is on its way to mastery. His social achievement was to force recognition on a willfully reluctant world, and his scientific achievement was to describe the previously unstated. It remained for others to open up the psychology of sex, to dig beneath description to causes, to reveal the dynamism in the facts that were static for Ellis. There is a brave serenity in Sigmund Freud's mind too, but in the knowledge that supports it you do not find the hopefulness that is inseparable from Ellis.

Furthermore, though the great work has had an undeniably immense effect on society, one cannot be sure just what that effect is. The past fifty years have seen changes in society's understanding of sex, its attitudes toward sex, and even its sexual practices. Yet those changes are almost unappraisable, since no one can be quite sure, for all their vividness, just what they consist of, nor quite sure, for all their explosiveness, just how far they have gone, nor quite sure, for all their extent, just whom they affect. It is equally impossible to appraise the part played in these revolutionary changes by any single force, such as Ellis's research, of the great composite that effected them. Foremost in time, exhaustive in scope, a work of genius, his book was a principal equation in the intellectual foci; it has influenced, directly and by the most innumerable and circuitous indirections, millions of people who never heard of it, who could not understand it, but who think and act and perhaps feel otherwise than they would have done if it had not been written. But there is no way of telling how great a part it plays in those altered thoughts and actions; no one can assign a value to that x.

A boy or girl of seventeen puts an end to the inexperience, the intolerable mystery, that has been torturing him. A frustrated husband or wife seeks outside of marriage a sexual fulfillment he has not found in it. An unmarried woman enters what is called a free union. A boy or a girl, a woman or a man, adopts the course that is called promiscuity. By chance opportunity arrives among friends or acquaintances, and a momentary attraction, a sudden impulse of passion, a heightening of affection or admiration is yielded to. How, in 1939, does the event differ from what it was in 1839?

It might be rash to decide that the event occurs any oftener in 1939. One has a skeptical suspicion that the amount of sexual intercourse has remained approximately constant since Adam's time, that since Adam the sum has been the practicable maximum. And even if the statistics have been stepped up, it would be unsafe to attribute the increase to the spread of intellectual enlightenment. It may be not that Havelock Ellis permits but that the gods no longer forbid; for more than his half-century the fires of hell have been burning out. It may be that not the gods but the half-gods have ceased to prohibit: the parents who for many reasons have less authority than they used to have, who are more bewildered, have learned to be less despotic, have come to hold their peace whereas they used to speak from the whirlwind. Or it may be merely that the perfection of machinery has reduced to Woolworth levels the cost of appliances which make sure that, as sin no longer has any wages, so experience shall no longer have any consequences.

Yet these doubts are unquestionably too extreme. There is more "freedom" than there used to be, at least among certain classes, notably the adolescents of the bourgeoisie. Unmarried women and frustrated wives may make their trial for sexual sanity with fewer hazards of prejudice and fewer social penalties than used to threaten it. The casual, impermanent, trivial kinds of sexual experience meet no such obstacles and reproof as they once did, and certainly, discussion, representation, literature, and all other inactive aspects of sex have a far wider license than they had fifty years ago. (This last may be, however, merely the periodic phenomenon of an overstrained world, like the world of Charles II or that of the Directory or the Regency, which seeks relief in the smaller sexual stimulants.) What has happened, then, is that attitudes have changed, and it would be folly to deny that, on the whole, the change has been beneficial. It is a gain that some people are now able to work toward what they conceive to be their private happiness without feeling a private sense of guilt, and a greater gain that society does not rob them of dignity and self-respect. (But the skeptical may wonder if, even here, something has not been lost. Puritans are sometimes sound psychologists and a pleasure is likely to be greater if you are to be damned for it.) In effect what has happened is that the individual's private affairs have achieved a great measure of privacy, and the enlightenment preached by Ellis and his followers has removed a vast bulk of irrelevance from everyone's efforts to work out his destiny.

Mankind, however, seems no nearer than it was to the inner peace and outward mastery that Ellis believed in. Calvary is no longer degraded by the irrelevant execution of two thieves; but for the generality of mankind the way of the flesh remains what, for the generality of mankind, it has always been, a way of the cross. The ultimate traveler from Mars who is to pass judgment on human affairs will note that much, and will be unemotionally aware of other reactions as well. For all free-doms are stern, and every person of mature years has friends for whom this one has been disastrous. It has destroyed many lives by imposing on them one further choice which they were not strong enough to survive. From Mars, Ellis and the move-ment in which he was so conspicuous must sometimes look like one further item in the paralysis of the social will. The strength of conventions, prejudices, and intolerance is that they protect the weak by making up their minds and deter-mining their behavior from without. Some men might have been better workmen or thinkers if they had not undertaken to decide their sexual conduct for themselves. A society might be better armed against disintegration if it could conserve the forces which enlightenment dissipates. It was the strength of the old-time religion, however false, that it simplified the duty of man. It was the strength of the old-time morality, however unenlightened, whatever lives it maimed, that it was taken for granted. Enlightenment has increased the complexity of indi-vidual choice. It has forced a primitive animal already over-burdened by his own civilization to live, as Freud says, that much more beyond his psychological means. Sexual enlighten-ment has not been Micawber's half-crown that makes all the difference, but it is clearly an unallocated farthing in the sum that has produced bankruptcy.

Precisely there one identifies Ellis's limitation. It was a lim-itation of his time that it did not recognize the limitations of its material, the limitations of the human race. One thinks of him (in fading afternoon) as a crusader riding eastward out of the Victorian sunset, a last champion of his century's hope. To learn, to know, to declare, to let the light and air in would be enough! The fetid mass of irrationalities which he uncovered would yield to reason; turn it over often enough in open air and the spores of fear and failure must be killed. What was wrong was not the nature of man, which must be sound by all the criteria that could be recognized, but man's ignorance and the institutions which his ignorance had enabled his fears and cruelties to build. But there was an older affirmation — that in much wisdom is much grief and he that increaseth knowledge increaseth sorrow.

As Ellis came downstage in triumph there entered quietly from an upper wing the unobtrusive figure of Dr. Freud. He has only a small place in Ellis's page: Ellis welcomed and praised him but seems either not to have fully understood or not to have been much interested in what he was about. But it was that unobtrusive figure who revealed the linkages in the facts which Ellis had so magnificently assembled and who began to make clear what was behind them. The world which Freud opened up was far more desperate than any Ellis had ventured into, and the race proved to be far more limited, far more beset by forces beyond its control. To let the light and the air heal as much as they could, to let knowledge arm reason to the uttermost, yes — but Freud uncovered bounds beyond which healing cannot go and reason has no force. The goal of the freedom in which Ellis believed was apocalyptic: freedom as power in itself, freedom as invincible. Freud's was a humbler, sterner, sadder freedom: freedom for man to grapple with reality liberated from unconscious forces within himself. Ellis's was a freedom of hope; Freud's of fortitude. Ellis's turned Prospero alone and unconquerable toward the stars. Freud's merely gave Prospero weapons which he might use against the Caliban with whom he must live forever on his seagirt isle. Freud revealed the irreducible, the immutable, the insoluble, which for Ellis had always been the insubstantial fabric of illusion — and with that revelation the nineteenth century ended in the psychology of sex, and the twentieth came in.

Nevertheless, it was a great man whose death was published among these tables in dulling light, among people who had never heard of him and cared nothing for his death, but had something they would not have had of dignity and knowledge if he had not lived. They knew more about themselves and a great man lived anonymously in the pattern of their thoughts. There was confetti underfoot and colored lights would begin playing when the sun went down — a carefree scene in which he meant nothing at all. But something of the moment's color and desire was his.

Paradox on Betelgeuse

~~~~~~~~~~~~~~~~~~~~~~~~~~~~~~~~~~~~~~

SEVERAL DAYS before the twenty-first of September the Easy Chair, oppressed by the thousand uncertainties that precede the writing of a long-thought-over novel, sat down and tried to write a scene that would be useful some months later. The scene dealt with a great windstorm and, like most scenes, utilized some memories from childhood. It went badly; all scenes do before you get started in earnest. So the Easy Chair swore and tore it up.

This was in a little New Hampshire town in the Connecticut Valley, from which we were scheduled to move to Cambridge, Massachusetts, on Wednesday the twenty-first. Rain had been falling for a week, and about the time that scene went into the wastebasket the papers said that a hurricane was approaching the Florida coast. On Wednesday morning we started south but learned that the rain had brought the rivers up over their banks and closed the roads. There was nothing to do but go back, reoccupy the summer place, unpack the car, and curse the weather, which was only being true to the year's average. We spent the afternoon inspecting the Connecticut, which was booming but had not reached flood stage, taking pictures of it in unfavorable light, and fretting about the crisis in Europe, which grew more desperate hour by hour.

It had stopped raining at about eleven but started again toward four in the afternoon. At five o'clock the rain became torrential and by six the wind was savage. It was exactly sixten when a shrill squealing got into that wind. The lights went out, the water system and the kitchen range were disabled with them, and we found that the telephone was dead. We were not alarmed, however: gales are common in New England and the only novelty about this one was that it was coming from the south. We decided that the disturbance must have been set up by the hurricane which had missed Florida, and kept busy lashing down doors and shutters, searching out candles, and enjoying the noise of the wind. From an upstairs window we could see down the hill road to the village for the first time since we had moved into the place; but that seemed to mean only that a few trees had lost some branches and, besides, it was too dark to see much. The most startling moment was the discovery that a forty-foot creek was flowing across the rear lawn, but that was obviously run-off from the already saturated hills, and the house was too high for it to reach. Clearly this was a big storm, but at our place there was no reason to suspect that it was anything more, no hint of the death and agony to the southward and the destruction everywhere around us. I remarked to my young son that he had seen a sixty-mile gale. What he had seen was something more than twice that strong but we didn't know that. Before eight o'clock it was clearly diminishing and when we went to bed we were more gratified than not by a stimulating experience at a time when we had anticipated only boredom.

Waking on Thursday morning to a quiet and bright-blue world, one began to understand — slowly. Trees were down everywhere, so many of them that miles of the Connecticut

Valley could be seen below us. The Connecticut itself was everywhere: it looked, from a mile away, like Long Island Sound. All four of the roads outside our house were blocked by scores of tree trunks; and, picking our way slowly downhill to the village, we could see unroofed barns, blown-over sheds, hundreds of fallen trees, electric wires hanging from shredded poles. And the first really appalling discovery was the number of magnificent old elms along the main street that had been uprooted.

Comprehension of our town's plight was slow enough but realization that most of New England had been devastated took much longer. No one in the immediate vicinity had been killed; few had more than trivial injuries; though one saw trees down by the thousand, it took time to think of them as forest and orchard crops destroyed. All roads everywhere were blocked by trees, all except hill roads were under water in places, and most of the hill roads had gaping washouts in them. At first there was no communication outside except by such radio sets as were powered by batteries, which in the village meant automobile radios. The telephone company soon had a line working for a short distance and added to it all day long so that the radius of the attainable steadily lengthened. But, quite properly, the company had turned over its facilities to the telegraph company so that they could be used privately only at rare moments. It brought in little from the outside world. We were isolated by water and debris, a town pushed back into the eighteenth century by the severance of the twentieth century's nervous system, without communications, without transportation, without electric power, with only the smallest reserves of gasoline and oil. And, islanded and impotent in an area known to be frightfully devastated, we were ignorant and anxious.

It was reminiscent of war. All old army men knew that an indeterminable percentage of the news that came in by radio was pure rumor. We learned now of the tidal wave that had

ravaged the lower coastline of New England. But we heard
that Martha's Vineyard had been entirely obliterated, that
Boston was in ruins and was being patrolled by militiamen,
that many thousands had been killed. The only mention of
Cambridge all day long was a wholly false story that the great
Agassiz Museum had been destroyed. Many such stories came
through for which a minute subsequent search can find not the
slightest cause — famous schools destroyed, cities in ashes, a
hyperbole even worse and more chaotic than the reality. They
could not be differentiated from the sufficiently horrible accounts of what had actually happened. We were an outpost
cut off from the army while a battle of unascertainable but
gigantic size was going on.

And it was prophetic of war. Wind and water had done
only what a bombing raid would do. Even in this uncomplex
agricultural community the loss of electric power was paralyz-
ing, no trains could run, and it would take only a few days to
immobilize all automobiles, trucks, and tractors. There was no
lack of food and one knew that transportation would be re-
stored long before there could be; but the holes made in roads
by the fall of trees might easily have been made by shellfire.
There were no fires, but the same shell holes made plain what
would happen if there should be. And now the broadcasts
were talking about pneumonia and typhoid fever: why, yes,
every war begets a pestilence. They were talking also about
refugees, a shocking word to be hearing in New England.
Worst of all was the lack of news, of information, the terrible
questions terribly unanswerable: *Where else? How badly?
How many killed? What cities fallen? How great suffering?
Who?* Beyond that black wall of ignorance, how had the familiar and accustomed been changed, what had been lost from
one's own life, what friends were dead? The edge was whetted
by one's anxiety over the war that had not quite reached gunfire when the wires went out. Was there any sign of its abate-
ment so that we might hope to endure a month or so, a year

or so longer? Or, while we hauled trees off our roads, were the bombs falling that would begin the already universally accepted termination of what we had called civilization? Planes now began to go by overhead; one knew that they were taking pictures for the press or making surveys for efforts at rehabilitation; but he would not have been immoderately timorous who thought of a different kind of mission and glanced at culverts while his ear strained for the whine of falling steel.

Yet the civilization that passively consents to perish in war was reacting magnificently against natural disaster. The villagers had begun to clear away debris at daybreak, our hill road was open by noon, the trees came off the other roads faster than the waters receded from them. (Going up a back road to see about a friend, the Easy Chair was bidden by a road crew "Get an axe" — and got one.) The guards who had been watching the flood were combating it now, having had no sleep; electricians and telephone linesmen were everywhere; the whole township was noisy with labor. It was noisy also with fellowship; a complete neighborly co-operation had been set up automatically and those who most needed help got it first. More ponderously, the energies of government came to the support of individual and corporate endeavor. State and national officials were extemporizing plans of action and getting them started. By Thursday evening, twenty-four hours after the storm struck, even in this little town one had a vivid, an unforgettable appreciation of a stubborn, powerful, and courageous people fighting back.

We sat in a dark automobile and listened to a dozen radio stations telling the larger story — reports at last accurate of the devastation, instructions going out to the Army and Navy and Coast Guard and Militia, instructions to the emergency crews of municipalities and corporations, an endless succession of messages reporting the safety of individuals. Departments of public health broadcasting directions to sterilize drinking water and explaining the efforts being made to prevent disease.

The Red Cross mobilizing food and clothing. The Army providing planes and trucks. The States providing food. The towns and cities providing food, clothing, shelter, assistance of every kind. The Governors to meet to-morrow, the national relief officials on their way by plane, trainloads of supplies and materials rushing toward New England. The chaos of reports one tuned in on adequately represented the chaos of catastrophe, but what held one spellbound, the picture that formed in one's mind, was not chaos but heroic human endeavor, prompt, undaunted, and certain to succeed.

Next morning we drove to Cambridge without difficulty. It was a tragic drive. The face of New England had been changed forever. It takes two hundred years to grow an elm, the characteristic New England tree, and the elms were down everywhere. But it was not this ended loveliness that one mourned most. All pine groves looked as if a gigantic lawn-mower had gone over them, the maples that had produced the section's second largest crop were decimated, the orchards were uprooted or, where some still leaned or even stood, were stripped of fruit. With timber, sugar, syrup, and fruit gone, what would the farmers do, how could they survive? Well, one had seen them intending to survive, and the farms fell away behind and we came to increasingly industrialized districts with their more terrible wreckage. It was at last clear that this had been the most destructive storm that had ever struck a wide industrial area. How would these mills and factories ever be rebuilt? How many of them would not open again? How many would reopen in the South or the Middle West? What would happen to their employees, to their stockholders, to the financial and economic and social systems of which they had been a part? . . . What happens after bombardment?

But one had seen, had listened in darkness, had realized the community rallying. The storm had struck and at once all the implements and resources of civilization had acted to repair catastrophe. Why, yes, as the picture rounded out, there had been looting and pillage, there had been and would be hideous graft, the conversion of suffering and loss to private profit and political expediency. But also there had been, there remained, the energies of a people polarized to restore the stricken section. They would suffice. The damage was immeasurable, the suffering beyond comprehension, the loss incalculable — but the end was sure. For the human will had been awakened and concentrated on human need.

There were newspapers now and in their back pages one found reports from abroad. The bombs were not yet falling; not to-day, not to-morrow, and finally not this year. But eventually they would fall and nothing could be done about that, nothing whatever. Victory over hurricane and flood had been assured in the midst of a world helplessness which would make the victory mere irony. The human will had repulsed destruction by fire and wind and water but it acquiesced in world war; though it might mourn it could not act, it had only sadness and a little folding of the hands to sleep.

And as the days passed and the hurricane stories moved to the back pages, the front pages resumed their familiar aspect. Under stress of hurricane one had forgotten the less spectacular destruction of America, the millions made homeless by other causes than storm, who had lived for nine years and would live their lives out on emergency rations which had been imposed by no tempest blowing in. A sudden natural violence had made one forget the gradual settling of the nation toward entropy; effective response to a limited disaster had made one forget the erosion of the national will by universal disaster. Here for a moment the people had been fused together by sudden peril and effective action was being taken toward an end unquestionably successful. But the people's will had long since ceased to act on the slower violence, and against the nine years' peril, the future's, nothing was being done — or would be done.

Doubtless this would look like pure and limpid comedy if one could get far enough from it, as far, say, as Betelgeuse. From intergalactic space one could read those dissonant headlines — victory over disaster, acquiescence in war, courteous acceptance of the nation's deterioration — with no feeling except a dispassionate admiration for the ingenuity of Almighty God, who made man as he is. But here on this inconsiderable planet the irony was intolerable, the paradox too painful to be borne. On this planet it was a shattering shock to perceive at one time an aroused determination to defeat catastrophe and a universal acceptance of extinction. From Betelgeuse all lines would run the same way and look alike and nothing would matter either way. But even on Betelgeuse there must still be, beyond the air and ice, some appreciation of the wild, the paradoxical knowledge that one carried over for a moment from the hurricane to the greater death: the knowledge that this proved it need not be.

Wisdom Lingers

FOR THE last few days before Christmas the corridors have a blessed quiet and the campus is as solitary as it was in late August. The professors may sleep later in the morning, take an unregardful third highball in the evening, and help the children trim the tree without thinking of to-morrow's nine-o'clock lecture. Optimism comes back, and on December 26th the railroads carry a freight almost as genial as the one that crowded them on December 21st: the scholars are off to their trade conventions. The convention city has been chosen with proper regard to the average fare, hotel accommodations, the neighboring university, and geographical impartiality – not to mention the horse trade by which St. Louis will get next year's convention and Princeton a second vice-president. If it is Chicago this year, it is likely to be Baltimore next year; but if it should be Baltimore then the administration must be induced to put the local delegates on an expense account, at least those who are on committees and those who will read papers.

The professors are joined by their colleagues from the private foundations, from the research departments of the national government, and from the laboratories of big corporations. Post-Christmas week draws the learned together from all over the country, to exchange information and advice, to report on the year's work, to plan for the coming year — and beyond it as far as thought can reach. A layman in search of enlightenment could choose among at least two dozen congregations of wise men. No formula can be given here to guide his choice. The American Association for the Advancement of Science gets the best press and puts on the most interesting show. The American Historical Association has the best time. The American Sociological Society is usually the windiest and always the funniest. The Modern Language Association is the dreariest and most fretful. If none of these suits the layman's taste, however, he may try the Association for Research in Nervous and Mental Diseases, the Seismological Society of America, the Archeological Institute of America, the Association for Symbolic Logic, or the trade organizations of geographers, philologists, speech teachers (*sic*), physicists, geologists, chemists, mineralogists, metaphysicians, anthropologists, economists, paleontologists, psychologists, oceanographers, and many others.

Offstage a convention of the learned is just like a convention of shoe salesmen or investment counselors. In the hotel corridors and the delegates' rooms the same activity goes on, the renewal of friendships, the manipulation of influence for committee appointments and next year's program, reminiscence of livelier days when we and the world were younger, the nurture of candidacies for President in 1943. Anxieties swell and tragedy is close at hand. The dean has given warning that you must produce; perhaps a ten-minute paper will hold him off for another year or a thirty-minute paper turn the corner for good. Or the last year of your appointment is here, the appointment is not going to be renewed, and somewhere in this convention you must find a department head who is looking for talent. Or your feud with the vitalists or the revisionists must be settled now by a redistribution of committees. Or the inadequacy-feeling that is endemic among the learned comes to a head and can be assuaged only by permission to read a paper — any paper, a paper on any subject, embodying any data and conclusions so long as you are vindicated before your fellows by an exhibition of technique utilized and work done.

For the convention exists, ultimately, that papers may be read. The main body breaks up into sections of specialists, and in the meetings of the sections, so theory has it, scholarship renders account of its trust. Here the results of research are presented, here the progress of knowledge is declared. Here the learned communicate to one another and to the world the end products of their labor, from the earth-shaking to the inconceivably inane. And, since scholars have as much flesh as any man, the inane predominates. The layman can get a picture of the state of learning in America from the specialists' papers, but he will spare himself shock if he assumes that the median line of scholarship must be very much like any other median.

It was the American Speech Teachers who this year heard about recordings of Hitler's speeches. The records reveal that Hitler is frequently angry. His strong emotion and his use of the higher voice-level tend to put the German people in a passive state. Hitler, the paper concluded, frequently reaches a condition bordering on hysteria. . . . The Folklore Society learned that Mexican peasants have a contemptuous epithet for political jobholders. . . . A professor told the Student Union that "every classroom in the nation must be converted into an outpost in the struggle for democracy," and professors were saying things quite as silly as that in all the conventions. . . . Another one told the Archeological Institute that Virgil was the first modern, just as Bruce Barton used to tell Rotary International that Jesus was the first advertising man. . . . The

American Sociological Society heard that "American language behavior" is "a societal epi-phenomenon, a form of oral hyperkinesia, a kind of chronic and acute but highly contagious blabitis." That means that Americans talk a lot. It is typical of the sociologists' language-behavior and contains a stately academic joke, and it shows that the lust for semantics which recently raged through sociology did not strike inward. . . . Always excepting Professors of Education, sociologists tend to be the most pretentious of scholars. A certain insecurity, a repressed fear that their four-dollar words may not mean anything and that their shiny, scientific-looking gadgets may not make them scientists after all, produces an aggressive clamor that isn't hard to diagnose. They beat gongs to keep the spooks away. . . . Insecurity takes a different form in the Modern Language Association, where professors of literature grieve over the dullest of all papers read during this supercharged week. What depresses these scholars is a realization that their discipline is supposed to deal with literature, whereas of sixty-odd papers annually read to the society only about ten have any bearing on literature and only about five of those understand that it is an art, that it is related to the dreams and heartbreaks and aspirations of mankind, that the odd creatures who write it have the blood and emotions of living men. They feel that culture is in their keeping, just as Professors of Education feel that progress and revolution are in their keeping, and five out of sixty seem a small proportion and they fall into despair.

Well, dispatches come in from the frontiers of knowledge: Solomon's port on the Red Sea is being excavated. . . . The serpents carved on Roman lintels were meant to ward off evil. . . . Amish hymns have been recorded for the phonograph. . . . It is now clear that a British naval officer was lying, a hundred and four years ago, when he claimed to have invaded the Antarctic ice. The map he drew was phantasy and the sea he named after himself was discovered at his desk. . . . White Leghorn chickens have had their feathers colored with pigment taken, in the embryo, from a robin's wing. . . . Professor Yerkes says that his chimpanzees are very much like human beings, and no lover of justice rises to denounce this libel of a mild and prepossessing animal. . . . The Association of American Geographers hears that we have started on the hot-to-cold part of the weather cycle and so may expect the kind of events correlated with that half of the curve. During the next five or ten years, that is, the dictatorships will probably perish. . . . But this heartening news is contradicted at the Geological Society of America, whence word comes that the earth is growing warmer as it continues to emerge from the latest glacial period and that the attempts of the "have-not" nations to get more metals will soon lead to war.

But now of course we are in an area where knowledge wears brighter clothing. The planet Neptune began to be disorderly in 1925 and is now five seconds ahead of where it should be in its orbit. But that may be because the earth wobbles so much that an error was made in the observation — and, considering the earth since 1925, the suggestion sounds reasonable. The metal-bearing ores of the wobbling earth dwindle fast but might be conserved for another century, though because of armaments they probably will not be. But new oil fields are being laid down on the ocean floor off California and will be ready for use in a few million years. Study of the chromosomes has revealed a gene which accelerates the rate of mutation. The discovery helps us to understand evolution, supplies a new instrument for those who are studying cancer, and suggests that a new type of mankind may appear in time to mop up the mess. Photographs in color were taken of the recent lunar eclipse, and the earth's crust is rising toward its pre-glacial level.

A chemical called histamine, which is carried by the blood cells, produces anaphylactic shock and is held responsible for various sensitivity diseases, including asthma. (So the Association for the Advancement of Science heard in Richmond. But papers read to the Association for Research in Nervous and Mental Diseases recorded cures of asthma by psychiatric methods and suggested that some asthma may be psychogenic.) A better analgesic than morphine has been found: cobra venom, which does not produce insensibility but has a pleasant reaction and so fulfills one of medicine's oldest dreams. And the audience at Richmond saw a new kind of microscope. It focuses not light rays but electrons, magnifies up to a million times, and effects separations as small as one twenty-five millionth of an inch. They saw it reveal the shape of the smallpox virus and of the *Staphylococcus aureus*, which no optical microscope can make visible. And while they watched, its fluorescent screen picked out the atomic pattern of a tungsten crystal and with their naked, virgin eyes they could see residual molecules of air shimmer against the sides of the vacuum tube. . . . Elsewhere scholars might fret and chill with doubt of what they were doing, but not these scholars. Here was the advance of knowledge and a tool to carry it farther still.

They are a more serene, more confident group than their colleagues in the social sciences and the humanities. Physical and biological scientists, medical men, even psychologists know what they are talking about, as sociologists and their kin commonly do not. They know it is worth talking about, which is not a conviction that the members carry away from the Modern Language Association. They know that even the humblest paper of the humblest chemist reporting that one hundred compounds which mathematics said in advance could not be produced in the laboratory cannot in fact be produced there will be useful to someone, whereas the reports on cultural vestiges shown in the drawings on outhouse walls in Wilkes-Barre that humble sociologists compose and the studies of Cowper's syntax which the abashed M.L.A. produces will just be dumped forever on the garbage heap of a self-perpetuating vested interest. They see instruments of hope and growth and healing and mastery put at the disposal of the human race, if the race should ever care to take them up, and not even Professors of Education, who claim everything, can claim healing or mastery. And they know that sometimes in small, drowsy rooms where a few aging men gather, papers are read which will ultimately change the face of nature and the form of society. No paper read at the Modern Language Association or the American Sociological Society, past, present, or to come, will ever have any effect whatever on either nature or society.

But, out of their laboratories, the scientists also are uneasy. They were told in Richmond that they must assume responsibility for social changes produced by science (talking like a Professor of the Science of Teaching the Science of Teaching, the speaker remarked that the main duty of our secondary schools is to teach civics and manners, science and discipline) and they are willing and even eager to accept that responsibility — if they can find out how. That, however, is one research for which they have no instruments. One of the foremost physicists in the world tried to tell his colleagues how; but his speech had as little meaning for the layman as if he had been talking about the mathematics of cosmic rays, and had far less meaning for the physicists. Like all other learned societies, the physicists passed resolutions in favor of democracy and against absolutism, and dedicated themselves to free inquiry and social advance, and denounced the perversion of learning to evil ends; but in the bitter glare of the modern world they saw that a physicist was indistinguishable from a sociologist and even from a Professor of Education, except that, a million-power microscope in his hand, he looked more forlorn. He had only his microscope, and it would be quite as futile as a study of cultural vestiges in outhouses or one of Cowper's syntax when he took it out into the freshening winds and the rising waters.

Yet the physicist is not so forlorn as he looks, and the layman reflects, when the week is over, that the other scholars are not so disheartening as they seem in a close-up. It is a mistake to look at them in close-up, unless one sedulously remembers that no human activity is very impressive under a magnifying glass. The average of anything human is — a human average. Measured against eternity, measured against hope and desire, measured against even the scholars' own aspiration and pretense, most scholarly researches do indeed look trivial, futile, and ridiculous. But measured against history, even the slightest of them does not look so bad. For their kind has been certainly the cleanest and by far the most fruitful activity the race has given itself to, and has built the one Republic that has withstood darkness and storm. And when you turn away from human mediocrity to the best, you come close to what is just about the only source of hope the storms have not obliterated. They are plain, imperfect men, plentifully bewildered, plentifully mired in human ignorance and human stupidity, but they do their job, their job goes on in peace, it slowly widens, it moves along. Even the statistician of outhouses or of ethical datives works against chaos, works toward rationality, is a conduit of the mind's freedom, a tender of an imperishable item who, if he should fall, would bring all down with him. And the physicist's microscope may be but a small bastion against the winds and waters but you will find no other quite so large. . . . And they meet in freedom and in peace, and, meeting so, are an earnest and a prayer and — a fortress.

"*Liberal*" *Equals* N^{nx}

WILL THE average man be happier in the year 2000 than he was in 1936? Answer "yes" or "no."

Were the masses happier a hundred years ago than they are now? "Yes" or "no," please.

Will genuine individual liberty flourish under socialism as it never did before? Again, please answer "yes" or "no."

The definition of liberalism is about to be brought out of the uncontrolled speculation in which it usually pulsates into the scientific domain of quantitative measurement. These are only three of 106 questions, and it will be possible for you to give an illiberal answer to all of them and still come out predominantly liberal at the end. Nevertheless, each has a correct liberal answer, and the "perfect" liberal will return it in each instance, whereas the "perfect" conservative will return its exact opposite.

Well, what is the average man? What is happy? How happy was he in 1936? How do you know how happy he was and how do you measure happiness? How happy will he be in the year 2000? How do you know? If such questions restrain you from returning a "yes" to the first question, you are $\frac{1}{106}$ illiberal in your "social attitude."

Define the masses. How happy were they a hundred years ago, and how do you know? How happy are they now, and how do you know? You have got to know that they are happier now than they were then or your attitude is another $\frac{1}{106}$ illiberal.

You will see by the third question that we are going to have socialism — kind not specified. The verb is not the conditional "would" but the future indicative "will." That being settled, can you say in what degree "genuine individual liberty" has "flourished" up to now and do you divine how it is going to flourish under socialism? Does the adjective "genuine" bother you? Do you detect a theorem that some of the rights which you take to be liberty now are not "genuine" and so may be curtailed by socialism? Do you find "socialism" a pretty vague word? No matter. Assert that genuine individual liberty (three terms undefined) will (not would or might) flourish (whatever that means) under socialism (undefined) as it never did before (all variations compared, corrected, and adjusted) — or you will lose another $\frac{1}{106}$. A liberal will confidently answer "yes."

This is by no means all the prophecy and divination you must subscribe to in order to be a liberal; but let us go on to other tests. Could an average family income of approximately $4,000 be obtained if the productive equipment of the nation were operated at full capacity? (The sum arbitrarily chosen corresponds to that mentioned by one speculative survey. Other surveys have estimated it as from forty to four hundred per cent as great.) What does "obtained" mean or imply? Have you an opinion on the question? Is it anything but a random guess? Would you stake your judgment and integrity on that opinion? Are you sure you know just what productive equipment is or just what full capacity would be? Do not hesitate or qualify: you must answer "yes" or be illiberal.

Or try what is known in mechanics as a virtual movement. Would our national health suffer if physicians were made civil servants like the public-school teachers and placed on the government payroll? You may say that you have no way of knowing, that anyone's answer to the question is worthless, and that a question so stated is meaningless. But that won't do. In order to be liberal you must utter a firm "no."

Or let us try the hortatory. Should all foreign trade be a monopoly of the Federal government? If you are a liberal, it certainly should.

Should the Federal government provide to all classes of people opportunity for complete insurance against accident, sickness, unemployment, premature death, and old age? Yes; and if you switch governments or drop any kind of insurance from that list, or if you find the word "opportunity" open at both ends, or if you boggle at "complete," you are not a liberal.

Exercise in locating tacit assumptions and concealed theorems. Should all banks and insurance companies be run on a nonprofit basis like the schools? Liberals say "yes."

That one is easy. Analyze this one: Is the behavior of the capitalists doing more to discredit and undermine capitalism than all the activities of anticapitalistic groups? Say "yes" and do not ask who the capitalists are, whether it is certain that capitalism is being undermined, whom it is being discredited with, what the unit and method of measurement are, or what values we are to assign the variables in the mixed terms.

Even that one is not so celestial a marriage of *petitio principii* and the indeterminate term as this: Does indoctrination by conservatives play a smaller part in American schools today than radical propaganda? Do not wonder how anyone can tell, do not wait on definitions, do not let the shrieking fallacy trouble you. Liberals say "no."

Comic relief. Do most of the undesirable features of the

newspapers, the movies, and the radio come from their being controlled by profit-making corporations? Yes, indeed.

Let us close with miscellaneous specimens from absurdity's stratosphere. Should all farm mortgages be assumed by the Federal Treasury at an interest rate not in excess of one per cent? "Yes." Would the regular calling of conventions for the revision of state and national constitutions at ten-year intervals eliminate some of the evils of social lag? "Yes." Does the smooth functioning of a profit economy depend upon either natural or artificial scarcity? "Yes." For most people would the opportunity to exercise beneficial personal initiative be increased by life in a socialist State? "Yes." As soon as we create a high level of economic security for all, will the finer arts and graces of living blossom everywhere? "Yes." If you reach for calipers or litmus paper you are no liberal.

The Easy Chair assures you that it did not invent these questions, and that they are not meant, here or in their native place, to be either a libel on liberalism or a joke. They are fifteen per cent of a serious questionnaire, and these specimens are not unfairly chosen for asininity of question or inconceivability of answer. The questionnaire was composed by the John Dewey Society and was sent to ninety-three hundred "junior and senior high school teachers throughout the nation." The Easy Chair encountered it while studying the ideal world envisioned by the philosophers of education who tell us that they are going to remake society by means of Longfellow School. There is much in that vision which will curdle your blood, but it must be postponed for a time while we stand, hushed and uncovered, in the presence of this Everest of pure nonsense. This is no bush-league idiocy; it belongs to a select company of the most preposterous documents since the invention of paper.

What the purposes of the Society were, what the teachers answered, and what conclusions the Society drew are all matters of great interest. But such considerations are insignificant compared with the state of mind and the ways of thinking revealed by the phrasing of the questions, the establishment of the "norm" for its answers, and the Society's belief that the answers supply data of a factual and rational kind.

Mind you, this is scientific, as the philosophy of pedagogy understands science. In establishing its test for liberalism the Society might unthinkingly have used its own answers to the pregnant questions as a norm. But it saw that danger that way lay. Instead, it drew up a "liberalism-conservatism key" by calling upon "more than a dozen figures in American life, including a former President of the United States [guess!], three presidential candidates, Congressmen, publicists, etc." Who the group were or how they were divided between liberals and conservatives does not appear — science does things anonymously. But the liberals agreed unanimously about all but 34 of the 106 questions and there was only one dissenting voice in half of the 34 reservations. So "all items on which a pronounced majority of the prominent liberals agree were considered to be symptomatic of liberalism." Liberals, it appears, are those who can answer questions.

The Society tells us that these questions call for "judgments of value" rather than "judgments of fact," and so warns us that we must deal grandly with great ideas and wonderful conceptions not to be crabbedly challenged by statistics. Nevertheless, the word is "judgment," and both the answers to the questions and the conclusions which the Society bases on them obviously involve the process of judicious analysis and logical thought. The "attitude" appraised by this method is presented to us not as a misty creed but as a body of reasoned ideas susceptible to investigation and verification, a structure of propositions on the basis of which intelligent action is to be ordered. So the Society believes and asserts, and on that basis it analyzes and acts. Yet anyone who applies to the questionnaire either the simple realism known as common sense or the process of controlled thinking known as logical analysis must see at once that it exists altogether outside the domain of intelligence. It is not illogical, it is nonlogical: it has nothing whatever to do with logic. It is pure belief, pure wish, pure emotion. Far from defining "liberalism" as a certain body of ideas, which is what the Society thinks it does, it defines it as a set of sentiments quite unconnected with reality.

In the total of 106 questions there are hardly a dozen to which an intelligent man thinking carefully would care to give any answer at all. To the sixteen quoted here no answer which has meaning is possible: a "conservative" answer would be quite as nonlogical as a "liberal" one, and the "yes" and "no" asked for are equally nonsensical. Take the last one quoted: As soon as we create a high level of economic security for all, will the finer arts and graces of living blossom everywhere? Passing up the assumption that we are going to create a "high level" (try solving that for x) for "all," and granting that you and I and the girl next door can agree on what the finer arts and graces of living are, is our assertion that they are or are not going to blossom everywhere worth a single, solitary damn? Obviously, in a world of careful thinking it is not. We don't know, no one can tell us, there is no way of finding out; and so our answer can have no meaning whatever. But now let us abandon clarity and assign a value to pure wish — let us say that we earnestly hope and passionately believe that there is going to be a high level of economic security for all. We welcome that great dawn but we, nevertheless, recall the vulgarities of the radio and conclude that we may have to put up with an average lowering of the arts and graces. That also is pure guess, valueless as thought, devoid of meaning except as sentiment. But the test key shows that it is "conservative." That is, in order to be liberal you must not only hold an opinion that is pure wish and can be neither analyzed nor verified, but, of a good many opinions possible in that uncontrolled ether, you must have a particular one. . . . Clearly the test operates outside the domain of logical thought. Clearly the questionnaire is nonlogical, an exercise in sentiment.

So throughout. A few questions could in part be answered by people in possession of much factual information. Thus, "Could cheaper electric light and power be had if the industry were owned and operated by governmental units?" could be more or less satisfactorily answered. One would need vast information about costs, specific details about the kinds of units, the policies of management, the terms of funding and taxation, and many other variables and unknowns. But your answer or mine or a high-school teacher's, or a conservative's, or the Society's, is obviously worth nothing whatever as thought: it must be considered sheer sentiment. And "Is a classless society possible?", or "Should any person be permitted to have an income of more than $25,000 a year until such a time as the average wage earner receives at least $2,000 a year?", or "For most people would the opportunity to exercise beneficial personal initiative be increased by life in a socialist state?" — no one is capable of giving any intelligent answer to them, "yes," "no," "perhaps," or "I think so." And more than 90 of the 106 questions are of that kind — nonsense impermeable to logic or meaning.

Taken as it stands, the questionnaire reveals a good deal about the sentiments of those who made it up, those who were selected as the norm, and those who answered it. As such it is a laboratory specimen of great interest, and if it were studied as a report on sentiments — which, very likely, are more powerful than ideas in social actions — it might yield valuable results. But the John Dewey Society does not accept it and study it for what it is, a document in the sentiments, but accepts it and proposes to act on it for what it is not, a document in ideas, a test which reveals the social opinion of those who took it, a factual exhibit in social thinking. This, says the Society, indicates the structure of ideas by which our teachers are governed. It does nothing of the kind. This, says the Society, gives us factual data about social thinking. It does not.

As for liberalism, let us not make a fetish of a word. If the Society cares to call "liberals" people whose sentiments about these unanswerable questions, unconscious assumptions, sleeping theorems, and meaningless propositions roughly agree with the "key" to this questionnaire, it is certainly entitled to. Those who think of liberals as people who try to apply logical and experimental knowledge to social problems may easily see that such people are not even approached by the test. Let us designate them by some other term. But let us make it evident that the two words are unrelated and are applied to separate groups.

And let us remember the John Dewey Society's complete self-deception in this enterprise. Our philosophers of education promise us that they are going to remake society by means of the schools, on the basis of their vision and scientific knowledge. Well, here is a specimen of their equipment and method — a monstrous experiment in complete meaninglessness, believed by its authors to produce experimental knowledge, and incorporated as such knowledge into their program of regeneration.

God help the Republic! It still lives — but for how long? Is there not some way of compelling Teachers College to paste labels on the enterprises of its stepchildren? Suggestion for one label: Not to Be Transported across State Lines. Or, more simply: Perishable.

The Fallacy of Excess Interpretation

~~~~~~

SOME TIME ago a syndicated comic strip transferred the adventures of its characters from the other side of the moon to the world of labor disputes. It showed a noble factory owner ruined, some high-souled nonunion workers deprived of employment, and the national safety imperiled by the action of some villainous union men who were incited to revolution by miscreants in the pay of an unnamed but not disguised organization. The public objected, as it is likely to when its amusements are adulterated with moral fervor, and the comic strip abruptly went back to the moon again.

At that time an indignation ran through liberal circles, which asserted that this was flagrant propaganda, part of an overt conspiracy between newspapers and our financial masters. The Easy Chair was skeptical. Not promising to believe in the existence of that conspiracy, it thought that the conspirators, if they did exist, would probably be more intelligent than the allegation credited them with being. If this was indeed propaganda, then it probably flowed spontaneously from the crusading sentiments of the man who drew the comic strip, not from the plans of some Secret Seven meeting at midnight in a bank vault. But was it propaganda? It looked more like a bad guess. Since the first necessity of a comic strip is to reflect the sentiments of its readers, this crude parable was probably based on the estimate, promptly proved wrong, that the public was in a mood to have the labor unions denounced. If it assumed agreement in advance, then clearly it was not propaganda. But such speculations were hazardous, for comic strips exist in the field of popular art, and that field is complex beyond the assumptions of the unwary. All interpretations of it are precarious, and all solemn ones are wrong.

Exactly that same charge is frequently made about the movies, and people who have liberal ideas in matched sets commonly believe that such gentlemen as Sam Goldwyn are in more or less open conspiracy with our masters to lull the people asleep. According to this view, the movies have become the opium of the masses and are constantly used as an instrument of propaganda for the established order. And in its March release the Institute for Propaganda Analysis undertook to investigate the charge. It was a promising venture, thoroughly in the public interest, but the Easy Chair is constrained to report that the results of this first essay are not impressive. The Institute's literary ideas are badly scrambled, its test for propaganda is itself a carrier of propaganda, and it ignores what should have been its first consideration, the nature of popular art.

It would be interesting to examine the Institute's remarks on the newsreel of the *Panay* sinking, which end by demonstrating (though the Institute seems unaware that they do) that propaganda for war may be an effective deterrent to war — an exceedingly interesting finding. But there is space only to consider the nub of the matter, the ordinary feature movie. The Institute sternly reminds us that "the greatest literature

. . . enlightens while it also entertains." That is more or less true but painfully irrelevant as well, and it introduces an element of wild unreality as well as a moral consideration which impedes the finding of facts. And one's suspicion that the Institute's critical judgments need renovation is confirmed when it praises the "delightful fantasy or humor" of "It Happened One Night" or "Mr. Deeds Goes to Town," but goes on to condemn other pictures as "vehicles for pseudo-realities, incorrect generalizations, and misleading stereotypes." Those two pictures were certainly delightful but their alleged realities would not bear much strain, their generalizations have holes in them here and there, and one may not comfortably stand on them shouting "stereotype" at their competitors. This part of the Institute's analysis could have used an experienced literary critic.

It is a graver defect that the analysis of propaganda is itself a form of propaganda. The Institute has a conception of what the movies ought to be, and that conception dictates its description of what they are. It asks whether the movies shall "provide social illumination, contribute something to people's understanding of themselves and of the world in which they live." Without defining those terms, it obviously believes that they ought, and on the basis of that theorem it asserts flatly that "the industry seems to lag behind, and even to hold back the development of the public taste." It dodges another flat assertion but makes it by implication when it directs us to "ask whether the praise that has been given to the motion picture . . . on the grounds that it allayed social discontent, was not perhaps a factor in the situation." In short, the Institute believes that the movies are the opium of the masses and that our masters use them to seduce the public into accepting its own betrayal. At this point, does someone want to inquire what findings the Institute is going to bring in after it has finished the search it is setting out on?

It lists five categories of propaganda. The clinch ending

rarely shows us that young lovers are going to live on in a world of insecurity and unemployment. Movies of crime seldom point out that poverty is the cause of crime. War is made to seem thrilling and heroic. The movies jingoistically portray other races and nationalities and minority groups as inferior to native white Americans. And finally, in the movies, "the good life is the acquisitive life with its emphasis on luxury, fine homes and automobiles, evening dress, swank, and suavity." That is the weightiest accusation, and in support of it the Institute says, "When we note the heavy emphasis in selection of leading male characters from the commercial and professional groups, with almost no representation from the ranks of labor, we get some explanation of the lopsided notion of the world of workaday living held by many young people."

That last is a *non sequitur* of national-championship class, but it throws a highlight on the essential unreality of the whole set of assertions. The clinch ending, for instance – can we really treat it as designed to influence "other individuals or groups with reference to predetermined ends"? Does the emphasis on the "acquisitive life" serve the function that the Institute thinks it does? The instruments of analysis seem almost romantically irrelevant to the job at hand.

So, at least, the Easy Chair thought; and it determined to apply the Institute's eleven tests to an actual movie and see what happened. The nearest one was "Bringing Up Baby," featuring Miss Katharine Hepburn and Mr. Cary Grant, and since Miss Hepburn is the only movie actress who ever made the Easy Chair bawl (that was in "Little Women"), there was no temptation to go farther from home.

In "Bringing Up Baby" Mr. Grant plays Dr. Huxley, a paleontologist who is reconstructing a dinosaur skeleton and has completed it except for one bone. Here is a hero dedicated to the austere pursuit of scientific truth: this movie is squarely on the side of the good life. To be sure there is a love interest, but, since Miss Hepburn ultimately takes Mr. Grant away from a far less personable woman, it makes for enlightenment in eugenics. Miss Hepburn is the niece of a woman who may give a million dollars to Dr. Huxley's museum and who is sent a pet leopard. Miss Hepburn marks Dr. Huxley for her own the first time she sees him, though he can't stand her; great literature has also used that theme (see Shaw and Shakespeare). Theirs is a romance singularly full of incident. Miss Hepburn rips Dr. Huxley's coat off; he rips her skirt off. The aunt's dog runs away with the last dinosaur bone and buries it, and the lovers feverishly serve science by following him about and trying to cajole him into digging it up. The leopard escapes and so does another leopard, a wild one, from a circus. The tame leopard is fond of being sung to, so the lovers wander through the night singing "I Can't Give You Anything but Love" to lure it back. They fall over a great variety of objects, climb over many others, get dragged through a pond, and land in jail, together with the aunt. In the end Miss Hepburn breaks jail and lassoes the wild leopard, recovers the lost bone, brings it to the museum, climbs up the scaffold that supports the dinosaur, slips and falls on the skeleton, and utterly ruins it. So she and Dr. Huxley get married.

Omitting psychological subtleties, that is an outline of the story. *What*, says the Institute's first test, *what are the assumptions about life and human nature on which this film rests?* That pretty and vivacious girls are attractive, that what begins as anger may end as love (pure Freud), and that life and human nature have comic aspects. *What values or goals do the characters in the play consider important?* Above all else, the endowment of scientific research. *Do we think they are?* Unquestionably, but some of us would hesitate to lasso a leopard even for science. *Is this film a defense of things as they are?* It argues that things as they are should not be tolerated for a moment. *Is it an argument for change?* It asserts that we must shatter the sorry scheme of things entire and then remold it

nearer to the heart's desire. *Were the problems of the characters remote from contemporary conditions or were they
closely related to the realities of to-day?* The Easy Chair has
never driven down a country road at night without seeing
cars parked in the shadows. *Were the relationships between
the characters on the screen traditional?* As traditional as those
in "Hamlet." *Would they be acceptable to intelligent people
to-day?* The man who wouldn't accept that relationship with
Miss Hepburn if he had a chance to isn't intelligent. *Who
wants us to think this way?* Did you say "think"? *What are his
interests?* Hours of patient analysis reveal no interest that is
being served except the box office. *Do they coincide with the
interests of ourselves, of most Americans?* Unhappily, with
this question, the experimenter muttered "Oh, hell!" and gave
up. It is like asking whether a pound of butter is in the key
of B-flat or C-major. Why should "Bringing Up Baby," or
any movie, be an argument for change? Why should it be an
argument? And is it only foggy writing when the Institute
fails to distinguish between a traditional relationship and a
traditional treatment of a relationship, or is this a theorem that
traditional relationships are evil and the movies should attack
them? What other theorems and assumptions are implicit in
these questions? And what bearing have any of the questions
got on the audience's satisfaction in watching the delightful
Miss Hepburn get her man?

The tests for propaganda, in short, are unreal and approach
the movies on a level of phantasy. They are ineffective, irrelevant, the wrong tests. They imply a propaganda of the
Institute's own, "conscious or unconscious," but they completely fail to examine the nature of popular entertainment.

The Institute has a conception of the role which the movies
might play in American life. They might be a source of education, enlightenment, and liberalization. They might be a source
of beneficent propaganda — for only your propaganda is evil,
mine never is. They might be, specifically, an instrument of

social enlightenment. So the Institute's analysis moves on a simple fulcrum: if the movies are not educative and liberalizing and socially enlightening then they are propaganda. That is the fallacy of excess interpretation. But the analysis is not only fallacious: it is a form of propaganda. The Institute does not try to find facts except in its own service — it tries to influence us to a predetermined end, an end predetermined by what it thinks the movies ought to be.

We may observe that movie heroes are mostly young men in course of becoming millionaires, but to conclude that propaganda for the acquisitive life is responsible is to ignore the realities. Why are heroes millionaires? Well, why are all the heroines beautiful? More simply, what propaganda produces a strip-tease act in a burlesque show? Neither utility companies nor the armament manufacturers profit when Miss Corio takes off her clothes and, except for Miss Corio, the status quo is not affected. Perhaps it is wrong of the audience to like to watch her stripping, but it does like to. You must get rid of that liking, and you must get rid of the prince in "Cinderella," before you can get the young millionaire out of the program movie. He is not propaganda for the acquisitive life, he is just a durable part of popular entertainment. The prince, the millionaire, the beautiful heroine, and the lady showing her build have been fixtures in popular literature throughout history. They are not propaganda, they are just symbols, identifications, and projections.

Nor is there any gain for righteousness in labeling this literature wish-fulfillment and lambasting it with words like "stereotype" and "sentimentality." It may be regrettable that popular literature is sentimental and that only stereotypes succeed in it, but regret is irrelevant, and if it is wish-fulfillment for audiences to look at millionaires on the screen, the movies cannot be accused of propagandizing for the established order until such time as that wish may be extirpated. Furthermore, the Institute would be wise to determine whether, in the movies it praises, it was social enlightenment that the audience enjoyed or just excitement. If "I Am a Fugitive from a Chain Gang" is "notable" to the Institute because it seems to carry a social message, it also appalled certain other seekers, who found that it dangerously pandered to the public's taste for cruelty. Something seems to be wrong here, and possibly the first objective of such analyses should be the determination of facts. Just which was it and just why did the audience like it? Story or message, cruelty or the good life?

Chautauqua found that a time came when the popular audience wasn't finding as much entertainment in sermons as it used to and Chautauqua promptly displaced its preachers with royal marimba bands. Was it propagandizing for righteousness when it sent out preachers, was it propagandizing for the lusts of the flesh when it sent out bands? Or was it, each time, just following the box office? Is there a vicious conspiracy in Hollywood to lull our people asleep, or are there some more or less sagacious men doing their damnedest to produce movies that people will pay money to see? Wouldn't it be sensible to inquire whether the movies must necessarily follow the folk before asserting that they lead them on? Does the public know anything about art or does it just know what it likes?

Finally, has *King Lear* or *Prometheus Bound*, or even *Das Kapital*, anything to do with "Bringing Up Baby"? And should not the name of the Institute for Propaganda Analysis require it to keep a tight grip on its own wishfulness till after it has established its facts?

Good and Wicked Words

THE EASY CHAIR has read Mr. Stuart Chase's three articles on verbalisms with much interest and approval. How important the Easy Chair believes their subject to be is shown by the fact that it has devoted eight of twenty-six monthly essays here to various aspects of that subject, has touched on it in others, and, before taking over this department, published four articles about it in the body of the magazine. Everyone who tries to think effectively must constantly allow for the habits of mind which Mr. Chase analyzes, the structures of abstract logic which he describes, the personifications and abstractions and verbal proofs which he exposes, the misunderstandings to which they lead, the meaninglessness of much activity carried on in the name of intelligence and received as meaningful by most people. Everyone who deals with thought or with human beings must understand the errors produced by the universal disposition to accept words as things and logic as a functional relationship among things. Furthermore, since science has done more than any other human activity to extend man's control over his environment, and since it has done so, as we believe, largely because it has freed itself from verbalism, the conclusion is indicated that the widest possible extension of its method would be beneficial to mankind.

But the Easy Chair desires to suggest that that conclusion also must be limited, because it too is meaningless as an absolute. Mr. Chase's articles serve here as the basis of analysis, but the Easy Chair intends no rebuttal, having shouted with delight over the greatest part of them. But it is important to point out that everyone who undertakes Mr. Chase's search must sometimes succumb to the evils he is exposing, and to point out that the search itself has implications that Mr. Chase does not allow for.

Mr. Chase knows that nobody can be immune to verbalisms. He conscientiously warns the reader to expect unconscious abstractions, absolutes, and personifications in what he writes. Well, one of his most striking verbalisms is his use of the word "conservative" as an absolute. He shows that such terms as "labor" and "democracy" can have meaning only in reference to specific situations, but "conservative" seems to have for him an independent existence of its own. He says he is tired "of fighting things which do not exist." But he seems to be fighting conservatism, and no such thing exists. The word can have meaning only in specific contexts, only by limiting definition or in relation to immediate referents. Even in such contexts it can hardly have a qualitative meaning; it must be used quantitatively, as a percentage possibly, as a ratio with something else. Again, in discussing the verbal fallacy of the wage-fund theory, he says, "Working people in England and elsewhere had paid a bitter price for fifty years for a Law without scientific foundation." That is personification. Those working people may be said to have paid a "bitter" price for food or, if you like a more inclusive term, for the power and immunity of their exploiting employers; but they didn't pay anything for any law, sound or unsound.

Again, refusing to go to war on behalf of Russia, he acknowledges that he desires to see the people of Russia given every chance to work out "perhaps the most significant economic experiment ever undertaken." Significant to whom, in what circumstances, in relation to whom and what? The people of Russia are undertaking an economic experiment; so are the people of Germany, the people of Italy, the people of Spain, the people of Japan. These experiments may have enormous significance to the people who are undertaking them, to other people affected by them, to Mr. Chase, to you and me. But "most significant" is empty of meaning. "During Franklin Roosevelt's first Administration, conservatives and businessmen after 1933 opposed increasingly the extension of authority at Washington." But many "businessmen" whooped up that extension, saw chances to make profits from it, made the profits, and doubtless voted Democratic in 1936. There is no such thing as a conservative and, though there are certainly men engaged in various businesses, there are no such things as businessmen. Two personified phantoms and a concealed assumption.

Again, "by 1940 we may have political parties which will provide a real issue." Operationally, there were plenty of issues of 1936: for example, shall we appropriate less money for relief, change the method of administering relief funds, and change the methods of raising revenues to produce them? If that is not a real issue, we must look for real issues in another concealed assumption — which suggests that Mr. Chase's use of "real" is a verbalism. Lastly, take a good look at Mr. Chase's climax. "The controlling issue for statesmen, governments, politicians is to find the human purpose to be accomplished in the given situation." Human purpose or blab? In a given situation politicians or governments may act to advance the interests of A, B, and C, or of this class or that one, or a combination or compromise. If the action thus taken impairs the interests of D, E, and F, or of other classes, what is "human purpose"? The phrase is an abstraction and personification, pulsating with emotion. It suggests that another concealed assumption is interwoven here — or several of them.

The Easy Chair is not attacking Mr. Chase. It is pointing out that his quest is in part conditioned by other phenomena which, in these three articles at least, he ignores. And to ignore them is to impair the inquiry, for they are inseparable from its objective.

Let us do what experience has shown to be helpful, let us look for a state of mind. One has already been suggested by "real issue" and "humane purpose." Well, Mr. Chase tells us that, in the campaign of 1936, the opponents of the New Deal attacked Mr. Tugwell and defended Mr. Landon with a lot of meaningless (but, let us point out, effective) abstractions, personifications, and animisms. That is verifiably true. Note, however, that, though he says such attacks darkened counsel, he fails to remark that the supporters of the New Deal attacked their opponents with another set equally meaningless and even more effective. He says that the personification of corporations has thrown the economic mechanisms out of gear. That also is verifiably true, but it is true that such animisms as "the workers," "the underprivileged," etc., also assisted in that stripping of the gears, and Mr. Chase does not bring that fact to bear on his question. He says that "more than one-third of the people in America are underfed, inadequately housed, and shoddily clothed." He has never counted them, no one has ever counted them, and his statement is not meaningful but emotionally useful. The only word in it that can be operationally examined is "underfed," and an inquiry by nutritionists (granting they could agree on tests) would possibly reveal a certain percentage of "blab." "Inadequately housed" is open at both ends — inadequately by what scale, in relation to what facts, in relation to what specifications and persons? "Shoddily clothed" is meaningless though it appears to refer to garments.

Mr. Chase says that after divesting ourselves of abstract principle we can advance toward "making Adam I and his family more comfortable and more secure." What if the path we elect to follow ends by impairing the comfort of Adam II and robbing Adam III of security? He says, "Within the broad limits set by the technical arts and natural resources, we can have any kind of economic system which enough of us want." Who are "we"? Are the limits he mentions the only barriers? Suppose that the kind of economic system "we" want can be got only by fighting "them"? Suppose that the fight ends in a compromise short of what "we" want? Suppose that it goes on till social chaos makes "our" kind of economic system impossible? Suppose that different parts of the system "we" want are inconsistent with one another? Exercise for beginners in semantics: find the verbalism.

Does not all this look *as if* Mr. Chase's ideas, besides being employed in an analysis of meanings, were also in part controlled by an underlying predisposition? Does it not look *as if* wish, desire, and phantasy had sometimes penetrated the filter? Does it not look *as if* the conclusions (if not the search also) had some relation to an unexpressed system of theorems, assumptions, and purely emotional values, consciously or unconsciously held by Mr. Chase?

If there are such systems, if there are such relationships, if people's attempts to use words accurately are affected in such a way, then the application of semantics is more limited than Mr. Chase concedes. We have all known brilliant scientists who, when working in the laboratory with electrons or bacteria, rigorously controlled their behavior by making their language correspond to measurable things, but who, when they left the laboratory, behaved in the crude world like professional anti-Semites or Townsend Plan evangelists. Mr. P. W. Bridgman, the author of the very test which Mr. Chase uses, the operational test for meaning, wrote for this magazine an article holding up "intellectual integrity" as the hope of the world, but neglected to supply an operation which would reveal the meaning of the term. But also we have known mechanics, politicians, and athletic coaches whose judgment about what was wrong with an automobile, a ward organization, or a lame knee, and about the best way to treat the condition, proved completely sound, no matter what general ideas or meaningless words they used to rationalize it. Both of these classes of facts are important to psychology and to society.

That is to say, first, that many areas of human behavior cannot be comprehended in exact terminology — and there is no reason why they should be. In any act of judgment that involves skill or experience there are certain automatic or unconscious elements which precede the conscious ones in time, which can be expressed only in inexact terms, but which, nevertheless, contribute to the act's effectiveness. You prove that such effectiveness is independent of exact expression every time you employ your own skill or someone else's.

It is to say, second, that verbal proofs, general ideas, abstractions, personifications, and logical systems are bound up with human habits, emotional and irrational habits, which seem to be ineradicable. Only a very limited success can be expected in any effort to diminish their power. If you succeed in showing someone that he is using an animate abstraction irrationally, you don't cure him of irrationality, you only impel him to alter its form. Mr. Chase attacks conservatism and supports the good society with the aid of semantics; the anti-Semite finds a subtler argument to support his anti-Semitism; the Marxist revises the terms in which the theory of labor value is expressed; the "businessman" discovers some new ground for opposing political control over business. If you then attack these new verbalisms you may annihilate them in turn, but the sentiments they embody promptly set up other terms of expression.

It is to say, in the end, that the sentiments behind these irrationalities are tremendously important to society, and to
suggest that society is inconceivable without such irrationalities. The effort to eradicate them may be not only futile but
misconceived as well. If we say that something is socially
good or socially bad we are using terms that have no meaning,
but if we say that something is socially useful we are using a
term that can be given meaning. We can give it meaning by
performing an operation. Something is useful to "society" on
the average, to a statistical majority of the people who compose the society, to the rate of production or the per capita
wealth or the effective functioning of social institutions. It
is useful to certain people, things, or functions, in certain
specific ways and contexts at certain specific times.

Such usefulness may be quite independent of "meaning" and
also of our feelings about it. The slaughter of some thousands
of Catholic priests by the Spanish Loyalists (if it occurred)
may horrify you and me; but it may have been useful to the
society that did the slaughtering. Our horror of the massacre
of Jews in Germany or of Trotskyists in Russia has no bearing on the possible usefulness of the killings to the societies
that conducted them. And the massacres may have made those
societies more stable or more vigorous because of the irrationalities involved in them. Nothing could be more irrational
than the meaningless term "patriotism," but a society that goes
to war is more or less effective as its "patriotism" is more or
less vigorous. "The classless society," "Aryan supremacy,"
"mare nostrum," "the New Deal," "the full dinner pail,"
"rugged individualism," "the one big union," "the solidarity
of the working class," and similar phrases are meaningless by
Mr. Chase's tests, and various of them may variously disgust
you and me and other people, but they have been socially effective. Though they have no operational meaning, they have
produced measurable results.

"To balance the budget" is a phrase whose operational

meaning, revealed by simple bookkeeping, is the same as its common-sense meaning. For five years we have heard Mr. Roosevelt announce that he was going to balance the budget. For five years we have heard him exorcise his failure to do so by saying that he must first "balance the human budget." To semantics that phrase is meaningless, and in using it Mr. Roosevelt has behaved exactly like the advertising men whom Mr. Chase proscribes, or like Hitler talking about communism. Yet most Americans, Mr. Chase probably among them, accept it and can be directed and controlled by it. In other words, a budget is balanced if you say that you are going to balance it or if you say that you have balanced it in a human way. And, operationally, by saying so you get x foot pounds of work done.

There is no such thing as "truth." There is no such thing as "social justice." But in the areas here briefly touched upon there are phenomena which occur regularly, in patterns, and to some extent predictably. They occur in what *appear to be* interdependent, mutually functioning systems, and they occur *as if* they resulted from sentiments — instincts, emotions, complexes, patterns of response. Such sentiments find expression in such social myths as solidarity and Aryan supremacy, and that expression, though it has no semantic meaning, has effective meaning. It is desirable for social investigators to think about everything as objectively and accurately as possible, but it is also desirable to recognize that the nonrational is nonrational and that it is socially important. The trouble with Mr. Chase's otherwise brilliant analysis is that he *appears* (to the Easy Chair) to act *as if* he thought he could distinguish between good and bad irrationalities and *as if* he wanted to obliterate the bad ones because they are bad. But, in such contexts, "good" and "bad" have no meaning.

The Oncoming

ONLY THE faintest images survive of the first week of August, 1914. In a Rocky Mountain town one had graduated from high school, was in love for the first time, had a newspaper job reporting the games of a Class D baseball league and the Chautauqua lectures. One scrawled AP war stories on strips of press paper and hung them from twine in the office windows. Unexcited, hardly interested, amiably chatting groups gathered on the sidewalk to read those bulletins — smaller, much less passionate groups than those which would soon gather to follow the World's Series. The bulletins drew pictures of a storybook war in one's mind: Uhlans against the Belgian sky at twilight, cruisers making out to sea with their lights doused, dust-gray columns deploying into line through ripening wheat while sulphur-colored flowers of shrapnel bloomed above them. They were formal tableaux on a screen, picturesque, romantic, tinged with Sir Lancelot; they were pretty under the box elders but meaningless and without importance; they were as far away as Saturn. This time it will be neither distant nor romantic, even to boys.

It had moved from Saturn to a Europe that was not quite so far away, seventeen months later, and in the rooms of Charles Townsend Copeland it finally crossed the Atlantic. In January, 1917, Mr. S. K. Ratcliffe was talking, late at night, to some Harvard boys. His musical, sensitively calculated voice brought another picture to Hollis Hall, English volunteers marching down to the ships singing "Tipperary," singing "Send father and mother, send sister and brother, but for God's sake don't send me." He made us see those soldiers going out to die and several times he paused, smiled in the lamplight, and said very gently, "I'll be seeing you young gentlemen in France before it's done." In moonlight a snow-crusted angle of the roof of Holworthy showed in Copey's window, and the voice went on whispering in yellow lamp-light. *It's really war, those singers are blown to hell now, and he may be right.* He was right and perhaps he did see some of us in France; for some young gentlemen who were in Copey's rooms that night are now just names on the roll of what is called honor in the church which Harvard built to commemorate its war dead.

There was a morning in early May, 1917. One crossed Boston Common and the Public Garden in spring sunlight, the trees budding, all colors clear and bright, flags everywhere — and for an hour or so something that is called dedication, something that is called sacrifice, something that is called patriotism, made a suffocating ecstasy in one's heart. One had enlisted to-day, would be in France to-morrow, would be dead, sweetly and decorously for one's country, by the morning of the third day. And that moment, scorned sometimes and jeered at, not believed in sometimes or shamefacedly denied, has never been altogether forgotten. And there was something besides bright colors and confused ecstasy: there was a swift, brief glimpse of a nation that has never quite existed.

Midnight in late December, 1918. One who had been for some hours an ex-lieutenant of infantry got into a dilapidated, oil-lighted day coach at Petersburg, Virginia. The town's lights fell behind and another ex-lieutenant said, "I know two that ain't going next time, me and the guy they send to get me." One agreed but hardly heard him, for there was a numb awe, a feeling recognizable as the end of disbelief, the turning of a deep tide back from death to life and to the possibility of belief in life. It is twenty-one years since that train rocked and groaned through the Virginia night.

The last two weeks of August, 1939. A small group of professional writers were gathered to instruct a larger group of apprentice writers, on a mountain in northern Vermont. The Gap opened westward on a vista of the Green Mountains and outlines of the Adirondacks beyond. There were days of clear sun; twice northern lights flared in the night sky; as the fortnight wore out the moon grew toward the full. In a Europe that was hardly a gunshot away the destruction wasted at noonday, and on the mountain we talked, because there was nothing else to do, about the use of words, and how to tell a story, and what the illusion of fiction is made of. We played tennis, went swimming in icy water, came together for a cocktail at dinnertime. We talked about the shadows of shadows, about writing, about the dreams that beget art, while death lowered over Europe. There was a deep insistence: hold trivialities to your heart, for they can be loved and cannot be taken away — tennis, the body's weariness, sleep, the voices of friends, patches of moonlight on the trunks of maples, ground mist across the valley when dusk comes.

One had always disliked automobile radios but had bought one just eleven months before, when a hurricane struck New England and only automobile radios kept a devastated village in touch with the world outside. We were prepared, we said eleven months ago, for the next hurricane. Now it was at hand. At intervals one walked away from the tennis, the cocktails, the talking, to switch it on and learn if the winds had been loosed. *Not yet. It is still, of a kind, peace.* The nerve had been pounded to paralysis, carrying no message to the brain of either horror or relief. One sat in the car listening, and one by one the others came out to listen too, and at length we shut off the radio and went back to the talking.

All day and up to early morning we listened to that voice coming from the cowl. Now it told us about the treaty of non-aggression between Germany and Russia. The nerve had been pounded too long and hard; only a little charge could travel its exhausted fiber. Dialectical materialism, one thought: thesis, Russian communism; antithesis, fascism; synthesis, this treaty. This was the identity one had often written about, one had discussed in the Easy Chair "that other fascism in Marx's cloth-ing." Then, as the nerve cleared: maybe one danger has been lessened for America, maybe two dangers, for our local com-munism cannot maintain its pale farce now, and what does the treaty do to Japan? Morning grew to morning and talk went on. One of us was sure that another deal was in the mak-ing, though this time they might have to get the armies into battle lines in order to put the deal across. Another was sure that those rudimentary Satans, the international bankers, had done all this of their own evil will, the taint of Adam's sin not having been washed away. And a third said, nothing will happen, all the great liners are sailing on schedule, Germany has insufficient trained reserves, not 1939 but 1943 is the war year. We went on talking.

It was an inconsiderable weight that snapped the string at last. War powers to the British government, a practical dicta-torship. But of course. If there was to be war there must be war governments, everyone knew that. Yet it was this bulletin that made the war real, as Mr. Ratcliffe's cunning voice in Hollis lamplight had made it real twenty-four years ago. In sixty seconds one of us leaped across the chasm to where others of us had been standing and, abandoning the cleansed idea of the Western democracies, was saying to hell with them all, who cares about the British Empire? who cares about Europe? how much of America can we save? His voice was shrill. *We shall all be shrill now, we shall watch the madness grow in one another.* A group of writers talking about art while war came. A group of friends reaching for one another in darkness.

How much of America could be saved? The lines of swift change will veer again now, to other changes, and all our desperations still unsolved. This makes it still easier to evade them than it has been. Here is a deadlier way to avoid the thinking and postpone the will which only could have helped us. And here is an exterior desperation. At this moment we are in the war, to stay. Whether formally remote or raising such armies as I was discharged from twenty-one years ago, we shall finish it — America will wage the war in one way or another and take the responsibility of fitting together what fragments of the world are left when it is finished.

The wolves will be prowling at once, one thought, the wolves, the jackals, and the rats. They will have good hunting and feeding on the edges of the fire; it is their big chance. Wrapped in the flag or in sheepskins, or just wolves, they will be hard to recognize. But he said *we*, many more will be saying *we* — for a while. There will be, for a while, more *we* in America than there has been. There will be a surge of willingness and common desire. Maybe something can be done with that; it gives us a chance as well as the wolves. There is that job to do, now that a voice from the air has destroyed most of whatever meaning was left in private lives and private jobs. There is that job, indefinable and incomprehensible, to be undertaken ignorantly and with resolution but little livened with hope, but to be undertaken. There is as much help for us as there has ever been for mortal man, as much and no more, there is as much courage, as much strength. And there is the misty glimpse, as above Boston Common, of a nation that has never quite existed.

(How the words came back! One had been at a play in the old Hollis Street Theater in April, 1917. Before the last act people brought in newspapers with big headlines, and afterward one went to the Nip and drank a glass of beer and read a long flimsy curling from a ticker, and the taste of that beer has always been part of the rhythms of the prose. *We are at the beginning of an age in which it will be insisted that the same standards of conduct and responsibility for wrong done shall be observed among nations and their governments that are observed among the individual citizens of civilized states. . . . We shall fight . . . for the rights and liberties of small nations, for a universal dominion of right by such a concert of free peoples as shall bring peace and safety to all nations and make the world at last free.* That made a pleasant promise when I was young and here is payday.)

God helping us, Mr. Wilson said, we could do no other. God helping us, we can now do no other — than what?

Still the final word had not come. At the week end two of us drove swiftly across New Hampshire, turning on the radio from time to time; the hills made reception bad and the jumbled bulletins that came through were still indefinite. Back to the Vermont mountain for a few days more, talking about art while the world broke up. The writers' conference ended and the radio voice was still guessing it would be peace. One drove southward to Boston and found it crowded with middle-aged men in uniform, the Veterans of Foreign Wars meeting in convention. On the night of August 31st they remembered their gunfire with a noisy program of skyrockets and aerial bombs, which woke one's nine-year-old son from sleep, and one listened to the radio till midnight, thinking of the armies that groped toward the battle of the Marne twenty-five years ago, and went to bed exhausted. So one woke early on the morning of September 1st, turned on the radio again, and found that it had happened while one slept. The newspaper on the doorstep said the same thing, and the nine-year-old boy came downstairs, saw the headlines, and asked, "Is there war in Poland now?", asked, "Why is there war?", and said, "War is terrible, isn't it?"

The thing had happened. There was war again and one's son was asking why. Upstairs his mother slept, and what had waked him last night was only fireworks set off for the amusement of old soldiers, though at that moment half a million children were being moved out of London in the hope that some of them might be saved from death. An American nine-year-old who could safely play in his back yard said that war was terrible and asked why there was war.

Tell him about those groups in front of the newspaper office tranquilly reading about a war as far away as Saturn . . . Mr. Ratcliffe in Copey's rooms . . . reading Mr. Wilson's speech in a saloon . . . walking dedicated to honor across the Common . . . leaving Petersburg for peace and the renewal of life. Tell him that my boyhood too had the promise of peace in it, that the love which begot him was an understanding that life is peace. Tell him that all boyhoods have the promise of peace and the promise of growing up to do something of one's will, achieve something of one's desire, be something of one's dream — and no promises are kept except as the dice may chance to roll. Tell him that the cost of any life, mine or his, is the price asked for it. Tell him that the price asked for any life is belief in a right and a truth that do not exist, conscription in a war against the uncomprehended for reasons never given — and that this does not matter. . . . Tell him that he may be sure of his family, that within a family there is love, willingness, life shared. There are other families, the neighborhood he plays in, the friends he has made — from street to street till some larger part of America is in his heart, which will always be too small to have the world in it. He will not grow up in the America he was born in, but neither did I or anyone else who has ever lived here; and if he cannot have the hope perhaps he can have the will to do more than I did in the shaping of his own America. Man by man, child by child, family by family, the job is to save something of the kindliness, the freedom, and the safety that are still ours. To save anything will be to save much.

To see to it that no children are bombed here. To save what we can and make what we can of what is saved. And — to strive on to finish the work we are in, to bind up the nation's wounds. Beyond that the issue of what we shall have to do as the war spreads is hidden. But the watcher on the walls knows that for an hour or so it is still possible to save something of America, and even finds a grave hope that for that hour or so there is a better chance than there was. For an hour or so. We can seize the hour or let it pass.

II

LITERARY CONVERSATION

FROM THE *Saturday Review*, SEPTEMBER 26, 1936

A Generation beside the Limpopo

TRANSITION adopts an upper-case initial and George Horace Lorimer has retired. Heywood Broun is writing for *Collier's* and Walter Lippmann will vote Republican. The recent reviews of *A Further Range* are being hastily revised because word arrives from Auden, Spender, Lewis, and Empson that Robert Frost is a proletarian poet, and a writer in the *New Republic* has spoken favorably of the American tradition. But the conclusive evidence that a caesura of some sort has been reached is the growing number of literary autobiographies. The Younger Generation and the Young Intellectuals have reached the age of reminiscence.

It would be easy to say, and is widely being said, that a literary generation is ending. An awkwardness, however, is at once encountered: nobody can decide just what a literary generation is. The time scale is ambiguous: the first novelist of the Younger Generation began publishing in 1900, its first poet died in 1886, and its twilight genius is only thirty-five.

No date can be agreed on for its beginning: Mr. Van Doren [1] believes that it began with the Armistice, but surely it was in full cry as early as 1912 and most of the rebellions for which it is celebrated were current during its early adolescence, among the muckrakers, the crusaders, and the *Ur*-Greenwich-Villagers of the preceding ten years. The end is also undetermined. We are told that the period closed with 1929 and the Wall Street crash, with 1932 and the bottom of the trough, with 1934 and the crest of the New Deal, and with 1936 and the possible success of Mr. Lippmann's candidate. But wherever you fix a date for the beginning of dotage, you find that nine-tenths of the reasonably good writing since that deadline has been done by men you have extinguished. Finally, only a resolute mind can keep from identifying a literary generation with a literary fashion, and a writer in *Harper's* recently established a periodicity of three and a half years for literary fashions in contemporary America. His curve was unnecessarily severe: literary fashions in contemporary America have a life of fully four years.

The heterogeneity of the human race, in short, nullifies the formulas of criticism, and all generalizations about a literary generation are faulty. The only sharp cleavage between 1936 and 1920 is in poetry: sixteen years ago poetry had to be pretty good in order to be praised, whereas nowadays it has to be fourth-rate or worse in order to get a hearing at all. Nevertheless, the fact that writers are now getting old who were leaders of revolt twenty-five years ago does make expedient the separation into a literary "period" of the time during which their mature work was mostly done. It is the third principal period in American literature, and all things considered, the richest, the most various, and the most interesting. Its best work falls short of the best of both the other periods: it produced no one who may be ranked with Emerson, Thoreau, or Mark Twain. It had even, by actual count, fewer first-

[1] *Three Worlds*, by Carl Van Doren.

raters than either of its predecessors: two poets, one novelist, and H. L. Mencken. But below the level of highest excellence it far surpassed both of them. There had never before been so much good writing in America, so many writers who knew their job, such a liveness and liveliness, so much genuine literature. It was our most cosmopolitan period — the time not only when American literature was least provincial but also when it for the first time achieved, in certain areas, leadership in world literature. And also it was our freest period, in that it won and for the time being at least kept the right of literature to deal with such subjects as it might choose to in such ways as might please it, exempt from social, religious, moral, and political aggression. That adds up to quite a bit. A period which was various and alive, which raised the common level of competence, and which established freedom as a fixed condition of American letters may be permitted the illusions with which it comforted itself.

You will not find those illusions discussed in Mr. Van Doren's book. A champion of the period who was one of its accepted critics, he shows its commonest weakness in leniently accepting its assumptions about itself. He is much better at the first of his three worlds, farm life and small-city life in Illinois. Those chapters have a reality that is never fully communicated to what follows them. They are stamped out of a profound and native experience, whose poignancy shows that it was more important than what came after it. They explain why Mr. Van Doren did not share the worst absurdities of the period, never found American life hideous or even dull, and rejected the clichés that so many of his colleagues built into a system of criticism. He knew in his nerve ends one segment of American life that most of his fellows only had ideas about. If more of that particular kind of knowledge had got into the literature of the period, less of that literature would now have the faintly archeological absurdity of a Godey fashion plate. It kept Mr. Van Doren amiable toward American life when indignation toward it was, apart from an unalloyed admiration of momentary masterpieces, the only mood that most critics thought proper to the period. But both his criticism and his autobiography are the poorer because he failed to make full use of the knowledge of experience when he moved from Illinois to his second world, the literary generation.

On page 251 you meet one characteristic of the generation in a revealing moment. Mr. Van Doren, noting that he has as wide an acquaintance with writers as any man of his day, makes a list of those whom he has nevertheless met only infrequently or not at all. There are fifty-five names on the list and something about that accidental grouping strikes home. For only five or six of them are eminent and only ten or twelve of them are important at all. What of the other forty? you wonder. And what of three or four hundred like them whom Mr. Van Doren probably has met? Good competent workmen, literary people doing a satisfactory job, giving the time back something of its tone and color, amusing it, holding up a more or less accurately surfaced mirror for it to gaze into. Several hundred of them — and all of them famous, admired, deferred to, sought after, coddled, and told that they are damned good and even great. Some of them rich, practically all of them in comfortable circumstances, most of them greatly overrated and all of them overpaid. This was the period in American literature which produced the most good writing. And it was also the period in which it was easiest for a writer to succeed, in which writing was most eagerly received and most lavishly rewarded, in which reputation was easiest to attain. Describing the effects of the boom on writers, Mr. Van Doren chooses to discuss only cocktail parties and the significant fact that many writers lost money in Wall Street. But the period of inflation began long before the boom and it principally affected reputations, not bank accounts. It was a period when any competent writer could support himself by his trade. But also it was a period when any competent writer could get himself respected and overvalued by critics and public alike. The public, in fact, was eager to recognize the talent of any writer who bothered to address it; never in the history of the world has literature stood so high in public esteem. . . . And absolutely rockbottom in the beliefs of the literary generation was the notion that art fared badly in America, that the country was anesthetic to literature, that the way of the American writer was bitter and intolerably hard.

America, they believed, was a gigantic conspiracy against art, thought, and the good life. Awed Rotary Clubs had raised purses to send some of the boys to college because they looked promising, others of them spent four years under the elms on scholarship grants, a good many first tasted the culture of France (their spiritual home) on funds supplied by foundations, and some of them, too lazy or too incompetent to write acceptably, have spent a lifetime as pensioners of endowments. But they perceived that the businessman who supported the funds was their ruthless enemy: he conversed badly about Matisse and so prevented them from living the intellectual life. They were permitted to be editors before they were dry behind the ears, bravely denouncing the manufacturer of gadgets in dozens of magazines which the Philistines bought by the thousand, though forbidding literature to exist. They were reviewing books at sixteen and reconstructing society at twenty-one, in a culture which respected and rewarded them more extravagantly than any other ever known on earth. Nevertheless art starved in America and the thinker was broken at the soda fountain and the businessman everywhere mixed Paris green with the bread of life. The literary generation knew, for theory told them so.

Even writers are heterogeneous, some of them swim against the current, and no generalization about the generation will hold. Mr. Van Doren finds the lowest common denominator in revolt, in the fact that his generation rebelled against practically everything. That denominator will do as well as any, if it be understood that most of the generation rebelled on rigorously theoretical grounds and displayed their greatest heroism in refusing to let the facts of experience, of immediate knowledge, of American life as it was lived round them, in any way modify or direct the teachings of theory. Another rockbottom principle of the period was that some vicious insulation had always separated the American writer from American life — be it cowardice, Puritanism, Philistinism, sexual timidity, the Methodist Church South, or whatever eidolon might be the target of the moment. Yes; and never was the insulation so complete as in the period 1912–1936. Mr. Edmund Wilson tells us that never in history had a generation so reviled its country; yes, again, and never had a generation so misrepresented it.

Recall the Young Intellectuals who in 1922, under the captaincy of Harold Stearns, gave the period its best joke book, who "wished to speak the truth about American civilization . . . in order to do our share in making a real civilization possible." While, they made quite clear, while there was yet time. (Since 1912 it has always been 11:59 in America, and only a few heroic literary folk to fend doom away.) They, like all American evangelists since Elder Brewster knelt on the Plymouth beach, bade us change our hearts for only in that way "can true art and true religion and true personality, with their native warmth and caprice and gaiety, grow up in America." These were stern men but they could also be benignant, and they had it in their hearts to give the Americans warmth and caprice and gaiety, to give them personality. While there was yet time.

And their equipment? The Young Intellectuals and the Younger Generation (let us thus distinguish the two groups whom Mr. Van Doren isolates in his period) were, most of them, characterized by a stupefying ignorance of what they were talking about, an instinctive fear of experience, and a vocational preference for describing America by gazing into the crystals of their souls. They knew no history. The American frontier was where Rousseau's disciples went; down to the Civil War American life was a simple unity of homogeneous people; the nation had never produced a reformer or a rebel; the begetters of the only true society on the continent were the Hopi Indians; since the Americans had never taken kindly to bells on the bottoms of their pants, it followed that the nation had no folk art; as late as 1935 we were told that Dewey destroyed Cervera's fleet; and wasn't it a shame that a potential artist like S. F. B. Morse was betrayed by our native materialism into inventing (*sic*) the magnetic telegraph? They had no sociology except Herbert Spencer, of whom they spoke very highly, and Thorstein Veblen, whom they misquoted so violently as to suggest that they knew him principally by rumor (and upsurgent youth, in 1936, here follows the elders' well-worn path). They had no economics at all (but in 1936 you become an economist by writing a novel). They had no travel in the despised hinterland: all they could find in The Small Town was the fraternal society and the lodge convention and the county fair. They observed the World's Series bleachers and decided that the Americans took their sport, as they took Life, vicariously, whereupon manufacturers of skis and tennis rackets and hunting equipment and automobiles shut down their mills. What they knew about agriculture was that an American manure pile (moved, in 1936, from Iowa to Idaho) was a symbol of spiritual squalor at whose steaming puddles Matilda gazed of a March morning with dumb and frustrate disgust, whereas a French manure pile meant the good life and the reality of human emotion in touch with the soil and therefore in touch also with the bloodstream of a liberal culture.

So they reported on America while there was yet time. But the America they reported on and saw collapsing every quarter-day was a derivative of theory and of dream — a province next door to Ophir, beyond the Hörselberg, somewhere along the Limpopo River all set about with fever trees. Wishfulness and a fine logic and a dread of experience were an effective insulation, and of the many paralyses they suffered, two were worst of all. They did not know the Middle West or the middle class. The clear-eyed, dauntless, and uncompromising youth of the We're Younger Generation, who will avoid all the errors of those who were young so sentimentally, are currently steaming full speed ahead in complete ignorance of the Middle West and the middle class.

There was also that personal devil, standardization. In Detroit Henry Ford (Ben Franklin's loathsome heir) was making cylinder rings which deplorably fitted any Ford cylinder anywhere, whereas each should have been unique and made by hand. (The generation's ambivalence toward machinery was another of its despairs.) Therefore you could not tell Portland, Maine, from Portland, Oregon, or from New Orleans — whose inhabitants all saw the same movies, thought the same thoughts, spoke with the same accent, lived in the same architecture, and voted the same way on another ol' dayvil, the tariff. The generation walloped America for failing to standardize on Matisse, and also larruped it for being so dreadfully of one piece. The whole nation was just one drab, gray monotone of thought, though in the next chapter it caught hell because no program of reform could be put through Congress since the sections would never agree on one. On page 5, a gum-chewing, movie-going standardization has stifled the priceless individuality of the immigrant cultures; on page 50, refusing its noble destiny as the Melting Pot, America remains just a polyglot boarding house. The generation was capable of many magnificent feats but of no other so arresting as this: that it could look at a chaos of races, cultures, creeds, traditions, philosophies, political and economic systems that has only once or twice been a nation and then only for brief periods of danger — and see a uniformity so dull that no artist could draw his breath there and no thinker find the courage to go on. The boys shuddered away from the Chicagoan for being a back-slapping, dynamic, uninhibited boor, and their nostrils quivered at the poison of a Bostonian's inhibition that said nay to life — and somehow, in the mystical reveries of the thoughtful, both were the same. They loved the South because it had a Cavalier tradition, reviled it because it came from the same oppressive mold as the Puritan neurosis, applauded the grace and realism and intellectual distinction of its aristocratic system, and wept over its native American violence in first flogging and later lynching its Negroes. What America most lacked and needed, they felt sure, was intimacy with the soil; nevertheless America was a nation of yokels dominated by the ignorance and superstition of the rural mind; and standardization made a Vermont farmhouse identical with an Arkansas share-cropper's shack, while the peasant manias of the upcountry were what kept us a backward people, though our gravest cultural defect was the lack of a peasantry.

So now, suddenly, requiems are being sung over a literary generation. There has not been time to give America a civilization, or even personality and gaiety, but there has been time for the boys — some of them — to grow older.

For one thing, they are back from Europe, and it was not only the devaluation of the dollar that brought them back. To be sure, a good many of them share a uniformity with the leopard and the Ethiopian that obscures the others. Thus, one type has been forced to wonder whether the trickle of books from the Left Bank really justifies the agonies of exile. Thought, he finds, will not sustain itself without material to work on; and books, he finds, do not write themselves, even when they are meant to make America the gift of gaiety. But this type has come home only to the Limpopo. He records that the French poor are graceful and have something to do and see and be amused by (Dr. Céline doubtless agreeing), altogether decorative poor they are, but in America the poor have no grace. Suburbia, he finds, is much worse. He confesses that time has taught him that men should make an ordered effort, should have a job to work at, should satisfy fundamental needs in marriage and parenthood and family life, should find the stability of living together and the symmetry of working in a community. Having learned that, he walks through suburbia where people have made an ordered effort and worked at their jobs and found the stability of marriage and parenthood. And he translates the symbols as just some ugly houses, and tells us that they have not the lift that ugliness has in France.

But age, agony, and Europe have taught some of the boys a different lesson. Conspiracy against the intellectual life? Well, they have seen some of the damnedest things done, in culture's truest home. Here in the suburbia of the standardized, the intellectuals are still publishing their brave manifestoes in uncensored magazines: in Germany and Italy a Philistine conspiracy that really knows its stuff has filled the cemeteries with those who tried to live the intellectual life. The manufacturer of gadgets is still conversing badly about Matisse, but the artist who cannot draw his breath here is still writing the kind of books he wants to write, whereas there have been some enthusiastic pogroms in the name of art on Moscow's golden shore. The American continent is still standardized, the money-changers having lain down with Father Coughlin while Rex Tugwell is leading both, and strong winds are blowing. But they are different winds from those which the boys observed in Europe and, at the generation's end, they have blown some of its phantasies away. A most astonishing revision has been going on.

The generation's finest critic was Mr. Van Wyck Brooks. He most brilliantly of all set out to find a usable past, most bitterly discovered that there was none, and most logically and rigorously worked out the generation's master idea, that American life stifled moral courage and spiritual greatness and true art. And lately Mr. Brooks has published a wise, profound, and very moving book in which he finds a usable past and turns up in the craven America the most astonishing courage in letters and leadership, the most amazing spiritual endeavor in the literary life, and the most astounding excellence of art in the wine of the Puritans. If one makes parallel columns of quotations from *The Flowering of New England* and from the books which Mr. Brooks was writing fifteen and twenty years ago, one beholds the best of the generation making a formal recantation.

The generation's finest novelist was Sinclair Lewis. He was also the one most alert to all the rhythms and overtones and shadows of the generation, and in him also, as in Mr. Brooks, one may plot the curve of a reversal. The butt of *Babbitt* became the hero of *Work of Art*. And when Mr. Lewis began to meditate on what could or couldn't happen here, midnight struck at last and all bets were off. For the savior of the good life, the Doremus Jessup who cannot die, is the editor of that *Weekly Dauntless* which Carol Kennicott despised, and when revolt breaks out against intolerable tyranny and standardization it first shows its strength in — the State of Winnemac. Gopher Prairie has become the hope of the world.

And so by 1936 the generation has arrived at the position from which Robert Frost started in 1913.

A vigorous and colorful generation, an emancipated and emancipating generation, the most interesting generation of our literature. But a wishful generation, impermeable to experience, separated by iridescent mist from the realities of men and women living on this continent, conjuring up an America of phantasy and out of theory, syllogisms, and boyhood lacks. And too soft. Times were too easy, success and reputation were too easily come by, it was too much respected and too gently handled by itself, by its critics, and especially by the public. . . . The times are harder now and Mr. Van Doren believes that his third world, including our post-depression literary youth, is tougher-minded. One hopes so but must ask leave to doubt. What can be discerned of a younger generation in literature does indeed regard its elders as sentimental, but alas that means not that it is more realistic but only that the foci of sentiment have changed with fashions. The Still Younger Intellectuals, producing for us still another kind of dissolute and collapsing America, may be reached at the old address, an ivory tower beside the Limpopo River, looking out to sea; and when reached there will be found in the familiar posture, gazing at their navels. The chief difference between them and their predecessors is that their theories will hold more gas and so rise higher from the common earth.

There is no sign yet that our writers are beginning to prefer looking at America and the Americans to approaching them with a set of preconceptions derived from a mystical trance. American literature is not, at the moment, preparing to be realistic about America. Nothing can be done to make it so, or very little. Criticism might stop helping writers admire their own beautiful ideas. It might begin to call mere gas by its right name, to designate guesswork as charlatanry and mystical nonsense as plain ignorance, to point out that misrepresentation, however generously intended, is just lying. But criticism cannot do much; let us, rather, invoke prayer. One who has the national literature at heart can pray that the Americans may stop greeting with patient courtesy whatever bilge literary gents offer them as descriptions of the nation, and let loose upon it the tonic stimulus of a belly laugh. And he can pray that writers may turn to experience, and away from books and theories — or, since that is praying for a miracle, that fortune may endow American literature with a good sociologist. God send the Republic someone who knows how the Americans live and can give the theories of the literary some basis in things as they actually are.

Plus Ce Change

~~~~~~

TWO BOOKS,[1] dissimilar enough, invite me to preach a sermon for the young. It begins in ignorance, since I have read only the first of the four earlier books by Mr. Rascoe listed opposite the title page of this one. But only the last chapter of his autobiography deals with the subjects to which Mr. Cowley's anthology is devoted, whereas the earlier chapters cover material common to us all and very useful to my principal point about the anthology.

To get to that point at once: Mr. Rascoe tells us that at the age of thirteen he had a job delivering morning newspapers in a Southern town. He got up hours before dawn, shocked himself awake with coffee, went down to the office and folded a couple of hundred newspapers, and then went out into the weather and hurled them at the subscribers' doors. How did he feel about this labor? He thought it was wonderful; it enabled him to earn money, it was adventurous, it gave him a

---

[1] *Before I Forget*, by Burton Rascoe; *After the Genteel Tradition*, edited by Malcolm Cowley.

good time, and he felt very proud of his achievement. Now if you will glance at *Look Homeward, Angel,* you will find that when Eugene Gant had the same job in a similar Southern town it seemed to Mr. Thomas Wolfe an affront to the human spirit which produced suffering hardly equaled since Calvary, if equaled then. This disparity teaches us nothing whatever about child labor or the newspaper business but, I think, it establishes that there are differences in literary temperament.

My guess is that Mr. Rascoe, as a practising critic, has allowed for such differences; my first objection to the thinkers who contribute to Mr. Cowley's collection is that they do not. I find no absolutes in Mr. Rascoe's book, and I suspect that he has been an *ad hoc* critic, holding to experience and letting the system go by default, dealing with the literature that came to hand in terms of itself. That is the habit of mind revealed in his reminiscences, and I am constrained to believe that it must have determined his critical work. If so, he is an altogether different kind of critic from those who reject the writings of their immediate predecessors (and Mr. Rascoe's contemporaries) in *After the Genteel Tradition.*

I shall be denouncing generalizations in a moment but I venture to make one now, that if there are marked differences between American literature twenty years ago and American literature as it now is, one of the most marked is the greater gusto of its earlier practitioners. Or some of them — for let us not forget that some of Mr. Rascoe's contemporaries held that literature should not make jokes. They were outnumbered, however, and there was a good deal of delight, excitement, high spirits, and sheer animal health in the literary world of 1920 and thereabouts. Some of the writers produced the most lugubrious books but they had a jovial time producing them, and much of that euphoria has gone from the literary scene to-day. I suspect that most of Mr. Cowley's colleagues would denounce it as levity unbefitting the present crisis; to-day a writer can enjoy himself only at peril of betraying the revolution. And yet, once said, this seems no novelty, for some thinkers in 1920 would have seen that he was betraying either Beauty or the Good Life, and this continuity is another point to make about the anthology.

Mr. Rascoe, in any event, appears to have had what Huck Finn called a noble good time. It carries over, in his autobiography, not only in the portion devoted to contemporary literature but even more markedly in the long and loving account of his boyhood. His book should be read for that account, not for its literary comments, which probably will be extended in later volumes. It re-creates the Southern town of the late nineties and after as well as anything I can think of in our literature, and makes one regret that Mr. Rascoe has never tried his hand at fiction. It is full of typical experiences that anyone of Mr. Rascoe's generation must recognize as in part his own as well. It makes first-rate reading, and one reason why it does is Mr. Rascoe's healthy zest in the society to which he belonged. Whoever else has been at war with his environment, Mr. Rascoe was not.

Now much of Mr. Rascoe's experience parallels that of Mr. Floyd Dell; at a greater remove it resembles what happened to Mr. Sherwood Anderson, and at a still greater one what happened to Mr. Edgar Lee Masters. Here are four literary men who grew up in somewhat similar localities not a generation apart. All have written their autobiographies, yet four more dissimilar stories, four more unlike interpretations of experience, it would be difficult to imagine. Why? The question is simple and transparent, and the complete answer to it is immediate and almost automatic. But it is also important and the answer is a fundamental which one kind of literary thinking, the kind represented by Mr. Cowley's anthology, dismisses or completely disregards.

After the Genteel Tradition is a collection of short critical pieces by various hands. It contains an essay on Ernest Hemingway by John Peale Bishop which is spectacularly good, probably the best ever written on its subject, and one by Hildegarde Flanner on Jeffers and Millay which, though by no means so brilliant as Mr. Bishop's, is nevertheless a first-rate treatment of its subject. With that sentence I am going to dismiss those two pieces, for they differ from the others in that they treat the writers they discuss in terms of the writers and their books, whereas all the other pieces in the book treat their subjects in terms of a theoretical system composed of abstractions which arise out of sentiment but are supposed to arise out of the absolute nature of things — and that is a kind of criticism which interests me a good deal. As specimens of the kind, these essays vary from the excellent, as in Mr. Arvin on Sandburg and Mr. Cowley on Dos Passos, through the perfunctory, as Mr. Chamberlain on Dreiser, to the hopelessly and grotesquely bad, as Mr. Lionel Trilling on Willa Cather. They vary not only in quality but also in statement and description, and in the information acquired by the authors as well. There are vast discrepancies in what the authors say about their common period and even in their bases of judgments, but it was right to publish the essays together, for, no matter how inharmonious extrinsically, they are unified by common sentiments.

The book undertakes to get into critical focus the last generation of American literature — defined as those writers who (*a*) lived through the war or the boom or both, or (*b*) haven't written books in which boy meets Party organizer. The generation does not include Robert Frost until page 230, where Mr. Cowley acknowledges that *North of Boston* is likely to be read for a while longer, and both its map and its climate have changed quite a bit since the last time an anthology got it into focus. But the Artist is still in torment, and the talk about him is still carried on in a domain where words, instead of standing for things, have an entity and significance of their own. And the generation is again shown to have, in the mass, betrayed itself and come upon frustration; though, again, there is still hope. For once more the fiddles are tuning all over America. Last time they never got beyond the tuning, but this time it is no fake and we are going to have a symphony, though of course it has not yet begun. What kind of symphony are we going to have? Well, literature is going to be about society. Literature in America has never been about society. The best thing about the generation treated by this book is that it once promised to be about society. The worst thing about it is that it did not make good.

In all this there is no exterior unity, but there is an imposing unity of internal sentiment, and the interesting thing is that it is identical with a powerful sentiment of the literature which these writers suppose they are repudiating. In order to pass judgment on individual writers, most of these critics have to characterize the period as a whole, and if you compare Mr. Louis Kronenberger's account of the times with Mr. Robert Cantwell's you will find serious incompatibilities, and if you then bring Mr. Peter Monro Jack's to bear upon the other two you are forced to decide that three periods, not one, are in dispute. Or take Mr. Cantwell's suspicion of the lower bour-geoisie which admired Coolidge and approves of Hearst; Mr. Cantwell resents them, presumably because they are the raw material from which (insert fascist) dictatorship may come. But when you get to Mr. Arvin, who writes about Carl Sand-burg, the lower bourgeoisie have become the people and they look altogether different. Nor is there any reconciling one appearance with the other.

This, of course, was also a dilemma of the generation whom Mr. Cowley and his colleagues are dismissing. On the one hand the people are wonderful, for truth and justice abide with them, and they are exploited by the evil men, and it is they in whose name the great society must be built. But on the other hand, the people are both vulgar and dangerous; their preferences in literature and amusement distress the critic; they give themselves up to beastly if not bestial ambitions; they follow after material ends by expedient or even dishonest means, and they become the mob whose violence threatens everything the critic believes in and may well wreck the great society. The dilemma glistens in every chapter of this anthology but no one resolves it, and no one reflects that in exactly the same way it frustrated much thought some years ago. It was the barrier, for instance, though Mr. Bernard Smith does not quite see it, which Mr. Van Wyck Brooks could not hurdle. Mr. Brooks demanded a genuine literature of American life, but whenever he encountered one he rejected it as coarse, vulgar, and unseemly. I cannot see that the group who dismiss him have improved upon his stand.

A fashion of the earlier enlightenment was to denounce American life as dull and contemptible, because it was materialistic, money-grubbing, standardized, inhibited, unrefined. The reason for this was that the Americans were inferior, if you belonged to that wing, or cowardly and puritanical, if you liked those epithets better. In any event, this fashion refused to apply the bell-shaped curve to the human race and concluded that things must be otherwise in France. The condemnation of American life still holds, though the terms have shifted to those of social injustice, the explanation now is that society is distintegrating, and the conclusion is that things will be otherwise in socialism. Yesterday what ailed the American, as our critics saw him, was suppression of or nay-saying to his natural instincts, and beauty and the Civil Liberties Union would cure all that. To-day his disgust of life is due to the malformation of society, and when collectivism comes in there will be no neuroses. . . . Has critical realism advanced? Or has a sentiment changed its skin?

Yesteryear we were commonly told that the American artist never lived up to his potentialities. A number of villainies were alleged: a hard crassness in American life ruined Henry James, a puritan-commercial culture emasculated Mark Twain, puritanism pure accounted for Hawthorne and puritanism mixed did away with Melville, provincialism slew its dozens and the bitch-goddess success her scores. Of the generation's own do their successors now return unto them, and their personal "promise that had seemed so rich" is almost always shown to have been frustrated or to have come to much less than it should. Most of Mr. Cowley's collaborators tacitly assume what he says explicitly, that this promise was slain when the war dissipated the writers' hope of helping to build the socialist commonwealth. Which is doubly odd: for nearly every book that he and his colleagues praise was written in 1920 or after it, and of all the writers they discuss only one, and he the least important, ever had any belief in or idea of the socialist commonwealth. At any rate none except Upton Sinclair ever put such a belief or idea into a book. Mr. Brooks spoke at intervals of a collective life, which he never defined and which he usually replaced with a society about which all we knew was that artists would be leaders in it, and Mr. Sandburg is, I believe, a Fabian — but even such loose visions as these failed to condition their books, and if socialism meant anything at all to the others it meant that women should not wear corsets and the state ought to set its citizens to dancing in cheesecloth on the lawn. The hard fact is that there was no general belief in a socialistic commonwealth among the literary people whom this collection examines, or among their generation. That belief is an invention of their successors.

It will be interesting some day to inquire why that particular explanation has been invented but let us now observe that with this correspondence between yesterday's and to-day's fashions in critical mythology we reach one of the falsifying forces in literary thinking. What is the promise of any given artist, how great is it, and how do you know? If you know what it is, how do you know what frustrates it? Such questions might well seem unanswerable but both generations answered them with confident certainty. The author of *The Adventures of Huckleberry Finn* was withheld from greatness because the pioneer tradition froze his personality at an infantile level; the author of *A Lost Lady* was withheld from greatness because the pioneer tradition ended and so she had left to her no source of strength and maturity. If the villain seems to face both ways, it is a habit of literary thinking to be ambivalent.

Such thinking loses sight of both the writer and the work, submerging first one and then the other in abstractions, and ignoring the world of experience in order to build these abstractions like bricks into a theory. The theory changes but the sentiments of which it is a rationalization remain the same from thinker to thinker and, it appears, from generation to generation. Thus the present anthology describes the — perfectly objective — data which it is considering in a variety of ways but there is a uniformity in the sentiments of the authors. What is actually written, you see, is pretty disappointing and you may choose the explanation that pleases you from a variety which mostly contradict one another, and you may be sure we are going to change all that.

There is an eidolon: The Artist. Usually he is endowed with supernatural powers but they count less than the fact that he has taken oath and veil, he is dedicated. What he is dedicated to changes as the theories change; it may be Beauty, the Individual, Detachment, Leadership, Culture, Collectivism, the Great Society, or the Good Life. But he is dedicated to some ideal end and he serves it by producing a succession of masterpieces. Yet it is only at the café tables of yesteryear or on the flag-draped rostrum of to-day that any writer is ever dedicated to anything, and in the world which living people inhabit masterpieces are so rare that if one writer out of a hundred can produce one of them in a lifetime he has won at long odds. Such imperfection distresses the literary thinker and he spends his energy explaining it away. He says to the writer: thou fool — or thou coward, or poor tortured victim of a cruel, puritanical, or capitalistic scheme of things. He says to society: O generation of Philistine or bourgeois vipers! He does not think of society as masses of people so absorbed in getting a living, rearing a family, and trying to have a moderately good time and build up a savings account that they can devote to literature only a few minutes now and then, and at such times prefer what he calls the literature of escape. Such a condition is intolerable to him and he erases it by deciding that in the great society, which is always a-borning, all this will be different. Once the labor pains are over no one will read *Photoplay* or even the *National Geographic;* children will begin with Waldo Frank instead of the Three Bears, only the birthdays of poets will be bank holidays, and at last the literary will be active leaders of society. Twenty-five hundred years of human history disclose no more than a half-dozen literary people who have meant much to society at large, and fewer than that who have had a decisive influence on government or events – but no matter, for that is exactly what is wrong with history and society. By to-morrow it will all be changed.

Still less is the literary thinker able to see John Doe, the novelist, as a man with children, a house in the suburbs, a golf membership, a heart murmur, and a fondness for pinochle, motoring, or talking with his friends – a man who usually works as well as he can according to his lights, the pressures put upon him, and the job and time at hand – who writes well sometimes and badly at other times, whose work is hampered and advanced by the affections and vicissitudes of ordinary experience, who by the grace of God sometimes writes above himself and by the guilt of the Old Adam is sometimes tawdry, trivial, and absurd. Somehow it is never alcoholism, a fondness for women, stupidity, or mere preference for a good time over art that makes a writer fall short of masterpieces – it is some defect in the eidolon which the literary thinker will never forgive and will understand only if he can transfer the blame to an inferior or a disintegrating society. Thus, since the world is full of books written by people whose dedication did not carry over from the café table to the ultimate performance, literary history is full of promises unfulfilled and potentially great careers betrayed. All right, how great should Mark Twain have been? Or Sinclair Lewis?

Again, as deduction from the eidolon and the dedication, and as projection of his sentiments, the literary thinker knows that books must be written in certain ways, and books which are not written in those ways are damned. The damnation remains constant because the sentiment behind it is continuous, but it is a commonplace of observation that the ways in which books must be written change not only from generation to generation but even from year to year. This step is but a logical prolongation of the original attitude, but it looks more absurd because it ends in the doctrinaire condemnation of obviously fine work. The theory is necessarily rigid; only certain ways of writing books, only certain ideas and accomplishments, can have grace. The books which abide by the theory are good, those that depart from it are damned. And among the damned you are certain to find some of the best work of the time.

Thus, it seems to me not only idle but downright idiotic to weep because *The Professor's House, Shadows on the Rock,* and *Death Comes for the Archbishop* are not thus and so. It seems to me that a survey of the last thirty years in American literature which ignores Ellen Glasgow and has only five words for Robert Frost may be as dialectical and portentous as you like but grotesquely fails to meet the primary test of intelligence. It seems to me that a system which will admit to grace only the intentions of Mr. Wolfe and the performance of Mr. Dos Passos, though it may have the beauty of a logically mortised and tenoned structure of abstract ideas, is grotesquely incompetent to deal with the fiction of our time. What is the trouble with Mr. Frost? Why, he abstained from the ideas of Robinson Jeffers and the techniques of T. S. Eliot, so he cannot have written poetry, for poetry can be written only in certain ways. What is the matter with *It Can't Happen Here?*

Why, Mr. Dos Passos presumably believes in collectivism and Mr. Lewis seems not to. What is the matter with *Shadows on the Rock?* Why, Miss Cather betrayed herself (though for her timidity society may also be in part to blame) by not writing a different kind of book. If you liked *Shadows on the Rock,* if you found it beautiful and poignant and wise, if it worked in you something of the mysterious fulfillment that is a quality of literature at its finest, why, so much the worse for you. Yah, escapist! *Shadows on the Rock* is not the kind of book that Miss Cather should have written, and so be damned to it. What kind should she have written? Well, Mr. Trilling knows. Theory has told him.

The theory killeth. It kills intelligence, and it does so by disregarding, out of the necessities of logic, the logic of sentiment, much and even most of the best work that is done. For some minds it has infinite resources of pleasure and reassurance; they derive comfort and healing from treating words as things and from erecting articulated structures of abstractions as a rampart against experience. Other minds prefer to take literature where they find it and let the theory go. We face here what may be a fixed difference in the pattern and organization of minds. Mr. Brooks once spoke of the malady of the ideal and I wonder if it is not also an occupational infirmity of minds more or less noble to be forever rejecting good work in the name of an abstraction, to be forever hearing the fiddles tuning for a symphony which somehow is never played. I wonder if health as well as intelligence is not on the side that common sense instinctively chooses, the side that takes literature as it is and works with it in its own terms, refusing to be omniscient about what it ought to have been.

Be that as it may, we should all be more comfortable if the plans for the great society were altered so as to require theorists to acquaint themselves with American literature not only of yesterday but also of the day before. It is only funny when Mr. Basso says that Herman Melville introduced declamation to American literature. Anyone may be permitted such a slip, but I don't think we should permit Mr. Chamberlain, Mr. Cantwell, Mr. Kronenberger, and Mr. Cowley to substitute their sentiments about the past for the past itself. They manage to box the compass with Howells — I suggest that they appoint a committee to read him and agree on what he is to stand for hereafter. It would be helpful if they would also read *Huckleberry Finn, Pudd'nhead Wilson, Moby Dick, Pierre, The Scarlet Letter, Walden,* seven-tenths of Emerson's essays, and the better half of Cooper, and then specify so that we all could see what is smug, Victorian, and evasive in them. Some of those who write about Henry James should also read him. And I am willing to draw up a miscellaneous reading list, like those used in college courses, to be used as a prerequisite to opinions about the failure of American literature to deal with social issues. It would be elementary but, in the circumstances, it would have to be. I have, however, no expectation that I shall be called upon to draw it up. For theory, the most useful way of making predictions, is also a useful way of moving backward. It would be comfortable and even inspiring if we were the first writers who knew about society. So why bother to find out what American literature has actually been when you have only to examine your formula to derive anything you want about it? Maybe it was not that way but, if it wasn't, quite clearly it ought to have been.

Autobiography:

OR, AS SOME CALL IT, LITERARY CRITICISM

MY dear Edmund Wilson:

Let me explain to the subscribers of the *Saturday Review* that I am abandoning my editorial anonymity because, in the *New Republic*, you have challenged me to "stand and unfold" myself. You want to know the bases, though I understand you to imply the singular, from which I am editing this magazine. If you are interested in knowing them, conceivably some of our subscribers are too, which justifies this answer. But I estimate that I should need at least forty thousand words for an adequate statement, and my editorial judgment is that the magazine cannot devote so much space to such an enterprise. You must take fifteen hundred and let the rest develop informally as I go on editing the *Review*.

Your article seems to me sensible and very fair. You are partly wrong in thinking of me as an academic: I was a full-time teacher for only the first of my seven years on the Harvard faculty, I have no graduate training or degrees, and such scholarship as I may claim is in the field of American social history. You ignore some rather important points made in my book about Mark Twain and, I think, misunderstand certain others. Let me say too, as gently as possible, that I think you take too seriously certain essays of mine which most people take, and which I intended, as jokes. You see, I never anticipated holding such an office as this and, when I was younger and much given to sin, I sometimes seized a chance to exploit the merely comic values. There are other assertions in your article with which I should take issue if I could have my forty thousand words, but I must disregard them here if I am to say anything about your central point.

You complain that you cannot make out, in my criticism at least, any unified, articulated system of ideas to which I am referring when I pass judgment on books and ideas. You ask me to forsake the seats of the scornful and state what my system is. What set of ideas do I champion? What generalizations do I stand on? What theory of the world, what metaphysics, what structure of abstractions? The answer is brief: None. I have no such system and I profoundly disbelieve in such systems.

For, you see, this is a demand for a gospel, and I have been acquainted with it since my earliest days. I was brought up in a religion which taught that man was imperfect but might expect God's mercy — but I was surrounded by a revealed religion founded by a prophet of God, composed of people on the way to perfection, and possessed of an everlasting gospel. I early acquired a notion that all gospels were false and all my experience since then has confirmed it. All my life people around me have been seeing a Light that, with a vision certified as excellent by the best oculists, I have been unable to see. At first astonishing contradictions in the reports they gave me troubled my mind but, you will understand, I came to conclude that absolutes were a mirage. And in my desert country mirages are also commonplace.

I distrust absolutes. Rather, I long ago passed from distrust

of them to opposition. And with them let me include prophecy, simplification, generalization, abstract logic, and especially
the habit of mind which consults theory first and experience
only afterward. That would have been the simplest way to
describe me for your purposes, since it accounts for most of
the objections you raise: that I have attacked a lot of people
whose ideas seemed to me out of touch with known facts and
common experience. People who prefer the conclusions of
logic to the testimony of their senses. People who do not recognize that the behavior of the human race cannot be accommodated to a syllogism. People who ask the race to be logical
about illogical matters and rational about irrational ones — and
who slump into despair and the lust for dictatorship because it
refuses to be. People who insist on applying deductive reasoning — and prophecy — in areas where it is the testimony of
experience and common sense that deductive reasoning and
prophecy have no force.

I am, if you must have words, a pluralist, a relativist, an
empiricist. I am at home with the concrete inquiries of historians and scientists, and uneasy among the abstractions of
critics and metaphysicians. I confine myself to limited questions; I try to use methods that can be controlled by fact and
experience; I am unwilling to let enthusiasm or desire or a
vision of better things carry me farther than the methods will
go by themselves. I rest ultimately on experience and, where
that fails, on common sense. No one need tell me how incom-
plete and imperfect they are, how misinterpretation and falsification betray them, how tentative, fragile, and unsatisfactory
the conclusions we base on them must be. I know: but they
are more dependable than anything else. They are, especially,
more dependable than gospels.

So I leave to others the elaboration of systems and theories
that transcend them, that go beyond. My job is to carry limited
objectives: to test the data that are presented to me and, so far
as I can, separate the factual from the illusory, the experi-

mental from the guessed, the verifiable from the hoped and desired. This will not get me far and, in the mass, it will not get the race far. But if it gets us only a little way, that little will be subject to use and control, and it will stand. At any rate, that is what I choose to do, leaving general ideas and systems of thought and theory to others. I can be fairly sure of the empirical fact — but I am even surer that the great system, however inspiring, animated by whatever nobility or benevolence or terror, is out of touch with things as they are. If the instruments with which you measure a continent are wrong by so little as one minute in a degree, still you will come out at the end with a grotesquely false description of the continent, and any maps you make will grossly delude those who try to follow you, possibly into catastrophe. But the instruments of thought which our system makers use must at best err far more than that one-sixtieth of a degree. As, perhaps, I shall be able to show you from time to time.

I wonder if you are not troubled because you understand this master condition of prophecy? You are something of a Marxist, but are not the seismic shocks in your association with other Marxists due to your perception of the difference between prophecy and experience? Your allies, who periodically become your enemies, look at the map which Marx has made of the present and the future, and where Marx says a mountain or a molehill must be found, they find it whether it is there or not. But sometimes you refuse to submit the testimony of your senses and your experience to the dictation of the gospel, and once more your allies excommunicate you. But sometimes you do not refuse. You tell me, for instance, that Marx and Engels exploded Utopian socialism almost a century ago. Oh, my dear Wilson! They merely asked us not to apply that label to their gospel. Is not Russia resolutely demonstrating to us that the dictatorship of the proletariat is no more than a Utopian vision? Or if you will not agree to that, what about the classless society? And you tell me that my outline of Mormon history exemplifies Marx. Perhaps, but the weightier consideration is that it exemplifies Pareto's criticism of Marx.

(I suppose that you and others will sometime force me, in sheer boredom, to discuss the application of Pareto to literary thinking. I am not much of a Paretian. I am mainly interested in finding out how useful Pareto's method of analysis may be in the study of American history; those who are working with his sociology regard me, rightly, as a dabbler. But meanwhile, if you will not read what Pareto says himself, preferring to get him from me, I wish you would forget the piece I wrote in 1933 for the *Saturday Review,* which was one of my unfortunate attempts to annoy certain literary people, and would consult the piece I wrote for *Harper's* when I was alarmed by the solemnity with which the earlier one was received.)

In literature, my first concern is the individual. What interests me is primarily the human emotions and experiences that have only a secondary connection with social movements. You are free to call this a fault or a deficiency in me, but remember that my religion taught me the principles of man's imperfection and God's mercy. The human tragedy does not seem to me an economic tragedy. Human courage, cowardice, tenderness, cruelty, ecstasy, hope, and despair seem to me to go deeper than an economic analysis can follow them. The struggle for existence seems to me deadlier and more hopeless than its economic constituent. My absorption is men and women in relationships which are immediately human but are economic only at many removes or at infinity. The grief of human life, youth and age, love and marriage and the talk of friends, how men conduct themselves under sentence of defeat — these immediately, of themselves, not as economic phenomena, are the values I consult. The literature that most interests me is the literature of man's loneliness and hope, his entanglement with the world, his words and consolations, his dismay under the night sky. Here also I avoid absolutes: there are other literatures, and you may have them, but permit me to follow after the kind I prefer.

As for America, let us go slowly. Many men are confident that they can sum up a nation and a people in one manuscript page, but I must refuse to try. I have no formula to explain the American past or present, still less the future; I have no logically articulated system of conceptions that will make all clear. The fault I find with the literary is precisely that they have such formulas and systems, and there is no difficulty in showing that they are grotesquely false. I can, and will, tell you something about what, in part, we are, and something about how, in part, it has come about — how in three centuries American life has been differentiated from other ways of life in the Western world. But these are complex things, far too complex for any system, and the most monstrous of all follies is to try to impose on them the pattern of our private wish. We must go tentatively, which is what literary systems do not do. We must be accurate, as they are not; we must make our descriptions exact, verify our conclusions, keep our ideas in continuous touch with experience and under the control of demonstrable fact. We must avoid certainty, unity, vision, and the loaded dice. Let who will devote himself to gaudy versions of America, past, present, or to come, that bubble up from hope, desire, or some splendid vision of an ideal end; my job is merely to expose all these as mirage and so bring the discussion back again to the world of experience. It is a humble job, but it is in the public interest.

In what I have studied and observed about America I make out, I think, some limited sequences of mutually dependent actions — here and there. They do not account for everything, they do not resolve chaos or dissipate mystery, but I think that they are, within their limits, trustworthy. Watch these columns, and from time to time you will see what they are. What you will not see is any claim of finality, any conclusive simplicity, any allegation that an induction is complete or that a series may be safely projected into the future. I will tell you a little but not much, and I will denounce everyone who I think tells more than may be verified. Meanwhile you are right in saying that I accuse American literature of the 1920's of, in varying degree but on the whole, misrepresenting American life. Why does that idea startle you? Everyone agrees that it was true of the 1830's, say, or the 1890's, when books also sold well — why suppose that it cannot be true of our own time? You are right also in saying that my sympathies are with the middle class. Your gospel tells you that it is decadent; my experience assures me that it is not, and my study of its history supports what I shall say about its energies from time to time. Your gospel also promises you, on the proved word of a logical demonstration, that the democratic forms are played out. But to a historian, to me, that is just one more prophecy, engraved on golden plates, that the world will end in 1843 or 1893 (do you want more visions of last things from my museum of exploded gospels?). So far as I can see, our native variety of conditioned chaos is continuing. You may prophesy, but I will not. I hear the voice of lamentation but it is past noon and no fire has come. Peradventure Marx sleepeth and must be awaked.

PREFACE   SOME TIME before Dos Passos's *Three Sol-*
CONTINUED   *diers* appeared, Mr. Edmund Wilson published in the *Liberator* a fine story about life in the A. E. F. I have never forgotten those doughboys jolting across France in a boxcar, and from the time the story appeared I have read everything by Mr. Wilson that I have encountered. I have frequently dissented from his ideas but I have always found him a very intelligent man and one of the few literary critics in America who make sense. For those reasons and for the further one that I was editing a family journal when it was written, the preceding piece treats him more seriously than

the context it was commenting on deserved. Mr. Wilson had undertaken to tell readers of the *New Republic* what I was all about, but he had done the job hastily and perfunctorily.

(I wonder if he had not been persuaded to help out the steering committee of the literary left in an emergency. It was a time when the New York literary scene was populous with young and older Stalinists who behaved a good deal like racketeers. I had annoyed them by remaining indifferent to a number of bad books which they had been instructed to rig a market for and by treating their activity precisely as I treated other literary fads. Literary Stalinism went the WPA Writers' Project one better; in the latter a journeyman soda jerker could become a writer by appointment of his ward boss, but in the former he could become a genius by appointment of the *New Masses*. I had pointed out that some of the *New Masses* geniuses had written stinking bad books; much worse, I had pointed out that some Trotskyists had written good books. There may have been no connection but several times a week for a couple of months before Mr. Wilson's piece appeared, various molls and finger men who did not identify themselves phoned to the *Saturday Review* to tell me that my pelt was about to be nailed to a barn door. Not Mr. Wilson's nor the *New Republic's* barn door — one that belongs to a man whom we will call Sandow. Sandow's piece did not appear but Mr. Wilson's did; and since the finger men stopped telephoning I concluded that Sandow had run out on the assignment. I don't know why he did and I'm sorry.)

Mr. Wilson was not sufficiently interested in the assignment to work it up. He ignored my best book altogether. He read my book on Mark Twain but read it so hastily that he missed the main point and misunderstood the parts he talked about, which were my remarks about the frontier and my contention with Mr. Brooks. He read most of my current book, *Forays and Rebuttals,* but he did not read all of it. Considering the demand he made on it, that was careless. For he wanted to know what kind of literary criticism I believed in and why, and I had covered the question in one of the essays he skipped — its title said clearly "Mark Twain and the Limits of Criticism." I should have picked up those points and made use of them if I had been answering Sandow. But I saw that Mr. Wilson had merely been in a hurry — he and I are the only critics in America who realize that writers sometimes are in a hurry. So I wrote the foregoing letter.

Mr. Wilson was satisfied. But a number of our brethren in holy orders were annoyed by my answer, as they had been annoyed by earlier homilies of mine and (together with Mr. Wilson) by one in particular, "A Generation beside the Limpopo," which is reprinted in this book. I had once proposed that we settle our differences by agreeing to define literary criticism as: anything that is over fifteen hundred words. They would sign no peace on those terms, however, and my letter to Mr. Wilson seemed to some of them deliberately insulting. Several of them fumed about it in various places and finally Mr. Bernard Smith asserted forthrightly what others had intimated: that if I insisted on being (as I had told Mr. Wilson I was) pluralistic, relative (that is, contingent), and empirical in my criticism, then I must certainly end, as I seemed to want to end, by making thought impossible. Now that is an impressive compliment and I must admit that it is partly true, though unfortunately in greater part it is wrong. The difficulty is that when Mr. Smith and I use the word "thought" we have different things in mind, and when we use the words "literary criticism" we feel different emotions. Ordinarily I am not sensitive to the epithets applied to me in print, but it is true that when I am called a critic I am more comfortable if sure that the one who applies the term means primarily that I write pieces more than fifteen hundred words long. And it is true that if a number of people whom it is amiable not to name would practise the principles of pluralism, relativism (that is, contingency), and empiricism, then there would be a lot less literary criticism in the world. And so much the better for us all, even if Mr. Bernard Smith had to stop writing books.

But mine is a helpful nature and if the brethren want more light from me, they can have it. Their bewilderment comes from the fact that they consider what I say too true to hold good; though they praise simplifications, they are disconcerted by simplicities. They learned in high school that platitudes like "Art is long and time is fleeting" are offensive, and they have concluded that truisms like the multiplication table must be false. From time to time in this book and other books I seem to be objecting to various things. It always turns out, however, that I am objecting to the same thing, a particular way of thinking. More accurately, I am not objecting to that way of thinking, which is all right in its place just as the culture of tropical fish is all right in its place, but rather to that kind of thinking when it believes or pretends that it is something else. . . . That is all, but it will not be enough for the brethren unless I enlarge on it. They are concerned with the bearing of what I say, or as they see it the lack of bearing, on literary criticism. So from now on let us work in literary criticism. That is, in autobiography.

I did not become a writer by first intention. My father pointed me toward a career which in my native West is respectable and sometimes profitable, that of a mineralogist. When I got to college I found myself capable of the necessary geology and chemistry but the career was closed to me forever when I began to study crystallography. The obstacle that closed it is instructive. You learn the shapes and structure and classification of crystals from large cardboard models; each model is exact and perfect, with all its angles, planes, and dimensions based on the theoretical absolute. They are type crystals, ideal crystals, and such crystals do not occur in nature. The gap between them and the crystals that do occur in nature proved too wide for me to bridge. I could memorize the cardboard ideal but I could seldom identify it in the wrenched, distorted, displaced, reversed, bent, crushed, and completely transformed crystal of actual rock. I could understand that the ideal was beautiful but I could not recognize it in the thing that had been subjected to the stresses of this world, and so I gave up mineralogy. Precisely the same defect has kept me from recognizing the dictatorship of the proletariat in Soviet Russia, the great dramatist in Eugene O'Neill, and the thinker in Granville Hicks.

Meanwhile college had developed in me a conspicuous expertness and two strong interests. It may sadden the brethren to be told that the expertness was in logic and metaphysics. Somewhere in the catacombs of Harvard my thesis on *The Critique of Pure Reason* and *The Critique of Practical Reason* doubtless still waits for someone to read it. It was a lovely thing, and evidence of my ability to adorn a chair of philosophy. I look back on that training in verbalism with regret for time lost, but it was not altogether wasted. It has enabled me ever since to understand foul and fatty prose. I can, for example, understand John Dewey and if I cannot understand Waldo Frank at least I can make out what he thinks he means. The strong interests were psychopathology and American history. The latter seemed to mean only a pleasant avocation but when I saw that mineralogy was beyond me I began to think of the former as a career. I began to associate with psychologists, translated *Traumdeutung* in 1916 (which makes me one of the first literary Freudians in America), and undertook to qualify myself for admission to a medical school. America's participation in the first World War closed that career to me. When the war was over I had lost two years and was both too old and too broke to go to medical school.

Let us avoid inquiring whether it was the taste for psychopathology that eventually took me into literary criticism. I came back to Harvard for my senior year and then found myself an A. B. and unemployed. I took a teaching job in order to earn a living. I had no preparation for teaching literature

beyond a lifelong habit of reading but it was, and widely remains, an axiom of the universities that anyone can teach English. Once a college teacher, I saw that it was extremely desirable to cease being one. I turned to the only facility I had:
writing. I published my first book in 1924, and three years
later I resigned my assistant professorship and set up as a professional writer.

I did not share the fantastic prosperity of writers in the
Twenties, but the profession has supported me in comfort and
I have found it, though this may be the psychiatrist speaking,
inexhaustibly amusing. I am a professional writer, a journalist,
and am proud of the craft. I am the kind of man who is temperamentally unable to refer to himself as an artist and is hard put
to it to maintain a proper solemnity when certain others pin
the label on themselves. Most people who call themselves artists are, I find empirically, bad artists. Journalism, I find, is
doing a given job as well as you can. The term is used with
contempt by bad artists but there are those who wear it like
a striped ribbon in their lapels.

As a journalist I have ranged pretty widely. I am an educated man and am willing to write about anything I am informed about and interested in. On occasions when we have
drunk beer together Mr. Elmer Davis (he and Robert Frost
are the literary people with whom I least need to define my
terms) has sometimes argued that he has a wider spread than
I since he has written a book about God and I have not. There
is a demurrer to that: I could write a book about God by
merely digging out that thesis on Kant, and I have written
verse whereas Elmer admits that he has not. Be that as it may,
a bibliography of my work would stretch a considerable distance — from *Liberty* to the *Psychoanalytic Quarterly*, from
coterie magazines of the fragrant Twenties which were issued
in editions of thirty-two on hand-made paper to their principal
emetic the *Saturday Evening Post*, from the program of the
Harvard-Yale game to the confidential reports of Consumers'

Research, from the private annals of the Social Science Research Council to the throwaways of a good many agitations. I have even appeared in the *New Republic*.

Nevertheless the bulk of my writing is fiction — at least two-thirds of it. I have written serious fiction for my own pleasure and in the wistful but almost wholly frustrated hope that somebody else might like it. I have written light fiction to make a living; it has supported my family and my other writing (except for two years as editor of the *Saturday Review*) ever since July, 1927. I have written both light and serious fiction under my own name and under various aliases — and, such is the depravity of this world, it is only under my aliases that I ever get triple-starred or even single-starred in Mr. O'Brien's presentation lists. Criticism is always changing its taxonomy but if you classify a writer according to the thing he writes most, then I am a short-story writer and a novelist.

Llewellyn Jones, Henry Canby, and the editor of the Evanston *News-Index* made me a book reviewer. A lifelong reader and a lifelong insomniac, I had to have books, and you do not buy books on the salary of an instructor in English, which in my time was seventeen hundred dollars a year. Mr. Jones (then of the Chicago *Post*) and the *News-Index* supplied them even up, one book for one review. I found that I could write a good many reviews while teaching six courses and writing a book, and presently my wife became literary editor of the *News-Index* and I wrote even more. Then Mr. Canby saw that my first book was getting good reviews and, in the optimism of literary editors which I was to acquire when I succeeded him, invited me into the columns of the *Saturday Review*. I liked reviewing and still like it. It is an intelligent job, and in the public interest. When you review a book you write about a *thing*, and you write about it for the information of others. You undertake to find out what it says — you read it in the way that Professor Adler has recently been recommending. Then you undertake to pass judgment on it —

whether its allegations of fact are supportable, how valid or how fallacious its ideas are, what relation it has to other books and to human experience, human behavior, and human dream. That is not an easy job; it calls for intelligence, for a sound knowledge of your subject, and for the kind of integrity that refuses to use loaded dice. When someone calls me a mere reviewer I feel no broken bones. As a former editor I can tell you that there are few good reviewers in the world.

How did I become a literary critic? Since the boys will not permit me to define criticism as reviewing that is continued in the back of the magazine, I must maintain that I have never been one. But the process that exposed me to the accusation was begun by Ernest Boyd, who asked me to write a book about Mark Twain for a series he was editing. The process was continued by Mr. Canby, who kept inviting me to write three thousand words (the length of a lead piece in the *Saturday Review*) about Sinclair Lewis, Pareto, Thomas Wolfe, the writers who called themselves the lost generation (John Chamberlain once thought that I belonged among them but Malcolm Cowley contradicted him), and similar topics for literary conversation. Finally when Mr. Canby decided to give up the editorial life I was offered, on the day of the Yale game, 1935, the job he was vacating. I twice thrust the crown away but by spring Caesar's weakness had undermined me and in September, 1936, I was consecrated and installed as a literary authority, with all the obligations and annoyances thereunto appertaining.

Long before this my literary conversation had annoyed the brethren. In my Mark Twain book I had denounced at considerable length the kind of thinking we have been dealing with here. Now there is this about literary people: some of them can't read at all, most of them read too fast, and practically all of them revise in the author's name as they read him. Thus, Mr. Wilson's piece took me to task for denying in my Mark Twain book the validity of psychoanalysis in criticism although, as he pointed out, I sometimes practised it myself. But an insurance company of Hartford, Connecticut, is bonded to pay Mr. Wilson a large sum if he will point out the passage in which the validity of psychoanalysis in criticism is denied. There is no such passage in the book. Instead there is a detailed refutation of one particular literary psychoanalysis. It is made in the simple exhortation I have made of many literary people: better know what you are talking about. I see no more reason for admiring ignorant and demonstrably wrong psychoanalysis simply because a literary man has produced it than for admiring ignorant and wrong dentistry or carpentry on the ground that the man who did it can write graceful prose. But literary people read hastily and know what you must have meant to say when you omitted saying it, and if you remark that an apple has specks in it you must have meant to plow the orchards of America under, including the peaches.

As it happens, I am consulting literary historian to three psychoanalysts who are engaged in the study of literature, two of whom will soon publish some results. Also, I have followed the literature of psychoanalysis since my undergraduate days. Also, as Mr. Wilson observed, I am sometimes willing to approach literature with such psychoanalytical instruments as I am capable of using. But I urge on my friends in the profession and try to enforce on myself the principles which grieve literary critics when someone mentions them. I point out, that is, that the method of psychoanalysis cannot be applied to literature in the circumstances that make it effective in the consulting room; there is no way of using trial and error, there is no way of checking one's conclusions by the observation of emotion and behavior in the subject, there is no way of chasing a phenomenon through successive disguises till you know what it is. As a consequence of this hard fact, many of the results possible in the consulting room are impossible in criticism, and you had best be modest and tentative about the results that are possible. There is an irreducible minimum of speculation in anything that psychoanalysis can say about literature, so long as it cannot study literature in the clinic's dynamic relationship with authors. Certainty is impossible; at best one can indicate only probability and one can indicate that only in favorable circumstances, in the pattern rather than the part, in the large outline rather than the specific detail. When the professional psychoanalyst approaches literature he must constantly remember that a book is not a patient. When the lay or literary analyst approaches literature he had better remember, first that he is not an analyst and second that he is entering a field where his activity can lead, and frequently has led, to the wildest nonsense this side of numerology. No analyst objects to that warning but it angers literary critics. For the fascination of criticism for certain minds, the attribute that makes it precious, is that it is one field of human thought where certainty is possible, where there are absolutes, where the aspiring soul may be comforted by the perception of higher truths.

The reader may check my principles and practice in this book. When Havelock Ellis died I wrote "Meditation in Fading Sunlight" for the Easy Chair. To write it I called on what I knew about his books and the intellectual currents of which they were a part but made only one statement about his private life. (That statement, that he had a happy life, was a deduction soon to be in part refuted.) A few weeks later Ellis's autobiography was published and George Stevens asked me to review it. Reading it, I found a great mass of facts that had not been open to me when I wrote the Easy Chair, and saw that they could be understood *only* by reference to the Freudian hypotheses and that, when referred to those hypotheses, they revealed ironies so powerful that a conscientious reviewer must point them out. So I wrote "Widower's House." It is a frank application of psychoanalytical principles to a book. It supplements "Meditation in Fading Sunlight"; it confirms several judgments arrived at by other means; it does not supersede the earlier article. It says, this is what I find in Ellis when I apply Freud to him. It does not say, this is Ellis, but rather, this is, apparently, a striking part of Ellis. I believe that it is sound — I believe, that is, that it gets closer to Ellis than I could have got by any other approach. But it is tentative and essentially speculative. I muster the facts that Ellis states and I apply to them several hypotheses of psychoanalysis, which in turn rest upon thousands of observations of human behavior made in the consulting room and summarized, not legislated or revealed, for use, not prayer. This is an instance where, I believe, the method is useful to criticism for the simple reason that no other method can be applied. . . . I am sufficiently a Freudian to admit that the piece has an added fervency in that Ellis's autobiography revealed him, to my considerable shock, as the kind of mind I am temperamentally at odds with, the ideologue's mind, the mind which wants to rationalize the irrational and prefers abstract general principles to the teachings of experience.

There are other areas of literature in which, I believe, the psychoanalytical hypotheses are more legitimate and serviceable, notably the complex problems of artistic creativeness. The analysts I have mentioned are working with those problems, and there are a couple of pieces in this book in which I mildly try my own hand at them. And I may announce here that I have found in the unpublished Mark Twain papers a bulk of material which, like Ellis's autobiography, can be best understood by reference to psychoanalysis, and that I am going to do exactly what I denounced Mr. Van Wyck Brooks for doing — I am going to study them psychoanalytically. This should interest Mr. Wilson but it is not a recantation. The question will remain the same, and if I cannot use the hypotheses on Mark Twain more effectively than Mr. Brooks did, then someone else will be quite right in ridiculing me.

All this should dispose of Mr. Bernard Smith's accusation that I am opposed to abstractions, theories, and simplifications. I have never written anything which, if read in relation to its context, could justify that accusation to anyone except a critic who was bent on finding my higher meaning where he had concealed it in advance. Human patience is short and space limitations impose brevity on journalism, and one cannot always be repeating definitions. I frequently say "theory," for instance (as in "A Generation beside the Limpopo"), where an earlier definition or the context itself makes clear that I mean "theory derived by deductive reasoning from abstract general principles without reference to the relevant facts, and used in the further elaboration of a theoretical system in such a way that, whether deliberately or inadvertently, it contrives to ignore certain demonstrable facts which, if they were taken into account, would vitiate the theory." I am used to a kind of thinking which abides by definition.

Therefore let it be said flatly that I have not objected to the use of abstractions but only to the use of abstractions in the illusion that they are bricks, girders, and tie bars. I have not objected to the use of theories but only to their use in ways that produce what are called higher truths. I have not objected to simplifications but only to the use of simplifications in order to satisfy the lust for oneness by denying facts, experience, and common sense. My objections rest on the observation that such ways of thinking produce confusion wherever they are applied and on the belief that criticism has no privilege of confusing us.

My opponents also object sometimes — when the principles are applied homeopathically and they find themselves in congenial company. My letter to Mr. Wilson alludes to the Pareto episode of the long, long ago. (As I told Mr. Wilson, though I learned much from Pareto I was never a member of the movement but only a kind of co-operating press agent.) The boys found no higher truths in Pareto and John Chamberlain (who has since learned the pleasures of the word "pluralism" which exasperates Mr. Smith) worked out an astrological equation which showed that if Pareto equaled *a*, then William Graham Sumner equaled exactly 48*a* with no remainder. Later, Thurman Arnold's *Folklore of Capitalism* came out and the boys saw at once that it was magnificent. Mr. Chamberlain has been using it ever since; it convinced him that some of the things he had previously been saying were just magical incantations. You produce Mr. Arnold's book by taking one drop of Pareto's first volume and diluting it with one liter of distilled water. (I should not like to be held to this assay, which is on the conservative side. Probably this solution should be diluted to the second attenuation.) Mr. Arnold becomes a seer and a prophet by telling the boys that some of the things they say have no meaning outside their own sentiments. But when I say the same thing I convince Mr. Bernard Smith that I have made thought impossible.

Then there was the discovery of semantics that flurried the dovecotes in the familiar way. Presumably the boys read Francis Bacon when they were undergraduates and, being seekers after truth, they must have read some of his successors. I don't know whether the Baconian tradition made thought impossible but the record shows that eventually Mr. Stuart Chase ran smack into Dr. Percy Bridgman and saw a great light. Dr. Bridgman had been practising his good works in full view of the public for many years but he made no impression on the boys till Mr. Chase took him in hand, diluted and emulsified him, and resolved to bring in a glorious new day of verbalism by telling the world it must eschew verbalism forevermore. For a while all the brethren were semanticists, and it is unfortunate that we have not learned what Dr. Bridgman and Mr. Richards thought about it. It is one of the recurring phenomena that make the literary life rich with amusement. In our time has anything been more entertaining than Mr. Chase's conversion? One doubts it — till he remembers how, when Stalin twitched the trapeze away, Dr. Frederick Schuman transformed a simple back flip into a triple somersault and came up with a copy of Machiavelli in his hand. Yes, that was funnier.

What is truth? What is a higher truth? What is a twelve-inch steel rod? What is your blood count? Those questions are of two different kinds and the kind of thinking I have objected to, in criticism and elsewhere, finds answers to the first kind. The kind of thinking which Mr. Smith says would make thought impossible does not know the answers to the second kind and is not interested in them. If you ask qualified machinists to make a twelve-inch steel rod for you, no one will take the contract. You will be offered a rod that can be passed between the jaws of a micrometer set at 11.9 and 12.1 inches; or at greater labor and expense, one that can be passed between more delicate jaws set at 11.999 and 12.001 inches. There is no twelve-inch steel rod and there never will be. Oh, sure, there is a piece of calibrated steel somewhere that is twelve inches long — but those twelve inches are contingent, it is twelve inches long by definition when the temperature is figured to two decimal places and the barometer has been read against a calculated variation, and be it further provided that you will not mention the earth's relative motions. But when someone comes into the room or the wind shifts or someone changes his position in the room upstairs, when you calculate the third decimal place or allow for the relative speed and positions of the earth, that piece of steel is not twelve inches long any more. The machinist is content with his empirical rod but criticism says "Good God! Can such things be?" and breaks its heart because it has been denied an absolute.

Or when you complain of feeling tired, a physician counts the red cells in a smear made from a drop of your blood. He tells you that there are 4,500,000 per cubic millimeter. That answer serves his purpose but it gives literary criticism the screaming meemies. For 4,500,000 is a lie. The brethren hold out for 4,351,628 and are willing to die for it, though your doctor is satisfied to work within ten per cent of a statistical average and knows that he can never possibly get closer than five per cent. He knows that there is no absolute number of those cells per cubic millimeter. He knows further that the 4,-500,000 he gets will be 4,250,000 when his assistant counts the same specimen under the same microscope against the same scale, and will become 4,750,000 when the man in the next office comes in to take a look at the slide. He knows that his count is relative to how much sleep and how much liquor you had last night, what you ate for lunch and when you ate it, whether you quarreled with your wife this morning or read that the Germans had sunk a British cruiser or bawled out your secretary. If he gets 4,750,000 when he makes another count on the following day, he keeps a tranquil mind. He is not interested in the higher truth about your red count or even in the truth about it. He is interested in finding out whether you need iron or liver extract or a couple of weeks at the seashore — or, since he is a thoroughgoing empiricist, whether you need a different secretary, or a different war, or even a different wife.

But there is a kind of thinking, in literary criticism and outside it, which knows that your blood count is 4,351,628 without relation to anything but eternal truth. Whosoever shall say otherwise is in danger of hell fire, has not written a good book, and must be suppressed for the good of society. How does criticism know? It has found that number in Isaiah, Plato, Marx, Hegel, or Thomas Aquinas, and it has proved by deduction from first principles that the number is implicit in the moral order of the universe and the economic order of the perfect state. You and your physician are living a lie, and cynical approximations that may do for the diagnosis of anemia or the determination of a star's parallax, or for the manufacture of a cylinder ring within a tolerance of two ten-thousandths of an inch, are the entering wedge of compromise, which God forbid. Criticism abhors the table of logarithms because it is calculated to five places with the intention of ignoring what may lie beyond, and that is a betrayal of the ideal. Criticism rejects Sinclair Lewis because his books do not show a blood count of 4,351,628 and Robert Frost because he is not twelve inches long. When criticism says twelve inches it means twelve inches.

So far that is all right with me, though I personally find tennis and the circus better fun. I don't object to the brethren's living in a world where blood counts come out even and steel rods are twelve inches long. But my sense of propriety becomes active when they take that twelve-inch rod, which does not exist, apply it as a measuring rod to things that do exist — and then as a result of those measurements order me to believe and behave in specified ways, order a novelist or a poet to write books in specified ways or else, and order society to reconstruct itself according to syllogisms premised on a meaningless reading. My feeling for amenity is offended by such thinking, whether a literary critic or someone else does it, and I begin to protest because I know what the next step is.

For nonexistent measuring rods can be applied only in theory, only deductively — in the elaboration of systematic general ideas which may fit together perfectly but cannot be checked by reference to fact, experience, and common sense. I have a greater respect for both literature and criticism than the brethren have — I take them seriously whereas the brethren take them frivolously and capriciously — and I object to the critic who devotes himself to such deductive elaboration, though I do not object to him till he reaches the point where he insists that his unreal structure shall have priority over empirically known things. Why do I object to him when he reaches that point? Because at that point his activity becomes dangerous. When an unreal structure conflicts with real things it can be given priority over them only at certain cost. That cost includes delusion, a lust for machine guns, and a helping hand to dictatorship. Idealism, whether moral or metaphysical or literary, may be defined as a cross-lots path to the psychopathic ward, Berchtesgaden, and St. Bartholomew's Eve. Absolutes mean absolutism — not logically but empirically.

Neither theory nor deductive reasoning is objectionable *per se*. You and I rely on them when we mix a cocktail, when we start out on a motor trip, when we stay in bed because a frontal sinus has begun to kick up. The race at large relies on them when it glances at a clock or picks up a telephone, and is able to use the telephone because some parts of the process that developed it applied them. An engineer uses theory and deductive reasoning when he designs a gang drill or a subway tunnel. Your physician uses them when he decides that a pain in your ear can be referred to an infection in your sinus. But when an X-ray negative shows that there is no infection there, he decides either that his data were faulty or that his method went wrong — not that since his theory and reasoning are infallible your sinus has an infection and you are a heretic. If he passes you on to a psychiatrist, the psychiatrist uses theory and deductive reasoning when he decides that the pain in your ear can be referred to your juvenile envy of an older brother. He checks that decision not by clapping you into a labor camp as an enemy of truth and suppressing your book on the ground that his theory is infallible, but by making a series of observations of your behavior. If the observations conflict with his theory, he sacrifices the theory, not you or your book. But the kind of thinking we are talking about does not behave in that way: the theory is true and the reasoning is right, and you must conform to them or here come the storm troopers. That kind of thinking is immortal, and in all history it has never abandoned a premise or changed a conclusion in recognition of a fact.

The engineer's theories are summaries of facts, observations, processes, and operations, and he is not in love with them. A physician's theories are a convenient expression of what has been observed to happen in stated circumstances, and the salvation of your soul does not depend on them. A psychiatrist's theories are statements of experience, shorthand for what many observers have reported about many people, and he changes them when more complete statements of more numerous observations make it expedient to change them. Such theories are a bridge from fact to fact. But there are other theories which make a bridge from idea to idea, unreferred to fact, unmodified by common sense, and unconditioned by experience. They may be logically unassailable and they seem to be orgasmically pleasurable, but they do not stand for what is and what happens. It is desirable to recognize them for what they are, whether we encounter them in literary criticism or somewhere else.

We might examine as a specimen the picture of Soviet Russia which some of the literary brethren and their affiliates composed by deduction from Marx and other systems of ideas in defiance of observed fact, human experience, and the testimony of common sense. They got that picture by marrying idea to idea and breeding, as always in that marriage, a hallucination. The Russia thus produced was outside the world where things exist and happen. Elsewhere the law of falling bodies might hold good and water might boil at an observed temperature and blood might flow from a cut and the clouds return after the rain, but not in the ectoplasmic vision called Russia. Russia was what theory said it must be. To that phantom they progressively sacrificed their intelligence and when need be their integrity, as some of them are busily confessing. It was a product of pure thought, of theory and deduction, of gospel, of revelation, of doctrine accepted. Whenever it encountered a fact, they got rid of the fact by means of an abstraction. Finally, however, a fact happened to hit the hallucination square in the kingpin and it collapsed. Some of the thinkers are explaining that the picture is a higher truth nevertheless, others are rearranging the fragments of delusion in a new picture, and there are some others. I know what they think of their own books, looking back on them now, but I wonder what their sons will think of them twenty years from now. And if you look at these particular brethren from one angle their heartbreak is affecting, but from another angle they are, like any ideologue clasping a broken syllogism to his heart, just funny. It is not important to remember anything about them except this: that, like all other servants of the ideal, they reached for a machine gun.

But let Russia go. That kind of thinking is eternally the same, whether applied to Russia, to Mr. Lewis's new book, the Albigensian heresy, the World of Tomorrow, or is a third term right or wrong? It is, as I tell Mr. Wilson above, the thinking that holds to gospels, that rejects the crystal as it occurs in the rock and worships the cardboard ideal. It is the kind of thinking which, when it undertakes to find out how much a five-pound bucket of water will weigh after a one-pound trout has been added to it, works out the answer by a syllogism based on what someone has said it ought to weigh according to first principles. It is the Holy Hardshell Roman Methodist Church of England, Marx, Plato, Health, and Q. E. D. On a humble, harmless level it tells you that you must not like Red Lewis's book because first principles and their logical implications show that he ought to have written some other book. It moves on to a more arrogant, more dangerous level and then tells you that you must shoot somebody because some beautiful words have been worked into a system of higher truths, and if you won't shoot him then you are a fool, a liar, a heretic, and an enemy of the state. It is quite true that, at all levels and in all ages, this kind of thinking finds numerous supporters among high-minded, generous, and self-sacrificing men. But experience shows that on all levels and in all ages, also, a machine gun is set up at the core of every higher truth thus revealed, and that it is dangerous to let even a generous man get his hands on a machine gun. There are various expedients for keeping generosity and its machine gun separated. One method is to place a forked stick over the neck of a higher truth and to set up a yell for the facts.

If Mr. Wilson will glance at my book about Mark Twain

with this in mind he will observe that I there pinned down a higher truth with a forked stick and yelled for the facts. A number of the brethren have denounced that book in the eight years since it was published but there has not yet been a single appeal from the facts it presents. And if Mr. Bernard Smith will reread my letter to Mr. Wilson in the light of this simple exposition he may revise his notion that I hope to make thought impossible.

I do not know where, verbally, this brings me out — whether it qualifies me to be a literary critic or denies me that enchanted label from now on. I don't much care. As I have remarked, by the taxonomy of space rates I am two-thirds a writer of fiction. For the remaining one-third any label will do, if we define its terms. If literary criticism is anything over fifteen hundred words, which is a sensible definition, then all right, I am a literary critic — operationally, by writing this essay, if by nothing else. Otherwise I should prefer the labels previously mentioned, history and psychiatry. But whatever I am called I am content to be one whose literary conversation recommends experience and common sense as guides. I shall be content to have my sons find that recommendation in my stuff twenty years from now, and to observe that I made it in time of tribulation. I have told Mr. Wilson that I know how fragile and disappointing experience and common sense are. They are a feeble light in this dark age. But the cry for other guides is, as it has been in all darkness, a death cry. Elsewhere in this book I quote what John Dickinson told the Constitutional Convention when it met to make a nation out of chaos, "Experience must be our only guide. Reason may mislead us." In the last few years even the literary, even Dorothy Thompson, have begun to study that Convention. It followed John Dickinson's counsel, as against the ideal visions of the best machine gunners of the day. And there came out of it a nation, one that the literary of all succeeding generations have easily demonstrated to be far from perfect but one that has endured and looks better to-day than any other. At about the same time there was, elsewhere, an attempt to establish a nation on reason and the ideal. There came out of it, it is true, a brief Rule of Reason that was very fine, but there followed after what we have to-day the best reasons for recognizing as the consequences. There followed, as there have always followed, Terror, and Thermidor, and the whiff of grape.

FROM THE *Saturday Review*, NOVEMBER 21, 1936

Monte Cristo in Modern Dress

~~~~~~

YOU WILL find the majority opinion in nearly any paper you may pick up. Unquestionably most of the critics and most of the public who think about literature at all will regard the award of a Nobel Prize to Eugene O'Neill as a gratifying recognition of a great dramatic talent. A minority will not, however, and because what may be a signal weakness rather than a great strength of our literature is involved, the *Saturday Review* cannot let the occasion pass without expressing that minority opinion. For the Nobel Prize, although it was once awarded to Rabindranath Tagore, is supposed to recognize only the highest distinction in literature, and Mr. O'Neill falls short of that. He falls short of it both absolutely and relatively. Whatever his international importance, he can hardly be called an artist of the first rank; he is hardly even one of the first-rate figures of his own generation in America.

Mr. O'Neill's good fortune has been his misfortune. He came to Broadway from the little theater of cheesecloth and mandolutes at the exact moment when the preciosities of coterie art in general were caught up on the impetus of a national movement. That impetus alone would have conferred success on the mechanical novelties that he brought with him from Washington Square — the off-stage tom-toms, the timed throb of engines and dynamos, the masks alleged to be ever so meaningful, the sirens blowing in the fog. But he also brought with him more important guarantors of success, a training in dramaturgy supervised by George Pierce Baker, and, even more important than this, an instinct like his father's for the theatrically effective. Calling on all these, Mr. O'Neill composed some very good early plays; some of them remain among his best work but it would be absurd to call any of them great drama, and they cannot have figured in the Nobel award. A restless and extremely energetic intelligence, he was already beginning the experiments that were to confuse and confute him when his alliance with the Theatre Guild began.

It is not alleged against the Guild that it created that confusion, but that it contributed more than all other forces to the inflation of his reputation which is so disproportionate to his talents and achievements. There is such a thing as economic determinism of reputation and surely that has had a part here; but a much greater part was intellectual and social determinism. A foundation engaged in the development of dramatic art, the Guild was under every obligation of sense and sentiment to discover a great native dramatist. Need we be surprised that it discovered him in Mr. O'Neill? Its great prestige, its power to compel the admiration of multitudes, its lavish resources for spectacular presentation and for publicity no less, and its austere authority as an arbiter of judgment combined to elevate him to a grandeur which neither criticism nor the public has ventured to impeach. He has had every kind of success that a playwright can have: money, fame, the best directors and designers and actors of his time, a sumptuous collected edition, a critical acclaim so reverent that the more recent treatises discuss him in language usually considered sacrilegious when applied to the merely mortal, and now the Nobel Prize. Here is a great triumph, but a very large part of it is due to prestige and publicity. At best he is only the author of some extremely effective pieces for the theater. At worst he has written some of the most pretentiously bad plays of our time. He has never been what the Guild and the Nobel jury unite in calling him, a great dramatist.

It is not a derogation but only a definition to say that workable theatricality is the measure of successful playwriting. In the theater the test is not: Is this true to the realities of human experience? Instead the test is: Is this fictitious representation satisfactory to the artificial conditions of the theater? With luck — or with genius — a play may pass both tests, but it must pass the second, and if they are in conflict, the first must yield. The theater is under many limitations: the exigencies of space and time; the dictation of the literal, which requires an actual Peter Pan to swing through actual air on the end of an actual wire in the presence of practicable props; and especially the necessary conditions of people meeting together as an audience, the lowered intelligence, the lulled critical faculty, the enhanced emotionalism and suggestibility of a group, the substitution of emotional accord for the desire to experience and understand that is fed by other forms of literature. Under all these limitations, the theater succeeds in its own terms. They are terms of the momentarily effective, not the permanently true or the permanently illuminating. Only small and superficial portions of human life can be honestly and thoroughly represented in such terms and under such limitations. Quite properly, the theater does not care. Where honest and thorough presentation of life makes available material, the theater will use it; where it does not, the theater must and cheerfully will depart from it for the sake of the theatrical values. They, the theatrical values, are concerned with something else.

A great dramatist, I take it, is one who has somehow managed to transcend the limitations of the theater and, while preserving the theatrical values that pass the second test, to add to them some profundity of human experience, human understanding, or human enlightenment that brings the art of the theater into the same area as the highest art of fiction or poetry. Those who have transcended them — we need name no more than Shaw and Ibsen — have done so by reason of great intelligence, great imagination, and great understanding. The whole truth about Mr. O'Neill is that his gigantic effort to transcend them has been of an altogether different kind. He is a fine playwright who is not sufficiently endowed with those qualities to be a great dramatist and who has tried to substitute for them a set of merely mechanical devices.

Let us recall his works. The charmingly romantic one-act plays were young Greenwich Village. They revolted against the dead theater of the day chiefly by means of sweetness. They were full of hairy chests, gentlemen rankers burning with despair, and a traditional rhetoric about the sea — the implacable enemy, the immortal lover who covets man, the inappeasable devourer, man's elder love, man's testing ground, the oldest mistress, the primal call. They had novelties of decoration but their effectiveness, like the dialects spoken by the sailors, came from time-honored tricks by which generations of playwrights had lifted the audience out of their seats for the tense half-second that means effectiveness in the theater.

A group of miscellaneous plays followed, some expressionistic, some realistic, some successful in their own terms, some obviously tending toward the confusion that was soon to follow. Two of them, *The Emperor Jones* and *Anna Christie*, are among the best work that Mr. O'Neill has ever done; of his other plays, only *Ah, Wilderness!* is comparable to them. *Beyond the Horizon* was still youthfully romantic in its conception of disease as heroic, and still very Washington Square in its clichés about sex-starved New England. *The Emperor Jones* was a triumphant experiment in the drama of phantasy, which may last longer than anything else he has written. It was a very effective assault on the emotions, and that path, if followed to the end, might have led him well beyond such work of his colleagues as *Beggars on Horseback*. But in *The Hairy Ape* it began to be apparent that expressionism and Washington Square, the masks and the ballet, the attraction of the allusively and immensely vague, were betraying him: already they seemed subtly counterfeit. *Anna Christie* was something else. It remains his most effective play. But note carefully that its effectiveness is theatrical — of the theater, not of life. The romantic conception of a prostitute, the Greenwich Village cliché of "dat ol dayvil sea," the flagrant falsification of life in the oath scene at the end were magnificent theater, magnificent craftsmanship, but surely they were an exact antithesis of great drama. It should be noted here, also, that with *All God's Chillun's Got Wings* he began the use of insanity as a solution of all dramatic problems, which makes for thrilling effects on the stage but falls short of explaining human life.

Mr. O'Neill then dived into the infinite. He undertook to transcend the theater, to break the shackles of mortality, to work with the immortal urges and the eternal truths. His characters would not be men and women merely, they would be Man and Woman, they would even be Earth Man and Earth Woman. And this mighty effort to be a great dramatist inexorably proved that he lacked intellectual, emotional, and imaginative greatness. In the theater he is a master craftsman. But in the cosmos he is a badly rattled Villager straining titanically with platitudes, and laboring to bring forth ineffabilities whose spiritual and intellectual content has been a farcical anticlimax to the agonies of birth.

Lazarus Laughed, The Great God Brown, Marco Millions, Dynamo — one or another of them must be the silliest play of our time. The gorgeous mounting which the Guild gave *Marco Millions* veiled the triviality of the play. Mr. O'Neill was trying to be a metaphysical Sinclair Lewis but he did not

(195)

make the grade. The play echoes a hundred forgotten mellers, trying to transmute them to poetry and philosophy. But the immortal wisdom of the East comes out very much like Sidney Smith's laundryman in the *Chicago Tribune*, and oriental loveliness and mystery have a heavy odor of Fu Manchu. *Dynamo* will long fascinate connoisseurs of the incredible and contains some of the most amazing nonsense ever spoken seriously in the theater. But one comes finally to the judgment that *The Great God Brown* is the worst of them. The design is once more to transcend, to Go Beyond — by means of Cybele the Earth Mother and Dionysus, the spirit of anarchic joy that treads down the stale conventions of this world, and the frustrate human spirit tortured and betrayed. But the result is uneasily one of a Model T Euripides — and a feeling that if George White ever set out to do a March of the Earth Mothers, it would look very much like this.

Mr. O'Neill has called himself a poet and a mystic. In these plays he is trying to press beyond the theater into great drama by means of poetry and mysticism focused through symbolism. But it is the very essence of symbolism that the meaning symbolically conveyed must be a distinguished meaning — a meaning profound and exalted — or the result will be preposterous. And Mr. O'Neill has no such meaning to convey. He has only a number of platitudes which would be comfortably accommodated to the one-acters of Washington Square from which he graduated, or to Dads' Night at a prep-school drama festival, but which come out flat and unchanged through as elaborate a mechanism as was ever devised to amplify inanities.

The same lack of profundity, subtlety, and distinguished imagination is quite as clear in the next cycle where, turning from symbolism, Mr. O'Neill occupied himself with racial myths and the unconscious mind. Probably the Nobel award was based on *Strange Interlude* and *Mourning Becomes Electra*, and yet these plays only emphasize what the others had made clear. Here all the strains meet and blend — the novelties of the little theater substituting for knowledge of the human heart, dodges and devices, a fortissimo assertion of significance, and a frantic grappling with what seem to be immensities but turn out to be one-syllable ideas and mostly wrong at that. The biggest wind-machine in our theatrical history is used to assist the enunciation of platitudes. Mr. O'Neill is dealing with ideas that elude him and straining for achievements beyond his power. Now it may well be that what he tries to do in these plays cannot be done in the theater at all. But a more flagrant point is that the significances he announces to us are elementary and even rudimentary. The intention is again cosmic but the meaning is very simple indeed, and though the effects are sometimes marvelously successful as theater they are false as life. Many times these plays reach the highest possible level of theatrical effectiveness, by reason of a superb craftsmanship working for the ends of the theater in the theater's terms. (With an overtone from many generations of sure-fire stuff, and the ghost of Monte Cristo raising a finger aloft and intoning "One!") But it is just that — it is not something more. Malicious animal magnetism destroying an unloved husband, a box of poison pills on papa's corpse — that is an expert playwright bringing the audience out of its chairs for the golden half-second. But it is not a sudden flood of light cast by genius into the dark recesses of the soul — it is not great drama giving us understanding more abundantly. Mr. O'Neill intended it to be that, and the burden of the Nobel award is that he succeeded. But what does he tell us, what does he show us, that we did not know before? Wherein is his wisdom, his revelation? Nowhere do we encounter the finality or the reconciliation of great art, nowhere is any fragment of human life remade for us in understanding and splendor. What he tells us is simple, familiar, superficial, and even trite — where it is not, because of a shallow misunderstanding of Freud and a windy mysticism, sometimes flatly wrong. It is not great drama for it is not great knowledge. You may add a new volume to the

Rover Boys series by setting the action in the unconscious mind, but they will still be the Rover Boys.

Mr. O'Neill has given us many pleasurable evenings in the theater, though he has also given us some pretty tiresome ones. But he has never yet given us an experience of finality, of genius working on the material proper to genius, of something profound and moving said about life. Just why, then, the Nobel Prize?

FROM THE *Saturday Review,* NOVEMBER 4, 1939

Widower's House [1]

~~~~~~

I T WAS natural to expect that Havelock Ellis's autobiography would be so frank, so searching, and so profound
that it might be compared with the masterpieces of St. Au-
gustine, Casanova, and Rousseau which, he says on page *vii*,
he had it within him to surpass. The man whom H. L. Mencken
called the most civilized Englishman of his time, the author of
one of the most fruitful scientific works of the last half-
century, an intelligence which harmonized the highest qualities of both the scientist and the artist, a distinguished writer
— surely such a man, when he should undertake to appraise his
experience, would write a masterpiece. Probably it would tell
the story of his research, as fascinating and turbulent as any
in the history of science. Probably, since Ellis had written *The
New Spirit* and *Impressions and Comments*, it would be a
measured judgment of his era. Probably, since he was intimate
with many of the most distinguished people of the time, it
would include a gallery of important portraits. And certainly

[1] See also "Meditation in Fading Sunlight" and "Autobiography."

as the life story of one who "had helped to make the world in the only way that it can be made, the interior way, by liberating the human spirit," it would describe the process of that liberation.

Well, Ellis set out to write a "Pilgrim's Progress of the soul," spent thirty years shaping it to his desire, and, when he finished, had indeed written a masterpiece. But it is in no particular the kind of autobiography one expected. All that he says about his era is that he was a child of it. James Hinton, Edward Carpenter, and Arthur Symons appear in person occasionally but few of his other associates are named and none are characterized; Ellis seems to have lacked not only the ability to write about friendship but even a sense of its importance. More surprising still, there is little about his life work, *Studies in the Psychology of Sex*, apart from repeated assertions of his dedication to it. He repeats the story which he had already told, in the final edition, of the bizarre events that attended the English publication of the first volume, but he says nothing about the work itself, nothing about its pioneering in forbidden fields, the passions it aroused, or the vast influence it has had. Of the labor or the warfare it involved there is not a single word.

It is not that kind of autobiography. It begins with a laborious study of Ellis's ancestry as dull as anything you will find in a year's reading. It goes on with a duller and more absurdly solemn narrative of his boyhood and youth. But then it becomes the book which the whole burden of his experience determined it must be, the story of his marriage. And from then on it is a tragic love story — and it is woven of ironies so terrible and so poignant that they carry the reader beyond criticism, beyond judgment, into the region of humble tears which only great books ever touch. But there are times when it seems in danger of turning into a joke book.

That story and those ironies leave the reader, I repeat, in a mood of grave humility. For Ellis was a great man and did a great work — and his confessions end by making more obscure, more unintelligible, than they were before the ways of human greatness in this world. For the man who helped to liberate the human spirit did not understand himself. The man who spent a lifetime studying women was blind and stupid about the woman he married, who is the obsession of this book. The man who devoted his life to studying sex, and fighting to dispel the pruderies with which Christian and Victorian ethics had surrounded it, depreciated sex in his own thinking and believed that it had not too much to do with passion and little to do with love. The first scientist of sex was not only under-sexed but was, the conclusion is inescapable, afraid of experiencing sex.

Those are formidable paradoxes in this bewildering book. But there are others, and the one that goes hand in hand with you from the first page hinges on Ellis's complete lack of humor. The faculty was not even vestigial in him, it simply did not exist, and in the first third of the book, before the tragedy of his marriage is apparent, his most heartfelt solemnities reduce the reader to uproarious laughter. It is hard to remember that this is a great man writing when he judicially identifies himself with the exact geographical center of the British genius. It is almost impossible when he gravely (and repeatedly) tells us that women have called him, the least faun-like and least satyr-like of men, a faun and a satyr, that he is mischievous and resembles Tolstoi and embodies the Spirit of Man, that his cast-off shirts have a distinct odor of cedar, and that Olive Schreiner said that his "nude form was like that of Christ in the carpenter's shop in Holman Hunt's 'Shadow of the Cross.'" And frequently it is altogether impossible, as when he remembers that certain practices he was given to at about the age of twelve were scientific experiments in the height of the urinary stream. One howls with laughter — for a while. Then one realizes that this tone-deafness is only one expression of a tragic defect: that this student of human behavior had little understanding of and no skill in personal relations, and that the algebraic cast of mind which it signifies explains why his marriage failed, why there is only talk about friendship in his book and no friendship, and why his great work on the anthropology of sex was never in the least what he called it, a psychology of sex. His humorlessness was the mark of a man who devoted himself to studying human emotions but was deficient in them, misunderstood them, and was bewildered by their failure to equate with rationality. It is the key to Ellis's life and to his work as well.

He was a romantic rationalist. He was like a character in Bernard Shaw's novels and in the half-dozen of his plays which resemble them — where people reason out the world by syllogism and arrive at a fantastic parody of experience. He was a late nineteenth-century man of good will and good works, a member of the Fellowship of the New Life from which the Fabian Society stemmed, an ideologue on a heroic scale, a yearner and a throbber in terms of the highest intelligence. And when you think of the Fabians you suddenly realize that you understand him — and that he enables you to understand the Fabians better than before. The book reinforces a suspicion long vaguely felt, that there would be profit in studying this whole area of British thought and politics, Shaw's plays, the Webbs' economics, as a phenomenon of sexlessness. Is not the central energy of the whole movement a wish that people would stop having feelings? When the Webbs draw up a constitution of Great Britain or approve the freedom accorded thought and speech in Soviet Russia, when Shaw makes the world happier by socializing parenthood, we are on all fours with Olive Schreiner's incredible advice to Ellis that he go abroad so that his wife may be undisturbed at the crisis of the quarter-century of torture which his rationality has inflicted on her. It is clear which feeling mankind would be best advised to give up first.

The only psychologist directly referred to in the book is Adler, who, remember, developed the theory of organ inferiority. The man with defective eyes becomes a painter, the man with weak legs becomes a sprinter. Well, the man who could not understand his own motives or those of the woman who was the center of his life became, so he thought, a psychologist, and the man of weak sexual potency became the first scientist of sex. He does not mention the Freudian theories by name but is at pains to deny that they are applicable to his childhood and youth. There was, he says, little or nothing in his early experience that implied sexual curiosity or sexual feeling — and he records innumerable data which Freudians will have a happy time exploring. That repression is not hard to understand, but it is astonishing that the author of *Erotic Symbolism* was never aware of what his own terminology calls fetishism in his love for his mother and his wife. He extensively discusses the weakness of his sexual impulses — but then he goes on to describe himself as a great lover, wholly failing to perceive that his love was fixed at a juvenile, even infantile, level. There are throughout an amazing naïveté and an amazing blindness in his introspection, and when he comes to the certainly psychopathic elements in his marriage his ideas are crude and desperately unrealistic. This is not the place for an extended inquiry, but there must be some characterization of the partners in the marriage which he rightly regarded as the center and significance of his life. In no other way can the love story be understood — and, make no mistake, it is a great love story greatly felt and greatly revealed.

It was a marriage of true minds, which is at once the core and the tragedy of it, and a true marriage as well, fused in an agony of frustration that made all the rest of their experience unimportant. When he met Edith Lees, Ellis had begun his long study of sexual behavior — and his sexual development had been permanently arrested at a narcistic level. He tells us that throughout his life he was intoxicated with love, but of sexual experience he had had, when he married, nothing that went beyond exhibitionism. His youth had been dominated by his mother-phantasies; he had had a number of fervent but inactive love affairs, of which the most notable was the grotesque one with Olive Schreiner. (Let's be specific: Olive appears never to have been his mistress in the complete physical sense, he and his wife found marital relations distressing and gave them up after a few years, it is clear that sexual intercourse played only a small and dubious part in his ecstatic relations with other women.) He had strong sexual exaltations but they rose for the most part out of substitute gratifications and they led him through wholly intellectual excitements into a fleshless mysticism which he identified as the ultimate joy of love.

All this clears up two ambiguities in the *Studies.* The thing you encounter least often in those seven volumes, whether in the endless data Ellis assembled or in the case histories he used for illustration, is the simple lust of the flesh, the immediate and unmodified desire of man for woman, the normal wish for pleasure as an end in itself, the normal impulse toward procreation. And, magnificent as the seven volumes are in their encyclopedic exposition of the facts of sex, they usually lapse into mysticism when they try to fit a hypothesis to the facts. The autobiography shows that there is little desire in them because Ellis felt little, and the psychological theorizing is mystical because in his heart the champion of the flesh had repudiated the flesh.

Edith Lees was a writer and lecturer, a social worker, an ardent communicant in the Fellowship of the New Life, an almost perfect exemplar of the theories which the advanced intelligence of England was shaping toward the end of the century, a New Woman out of Ibsen, Grant Allen, and Bernard Shaw. (Or out of Shaw alone. You meet her many times in the beskirted but epicene figures who debate their way through *The Doctor's Dilemma, Getting Married, Misalliance, Fanny's First Play, The Philanderer, Widowers' Houses.*) Her childhood had been maimed by the hatred of a tyrannical father and, classically, by the persecutions of a step-mother. Ellis comes closer to the psychology of sex than any-where else in the book when he says that her father's antago-nism had given her an inferiority complex, but he never takes the further step which would have enabled him to understand her. Pathologically independent, fiercely antagonistic to all male images and manifestations, she had inevitably formed her-self in the image of her father and was, though as yet only latently, a homosexual. The stresses thus set up had made her also a hysteric and hypochondriac.

Psychologically, each of these ideologues found in the other exactly what he needed. Ellis could love only a woman who would preserve inviolate the infantile narcism which pro-tected him from his own dread of adult sex. Edith, who was emotionally somewhat more mature, needed a man sufficiently male to defend her against her homosexual impulses but in-sufficiently adult to activate the ambivalent dread of masculin-ity that had been implanted in her.

So, after acting out three-quarters of a Shaw play in high-minded debates, whether they should establish an open and free union, whether it was better to cohabit privately, whether they should have children, whether the State had any proper interest in a contract which excluded children – they were married. And, being liberated intelligences out of a Fabian tract, they drew up specifications for the marriage. They would maintain separate establishments. Each would shoulder his own expenses. The individual must be protected in his in-dividuality, so they would separate for long periods, in fact they would meet only when mutually inclined. They would put jealousy behind them, as a barbarous and unemancipated emotion. Each would be free to cultivate his own interests, his own friendships, his own loves, and the other would co-operate as sympathetically as a Shaw hero. They would master life, marriage, and the problems of the individual with a set of bylaws as enlightened as the modern intelligence could frame.

Only the individual would not emancipate, the emotions would not conform, and forces which neither the Fabian Society nor the first scientist of sex ever took into account at once linked these two in a bondage so powerful, so terrible, and so beautiful that its detailed exposure makes this book a great document in human love. They were caught fast in a mutual need which time never lessened but only increased, which made everything else insignificant for both and inhibited Ellis from thinking about anything else when he came to appraise his life. They could meet, of course, only on an infantile level, only as children. On page after page of the letters which make up a large part of the book, each repeatedly calls the other "baby." Each is forever repeating his desire to be the other's child. Their love-making is the play of children, their tenderness is the mutual gratitude of children for help in remaining Peter Pan, the highest maturity that either could attain (Edith shows it oftener than Ellis) is the phantasy that he is the other's mother. Each was the other's ally against the terrifying necessity of growing up in a world of adults, and neither could tolerate sex except as it evaded its own necessities and provided a childish escape from the obligations of adult heterosexuality. Love was a license to be neuter, a way of staying safely sterile. There are words for it in *Studies in the Psychology of Sex.* There are more accurate words for it in Freud.

Secure in his younger infantilism, Ellis never thought the sexual act very important. It disgusted Edith and presently she suggested that they give it up but, significantly, when she later suggested resuming it he refused. It appears to have played some part in his subsequent affairs with other women but that part is ambiguous and must have been exceedingly small — and could probably be identified somewhere in the *Studies.* Edith, however, had a stronger drive toward maturity than he — and he failed her. Her homosexuality became overt and she had a continuous series of affairs with women. Ellis's prose veils them in the same mystical rapture she got from them, but it is clear that at least some of them were complete unions. Meanwhile the pretty diagrams they had drawn up for marriage were blown to tatters by the gales of experience. Her increasing, neurotic invalidism prevented her from bearing her share of the family expenses, and her will to be an independent spirit clashed agonizingly with her desperate need to be protected as a woman. The rational separations became torments of jealousy and unsatisfied, childish need for each other. Always an infant, Ellis was able to achieve an equanimity toward Edith's infidelities with women which must have seemed admirably advanced to the Fabians but is psychologically a type-symptom of emasculation accepted. (And how did the student of perversions miss the perversity in his identifying himself with the female lovers of his wife?) But Edith, always the more adult, though she struggled to maintain the proper Fabian complaisance toward his mild, conversational, and adolescent infidelities, suffered such a hell of jealousy, self-doubt, and displaced hatred as has seldom got itself into print. (And how did the student of sadistic violence miss recognizing hostility as one pole of their love?)

That this relationship was a great love affair, that it sustained them through the ghastly suffering it created, that it was so rich as to make all the rest of their lives poor, is evidenced on every page of the book, in words that transmit unmodified the despairing but bitterly sincere cry of the heart. It was a great love affair — but what a composite need misunderstood, desire unsatisfied, and hate unrecognized it was! They were welded in a desperation which was a flight from maturity when they were together and became a pathological anxiety bordering on panic the moment they were separated. They scourged each other with an endless questioning and protestation, an endless accusation, an endless reproach for insufficiency of love, an endless demand for love, an endless assertion of love, of protection, of suspicion, of understanding, of mystical fulfillment. They loved as children, even as frustrated and terrified children, but the childish love burned to incandescence. Quite simply, it was the meaning of life to Havelock Ellis, and the passages in which he reflects on it (so uncomprehendingly) have a nobility which cannot be impugned.

And yet! Edith emerges from these pages a figure of genuine tragedy, a woman who had elements of greatness in her and was crucified by life. Ellis, a much greater intelligence, a man who accomplished great things, is, however, wrapped in an ineffable irony. The book, in fact, is surcharged with ironies so acid that they seem cosmic. The rationalist who supposes at the climax of tragedy that he has transmuted his irrationality to reason, the self-styled great lover who reduces sex to conversation and discovers that the transcendence of passion occurs as the absence of sex, the husband who rejoices in perverse cuckoldry because he thinks it an affirmation of life's deepest freedom, the encyclopedist of sex who fears sex and fails to perceive its manifestations in himself — what comic dramatist would have created such a figure? He will go down in intellectual history as a man who fought a great battle victoriously and established a science which has the greatest possible import for mankind. But elsewhere in history he will have a different shape. He will be seen as inconceivably inept in the relationship which meant everything to him. A figure talking, talking, talking, trying to reduce the most powerful energies of life to the service of an empty and impotent sweetness of the mind, blackly misunderstanding the woman who was the center of his existence, and not only misunderstanding her but, with the unaware stupidity of a Shavian ideologue, destroying her. Frustration unperceived, tragedy diminished to simple self-love, a magnificent intelligence altogether confounded by its crucial experience — that is the man whom this book reveals, and reveals in a serene delusion that it is portraying a master of life. A man, in one illustration, who, when his wife was half the world away, could write to her, at the very moment when her health and sanity were breaking under the long accumulation of his failure as a lover and husband, that he was contracting a new, beautiful, and ever so Fabian relationship with another woman — who, after twenty years of living with her, could write such news in the placid expectation that she would be as delighted as any Shaw preface said she ought to be, and who spends many pages wondering just why and wherein he seems somehow, though with the purest intentions, to have been wrong.

Do not miss this book. It is instinct with the insoluble mysteries of men and women. It is a deep well from which everyone will bring up what he can, but something surely, that bears on the insoluble mysteries of human greatness. And it makes clear why the finest part of Ellis's *Studies* is not the volume called *Sex in Relation to Society*, as Ellis thought, but instead the volume called *Love and Pain*.

Witchcraft in Mississippi

IT IS now possible to say confidently that the greatest suffering of which American fiction has any record occurred in the summer of 1909 and was inflicted on Quentin Compson. You will remember, if you succeeded in distinguishing Quentin from his niece in *The Sound and the Fury,* that late in that summer he made harrowing discoveries about his sister Candace. Not only was she pregnant outside the law but also, and this seared Quentin's purity much worse, she had lost her virginity. In the agony of his betrayed reverence for her, he undertook to kill both himself and her but ended by merely telling their father that he had committed incest with her. This blend of wish-fulfillment and Southern chivalry did not impress Mr. Jason Richmond Compson, who advised his son to take a vacation, adding, in one of the best lines Mr. Faulkner ever wrote, "Watching pennies has healed more scars than Jesus." Quentin went on to Harvard, where, however, the yeasts of guilt, expiation, and revenge that are Mr. Faulkner's usual themes so worked in him that he eventually killed himself, somewhere in the vicinity of the Brighton abattoir. But at the end of *The Sound and the Fury* not all the returns were in. It now appears that only a little while after he was pressing a knife to Candace's throat — I make it about a month — Quentin had to watch the last act of doom's pitiless engulfing of the Sutpens, another family troubled by a curse.

Mr. Faulkner's new fantasia [1] is familiar to us in everything but style. Although the story is told in approximations which display a magnificent technical dexterity — more expert than Mr. Dos Passos's, and therefore the most expert in contemporary American fiction — and although the various segments are shredded and displaced, it is not a difficult story to follow. It is not, for instance, so darkly refracted through distorting lenses as *The Sound and the Fury*. Though plenty of devices are employed to postpone the ultimate clarification, none are introduced for the sole purpose of misleading the reader, and in an access of helpfulness Mr. Faulkner has included not only an appendix of short biographies which make clear all the relationships, but also a chronological chart which summarizes the story. If you study both of them before beginning the book, you will have no trouble.

Thomas Sutpen, the demon of this novel, has a childhood racked by the monstrous cruelties to which all Faulkner children are subjected. He has immeasurable will — like evil, will is always immeasurable to Faulkner. He forms a "design": to found a fortune and a family. In pursuit of it he marries the daughter of a Haitian planter, has a son by her, discovers that she has Negro blood, abandons her, and rouses in her a purpose of immeasurable revenge. He takes some Haitian slaves to Mississippi, clears a plantation, becomes rich, marries a gentlewoman, and begets Henry and Judith. At the University Henry meets his mulatto half-brother, Charles Bon, who has been sent there by his vengeful mother, who knows the secret of his parentage, and who is married to a New Orleans octo-

[1] *Absalom, Absalom!*

roon. Henry worships Charles at sight and helps to effect his engagement to Judith. Thomas Sutpen inconceivably does nothing to prevent the engagement till, just before the Civil War, he tells Henry the secret of Bon's birth, though not (and here again the motive is what Mr. Faulkner would call un-motive) that of his Negro blood. Through four years of war Henry remains jubilant about the contemplated incest, but when his father at last reveals the secret he cannot accept incestuous miscegenation, and so shoots Bon when he goes to claim his bride. Henry then disappears and Thomas Sutpen, still demonic, comes back to rehabilitate both his estate and his posterity. He informs the sister of his dead wife (who also was tortured in childhood and hates all men, though she con-trives to desire two of them) that if he can succeed in be-getting a male child on her, he will marry her. Being a South-ern gentlewoman, she declines, and Sutpen begets a child on the fifteen-year-old granddaughter of a poor-white retainer. The child is a daughter and so Sutpen's design is ruined for-ever. The grandfather kills him with a scythe, kills the grand-daughter and the child with a butcher's knife, and rushes hap-pily into the arms of the lynchers. The relicts then send for Charles Bon's son and raise him, a mulatto, with further tor-tures. He rebels, marries a coal-black wench, and begets a semi-idiot, the last of the Sutpens who gives a tragic twist to the title of the novel. The horror which Quentin Compson has to undergo occurs many years later, when this last Henry Sutpen has crept back to die in the ruined mansion, cared for by the shriveled Clytie, another mulatto of Thomas's get. Henry and Clytie are burned up in the final holocaust, the ritualistic destruction of the house of hell and doom that is in part repeated from *Light in August*.

Mr. Faulkner, in fact, has done much of this before. This off-stage hammering on a coffin — Charles Bon's coffin this time — was used to make us liquefy with pity in *As I Lay Dying*, where it was Addie Bundren's coffin. And when Addie's coffin, with the corpse inside, slid off the wagon into the flooded river, the effect then gained discounted the scene in *Absalom, Absalom!* where the mules bolt and throw Thomas Sutpen's corpse and coffin into the ditch. Much of Henry Sutpen's ambiguous feeling for his sister Judith was sketched in Quentin Compson's attitude toward Candace. When Charles Bon forces Henry Sutpen to shoot him, moved by some inscrutable inertia of pride and contempt and abnegation (or moved by unmotive) — he is repeating whatever immolation was in Popeye's mind when he refused to defend himself against the murder charge of which he was innocent, near the end of *Sanctuary*. These are incidental repetitions, but many fundamental parts of *Absalom, Absalom!* seem to come straight out of *Light in August*. It is not only that Etienne Bon undergoes in childhood cruelties as unceasing as those that made Joe Christmas the most persecuted child since Dickens, not only that he is moved by the same necessity to wreak both revenge and forgiveness on both black and white that moved Joe, not only that he commits some of the same defiances in the same terms, and not only that the same gigantic injustices are bludgeoned on the same immeasurable stubbornness and stupidity in the same inexplicable succession. It is deeper than that and comes down to an identity of theme. That theme is hardly reducible to words, and certainly has not been reduced to words by Mr. Faulkner. It is beyond the boundary of explanation: some undimensional identity of fear and lust in which a man is both black and white, yet neither, loathing both, rushing to embrace both with some super-Tolstoian ecstasy of abasement, fulfillment, and expiation.

The drama of *Absalom, Absalom!* is clearly diabolism, a "miasmal distillant" of horror, with clouds of sulphur smoke billowing from the pit and flashes of hellish lightning flickering across the steady phosphorus-glow of the graveyard and the medium's cabinet. And it is embodied in the familiar hypochondria of Mr. Faulkner's prose, a supersaturated solution of pity and despair. In book after book now he has dropped tears like the famed Arabian tree, in a rapture of sensibility amounting to continuous orgasm. The medium in which his novels exist is lachrymal, and in *Absalom, Absalom!* that disconsolate fog reaches its greatest concentration to date. And its most tortured prose. Mr. Faulkner has always had many styles at his command, has been able to write expertly in many manners, but he has always been best at the phrase, and it is as a phrase maker only that he writes well here. Many times he says the incidental thing perfectly, as "that quiet aptitude of a child for accepting the inexplicable." But beyond the phrase, he now — deliberately — mires himself in such a quicksand of invertebrate sentences as has not been seen since *Euphues*. There have been contentions between Mr. Faulkner and Mr. Hemingway before this; it may be that he is matching himself against the Gertrude-Steinish explosions of syntax that spattered *Green Hills of Africa* with bad prose. If so, he comes home under wraps: the longest Hemingway sentence ran only forty-three lines, whereas the longest Faulkner sentence runs eighty lines and there are more than anyone will bother to count which exceed the thirty-three-line measure of his page. They have the steady purpose of expressing the inexpressible that accounts for so much of Mr. Faulkner, but they show a style in process of disintegration. When a narrative sentence has to have as many as three parentheses identifying the reference of pronouns, it signifies mere bad writing and can be justified by no psychological or esthetic principle whatever.

It is time, however, to inquire just what Mr. Faulkner means by this novel, and by the whole physiography of the countryside which he locates on the map of Mississippi in the vicinity of a town called Jefferson. This community is said to be in the geographical and historical South and the Sutpens, together with the Compsons and the Sartorises and the Benbows and the Poor Whites and the Negroes, are presented to us as human beings. Yet even the brief summary I have made above shows that if we are forced to judge them as human beings we can accept them only as farce. Just why did not Thomas Sutpen, recognizing Charles Bon as his mulatto son, order him off the plantation, or bribe or kill him, or tell Judith either half of the truth, or tell Henry all of it? In a single sentence toward the end of the book, Mr. Faulkner gives us an explanation, but it is as inadequate to explain the tornadoes that depend on it as if he had tried to explain the Civil War by the annual rainfall at New Granada. Not even that effort at explanation is made for the most of the behavior in the book. Eulalia Bon's monotone of revenge is quite inconceivable, and her demonic lawyer is just one more of those figures of pure bale that began with Januarius Jones in *Soldiers' Pay* and have drifted through all the novels since exhaling evil and imitating the facial mannerisms of the basilisk. Miss Rosa (another Emily, without rose) is comprehensible neither as a woman nor as a maniac. Why do the children suffer so? Why did Emily's father treat her that way? Why did Sutpen treat Henry and Judith that way? Why did Judith and Clytie treat Etienne that way? Just what revenge or expiation was Etienne wreaking on whites and Negroes in that Joe Christmas series of attempts at self-immolation? Just what momentary and sacrificial nobility moved Wash Jones to kill three people? Just what emotion, compulsion, obsession, or immediate clairvoyant pattern of impotence plus regeneration plus pure evil may be invoked to explain the behavior of Charles Bon, for which neither experience nor the psychology of the unconscious nor any logic of the heart or mind can supply an explanation?

Well, it might answer everything to say that they are all crazy. As mere symptomatology, their behavior does vividly suggest schizophrenia, paranoia, and dementia praecox. But that is too easy a verdict, it would have to be extended to all the population of Jefferson, the countryside, New Granada, and New Orleans, and besides the whole force of Mr. Faulkner's titanic effort is expended in assuring us that this is not insanity.

A scholarly examination might get us a little farther. This fiction of families destroyed by a mysterious curse (beginning with the Sartorises, there has been one in every novel except *As I Lay Dying* and *Pylon*), of ruined castles in romantic landscapes, of Giaours and dark "unwill," may be only a continuation of the literature of excessive heartbreak. The Poe of *Ligeia* and kindred tales, Charles Brockden Brown, Horace Walpole, and Mrs. Radcliffe suggest a clue to a state of mind which, after accepting the theorem that sensation is desirable for itself alone, has moved on to the further theorem that the more violent sensation is the more admirable, noble, and appropriate to fiction. Surely this reek of hell and the passage to and fro of demons has intimate linkages with Eblis; surely Vathek saw this ceaseless agony, this intercellular doom, and this Caliph's heart transparent as crystal and enveloped in flames that can never be quenched. Surely; and yet that tells us very little.

Much more central is the thesis advanced in these columns a couple of years ago, that Mr. Faulkner is exploring the primitive violence of the unconscious mind. Nothing else can explain the continuity of rape, mutilation, castration, incest, patricide, lynching, and necrophilia in his novels, the blind drive of terror, the obsessional preoccupation with corpses and decay and generation and especially with the threat to generation. It is for the most part a deliberate exploration, Mr. Faulkner is at pains to give us Freudian clues, and he has mapped in detail the unconscious mind's domain of horrors, populated by anthropophagi, hermaphrodites, Hyppogypi, Acephalites, and cynocephalites. It is the world of subliminal guilt and revenge, the land of prodigy which D. H. Lawrence thought was peopled exclusively by beautiful, testicular athletes, but which is inhabited instead by such races as Mandeville and

Carpini saw. These are the dog-faced men, the men whose heads do grow beneath their shoulders, who feed on corpses, who hiss and bark instead of talking, whose custom it is to tear their own bowels. A far country, deep under the mind's frozen ocean. In Mr. Faulkner's words, a "shadowy miasmic region," "amoral evil's undeviating absolute," "quicksand of nightmare," "the seething and anonymous miasmal mass which in all the years of time has taught itself no boon of death."

Haunted by the fear of impotence and mutilation and dismemberment, hell-ridden by compulsions to destroy the mind's own self and to perpetrate a primal, revengeful murder on the old, cataleptic in the helplessness of the terrified young, bringing the world to an end in a final phantasy of ritual murder and the burning house — the inhabitants of the prodigy-land of the unconscious are also fascinated by those other primal lusts and dreads, incest and miscegenation. In Joe Christmas and Etienne Bon, neither white nor black, repudiating both races, inexplicably ecstatic with love of both, mysteriously dreading both, mysteriously wreaking revenge and expiation on both, we face a central preoccupation of Mr. Faulkner, a central theme of his fiction, and, I think, an obligation to go beyond the psychoanalytical study of his purposes. In spite of his enormous labor to elucidate these two mulattoes and their feelings and their symbolism in society, they are never elucidated. What is it that bubbles through those minds, what is it that drives them, what are they feeling, what are they trying to do, what do they mean? You cannot tell, for you do not know. A fair conclusion is that you do not know because Mr. Faulkner does not know. I suggest that on that fact hinges the explanation of his fiction.

It is a fact in religion. For the energy derived from primitive sources in the mind projects a structure of thought intended to be explanatory of the world, and this is religious, though religious in the familiar reversal that constitutes demonology and witchcraft. William James has told us how it comes about.

The simple truth is that Mr. Faulkner is a mystic – on the lower of the two levels James defines. He is trying to communicate to us an immediate experience of the ineffable. He cannot tell us because he does not know – because what he perceives cannot be known, cannot therefore be told, can never be put into words but can only be suggested in symbols, whose content and import must forever be in great part missed and in greater part misunderstood. This is a mysticism, furthermore, of what James called the lower path. There are, James said, two mystical paths, the one proceeding out of some beatitude of spiritual health which we may faintly glimpse in the visions of the saints. But it is from the lower path, the decay of the vision, that witchcraft always proceeds. And witchcraft, like all magic, is a spurious substitute for fundamental knowledge.

The crux of the process by which witchcraft came to substitute for the ordinary concerns of fiction in Mr. Faulkner's work may be observed in *Sartoris*. His first book, *Soldiers' Pay*, introduced the overwhelming despair finding expression in lachrymation and the creatures of unadulterated evil that have appeared in all his later books – curiously combined with the glibness and tight technique of magazine fiction. His second book, *Mosquitoes*, was his *Crome Yellow* effort, and had in common with his other work only a pair of lovers moving on some manic errand through a nightmare world. With *Sartoris* (which was published, if not written, before *The Sound and the Fury*), he became a serious novelist in the best sense of that adjective. He undertook to deal fairly with experience, to articulate his characters with a social organism, and to interpret the web of life in terms of human personality. Wherever he was factual and objective – in Loosh, Miss Jenny (who is his best creation to date), the unmystical Negroes, the crackers, the old men, Dr. Alford – he imposed a conformable and convincing world of his own on a recognizable American experience, in symbols communicative to us all. But he failed in the principal effort of the novel. What he tried to do, with the Sartorises themselves, was to deliver up to us the heart of a mystery — to explain the damnation, the curse, of a brilliant, decayed, and vainglorious family doomed to failure and death. And he did not do it. They were a void. We did not know them and he could not tell us about them. They were without necessity, without causation. When he faced the simple but primary necessity of the novelist, to inform us about his principal characters, he backed away.

He has been backing away ever since. All the prestidigitation of his later technique rests on a tacit promise that this tortuous narrative method, this obsession with pathology, this parade of Grand Guignol tricks and sensations, will, if persevered with, bring us in the end to a deeper and a fuller truth about his people than we could get otherwise. And it never does. Those people remain wraiths blown at random through fog by winds of myth. The revelation remains just a series of horror stories that are essentially false — false because they happen to grotesques who have no psychology, no necessary motivation as what they have become out of what they were. They are also the targets of a fiercely rhetorical bombast diffused through the brilliant technique that promises us everything and gives us nothing, leaving them just wraiths. Meanwhile the talent for serious fiction shown in *Sartoris* and the rich comic intelligence grudgingly displayed from time to time, especially in *Sanctuary*, have been allowed to atrophy from disuse and have been covered deep by a tide of sensibility.

Snow White and the Seven Dreads

IN ALMOST any town of five thousand that is fifty miles or more from the nearest city you will find the store of T. M. Kirby & Son, Office and Mimeographing Supplies, Papeteries, Favors, Souvenirs, Greeting Cards, Lending Library, and, decrescendo, Books. Toward midafternoon Ruth Martin comes into Kirby's, buys a box of correspondence cards and a dozen bridge pads, and pauses before a shelf labeled "Recent Fiction." Ruth is the wife of the cashier of the State Bank and Trust Company; she is thirty-four and has three children, the youngest of whom is four years old; she is an A.B. of State U., class of 1925; she is head of the local Episcopal charities, she once broke 95 at the country club, and, against Bob Martin's express command, she twice voted for Roosevelt. After twenty minutes of indecision she buys two new novels at two dollars and fifty cents apiece. One is the latest work of John Dos Passos, James T. Farrell, Thomas Wolfe, or Sinclair Lewis. The other is by a newcomer of whom she has heard only in the advertising columns of *Books*, which Kirby's gives away to all charge customers. A week later she has read both novels and Bob, who is fundamentally serious-minded and had a cold over the week end besides, has read one of them (the newcomer's).

Ruth's purchase and the fact that she will repeat it in a week or two are the foundation that supports the publishing business and the trade of authorship. Not her purchase, however, but her pleasure in the books concerns us here. Novels are one of the durable satisfactions in Ruth's life, and in the lives of several hundred thousand other Americans; but one who undertook to find out what that satisfaction consists of would get little in print to help him. Why do people read novels? What is this pleasure bound in cloth which they buy for two dollars and a half? Such questions usually evoke only the most perfunctory answers.

Professional and amateur literary people must be excluded from the inquiry. Poets read poetry by living writers primarily to resent it. Novelists feel a similar resentment of novels but sublimate it better, and have other motives besides: they read one another's novels to keep abreast of fashions and technique, to study the solution of professional problems, to appraise materials, to argue and agree and repudiate. The semi-literary, the dilettanti and hangers-on, read fiction in order to talk about it as if they were novelists themselves. The Martins have none of these motives, however, and few of the motives which literary people attribute to them. Novelists are never content to consider themselves mere entertainers who provide amusement for people's leisure and will tell you that readers come to them in search of truth and beauty and to acquire a philosophy of life. That is a very solacing thought for novelists to hold, but the Martins are not self-conscious about truth or beauty, and their philosophy of life — happily for the Republic — is imposed on them by forces far stronger than fiction, by family and friends, by school and church and other social institutions. Novelists also say that readers ask them to interpret experience, and here they are on firmer ground, though the interpretation asked of them is not the kind they usually claim to supply.

Ruth likes a good story of course and will talk about the two novels at the parish supper, and to that extent she is moved by the desire to be in fashion. But the privilege of keeping up with the Joneses in literature is a very slight privilege and she would not pay two dollars and a half for it, still less five dollars. She wants to keep up with the world but wants to do so by keeping up with the story of her own life, and what she asks of the novelist is not interpretation but information.

The clue may be found on simpler levels of fiction than Dos Passos and among more naïve people than the Martins. The aspiration of America is still upward, toward a better job, a finer house, a more powerful automobile, and in phantasy at least, which is to say in fiction, the aspiration is still reasonable. So there is a constant need to know what things are like on the next landing, that one may behave as if accustomed to it when he arrives there. The attendant at a Socony gas station derives from popular magazine fiction an immense amount of information about the surroundings he may expect to find when he is a field supervisor and, later, a district manager, and about the behavior appropriate to such surroundings. Most of all, information about rituals. How do people act at an executive's desk, at the country club, at a restaurant where dinner jackets must be worn? How do they talk and what do they talk about? What are fighting words here and what epithets treated on the floor below as insults are now to be shrugged away as mere good fellowship? What assumptions and beliefs does an initiate carry to a directors' meeting, a church wedding, the Kentucky Derby, the moment when an assistant's treachery is discovered? On his way up the Socony boy will have to know, and he turns to popular fiction in order to be prepared.

The Martins, however, need not call on James Farrell for information of that kind. If Bob were raised to the national Treasury to-morrow he would repair his ignorance by direct inquiry and Ruth would go to *Vogue*, the smart shops, and the manuals provided. It is rather an emotional preparedness they need. Life goes on, their own individual stories unfold, they are confronted from month to month with the manifold experiences of human maturity and decline — and with them comes the immortal human necessity, not of knowing how to act, since action is imposed involuntarily, but how to feel about them. If drift and circumstance transform Bob's flirtation with his secretary to a moment of authentic passion acted upon, if a star-crossed summer night finds Ruth and the rector of St. Anne's transfixed by the flesh's agony, there is a turbulence whose instant need is to be understood, to be given terms of the experienced, to be brought out of uniqueness into the humanly familiar. Fiction has been encouraged to occupy itself so largely with adultery not, as some critics hold, because it supplies safe gratification for wishes that cannot be acted upon — for Bob and Ruth can gratify such wishes with much more vivid and particularized phantasies than any novelist can give them — but because every strong emotion is both unique and intolerable to the individual until it is fitted into a pattern of the familiar; and, with the confessional and the conversation of old friends, fiction is a ready means to such assimilation. No one can stand unshaped emotion: it must be given shape, familiarity, a conduit of the known. So Ruth's requirement of the novelist as she approaches the rector's arms (or the grave of her first-born, a friend's insanity, or a doctor's diagnosis that she has cancer of the breast) is not What Shall I Do? — for her behavior is conditioned by forces no novelist can affect — but How Do I Feel?

A primary service of fiction is that it helps to answer that question, prepares Ruth and Bob for the whirlpools of their own feelings, ekes out experience by anticipating it and filling in its gaps. Ruth and Bob grow older, the children grow older too and turn against them or disappoint them or prove to be far otherwise than early parenthood had dreamed. What do I feel about all this? What is this agony or ecstasy? Their friends die and they see themselves plain, the coarsening of aspiration, the eclipse of hope, the details of loss and suffering and defeat and decay — and such achievements and exultations also as the human story contains. What do I feel about them? Delivered over to emotions that crucify and exalt him, the individual is helpless; all emotion happens to him for the first time and his great need is to know what it is, to give it contact and fixation in the known. Fiction is an effective way to close the circuit and bring the known in.

It is here, almost it is here alone, that the novelist may be trusted. Within limits, he can answer that pitiful question, How do I feel? Within limits, he can tell us what individual emotion is. When he moves on from there and tries to tell us what the world is like he is the feeblest of all diviners. An inquirer can get a more trustworthy interpretation of society, or any of its component parts and energies, from a dowser, a palmist, or an astrologer, and a far more trustworthy one from the bell-shaped curve or the toss of a coin. The novelist may sometimes describe the appearance of things with moderate accuracy (an accuracy impaired by his timorousness, ignorance, and lack of analytical capacity and worldly experience), though such surface descriptions are usually dead as fiction in so far as they are uncolored by the compulsions that make him an artist. But when it comes to explaining the world, to explaining anything beyond the impact of individual on individual and the emotion it begets, he has, in support of his compulsions, only hazily remembered and temperamentally distorted theorems learned in Sunday school, in college courses in ethics or metaphysics, or in some conversations about Plato, Spengler, or Marx which he participated in some years ago but didn't understand very well. If Ruth and Bob Martin relied on him for orientation in the world they would be farcically betrayed. But, not being of the literary, they do not: they go to guides who are not under compulsion, they go to the luncheon clubs and the saints and sinners of the parish guild.

But the Martins are not yet done with the novelist. If it is Ruth's deep need to know how she feels when the flesh wakens or the children stray, it is an even deeper need to slake desires and assuage terrors that never rise to the threshold of awareness. If a novelist is a person who by anatomizing his emotions enables her to identify hers, he is also one who sinks a shaft into his unconscious self for the stability of hers. It is this reason even more than the other that keeps Ruth reading novels, bad ones almost as pleasurably as good ones, plowing through fiction that is alien to her experience and opaque to her understanding, ineptly, tritely, repetitiously written. It is for this reason that publishers and novelists may count on her always to spend two dollars and half for another version of a fable already wearily familiar to her or so strange in milieu or treatment that she cannot come to grips with it.

We have heard much of wish-fulfillment literature and the literature of escape, yet in the naïve sense usually given these words they have only the slightest application to the people who read novels. A novel may be an escape for the novelist, but at best it can be no more than a brief holiday for the reader. No man ever escaped so believingly into a novel that he tried to kiss the heroine, and no woman was ever so engaged with one that the hero got into her reveries — which, if they must stray from Bob, settle on the rector of St. Anne's or some other person who is not type but flesh. And it is superficial to suppose that, toward the fulfillment of desire, any Ruth Martin in the world identifies herself as Scarlett O'Hara to the end that she may surrender to Rhett Butler. The energies at work are more complex than that — and darker.

For Ruth is grown up and grows older, and the reality-principle has triumphed in her beyond the power of any character in fiction to impair it. When the mysterious energies of the personality make an identification on her behalf it is not with one character or two but with the sum of all the characters in the book and with the relationships in which they are placed. They can make such an identification only on a level of the personality that is buried much deeper than the shadow play of phantasy. Among the mind's pre-Cambrian quicksands there is hardly even personality, and certainly there are not characters either of fiction or of the waking world; there are only wills, blind and frustrate, and a child crying in fear. It is the child who was left behind when Ruth grew up and is now only a wraith — a wraith not seen as Ruth goes about her daily life but heard as a voice whispering and an impulse exerted on all she does. There in that Lyonnesse of the soul, where the cathedral chimes toll under waves which no light penetrates, fiction does its greatest charity to the human spirit. It is a means by which the child to whom all time is one may find achievement, joy, expiation, and reconciliation. It is one of art's immortal handmaidens to the child who must not live and cannot die.

Thus Ruth Martin reading a novel about the rebellion of a generation against its parents is not only a mother in 1938 who greatly needs to know how she feels about her children's desertion; she is also a child in 1912 rent by will and terror to destroy a parent who died in 1918. If the novelist has gratified the mother in 1938 by displaying his own maternal woes, be sure he has also gratified her childish need by molding his own in images. Ruth will raptly follow, say, William Faulkner through a hell's broth of panic, mutilation, murder, and disembowelment that should disgust the gently reared parishioner of St. Anne's — because from severed roots far below the parishioner's introspection grow out just those monstrous blossoms in a child's terror and necessity. She will follow John Dos Passos through a chronicle of events she does not understand occurring to puppets that never touch her adult heart because over and over in that chronicle events and puppets symbolically evoke relationships, currents of desire thwarted or gratified, guilt felt and anticipated, fear assuaged and ecstasy achieved when the child who is now a wraith confronted the unknown, and because that child must still quiver with them in the void. She will follow the brutalities of *Studs Lonigan* and the delicate poetry of *Winter Orchard* with the same intentness for, over and beyond the fictitious events occurring to imaginary characters, both permit that spellbound child to raise a curtain, in safety and some comfort, on a theater where a child's dreads played out their drama years ago.

The mole, its forehead bloody from the spade's thrust, burrows deeper than the mind can follow it, but in every novel there are Snow White and the poisoned comb, there is a thumbling loosed with his sword in the giant's house, there is an impetus and handhold for the child Ruth used to be. If it chances to be a fine novel it will fuse these pitiful symbols with the real objects of an adult's world; but it need not be even a good novel to provide channels for the immortal cravings and surcease for the seven dreads. It need only attach the marionettes to their proper strings and turn out the lights, leaving the rest to childhood. For it is fiction's eternal charter that children accept fairy tales as true. And it is the reader's reprieve and absolution that novelists, whatever else they may be, are also children talking to children . . . in the dark.

From Dream to Fiction

WHEREIN does a novelist differ from the generality of human kind? Any layman who happens to know a novelist would probably answer that the most noticeable difference is conversational. Most people can talk impersonally for perceptible periods, whereas every topic you broach with a novelist leads straight to him or his books in a sentence or two, or at most a minute or two. This lay test, however, is crude and unselective. It does not distinguish novelists from other artists or even from other literary people. There may be a difference between the rates of personal reference at which poets and novelists operate, but science has not yet developed instruments sufficiently delicate to reveal it.

A distinction believed in by novelists themselves, their colleagues, the critics, and the textbooks is even more illusory. A novelist, they tell us, is an observer, a person who perceives the appearance of things more rapidly and more accurately than the layman can. This textbook definition has such a widespread acceptance that the aspiring young who want to be novelists go about with notebooks jotting down tragedies which they think they find in faces in subway cars and pausing in the midst of sunsets and symphonies to make notes on presumably significant details. By extension the talent is supposed to make novelists so exquisitely sensitive to human relationships that they cannot come into a group of people without at once intuitively perceiving the subtlest relationships, stresses and strains, hopes and frustrations, and unfinished dramas in that group.

Nothing could be farther from the truth. Novelists are among the least observant of human beings; they are practically impermeable by what goes on around them except as it can come through channels of personal reference. Embarrassing experience has taught them not to rely on even such routine functions of the sense organs as they share with lesser folk. The novelist's wife can tell tulle from chiffon at sight and can remember exactly what Louise had on the other night. The novelist cannot, and he has learned to appeal to her for costumes and to other authorities for all his supporting details. A sedentary and hypochondriac man, he has never seen the interior of a factory or been present when finks and strikers were rioting — and if he went out to see for himself would be too worried about accidents and head colds to keep his mind on what was happening. Those vivid impressions of industrial activity which you admire so much and those violent strike scenes come from the newspaper accounts which the novelist looked up and from his files of *Life* and *Fortune*. And you have probably admired a good many scenes of passion which, because the novelist's experience was defective, rest on researches of Havelock Ellis.

As for the intuitive recognition of human nuances, you could almost grade a novelist's talent by the degree of his insensibility to them. You could not hope to conceal a quarrel with your wife from a society reporter or your next-door neighbor, but it is safe from a novelist even if he enters in the middle of it. He will get there in the end and may find that quarrel very useful in his new book, but it will have no existence for him until he can relate it to himself. If Sinclair Lewis were to attend a Rotary luncheon it is unlikely that he could correctly report the color of his sponsor's hair, accurately outline the speaker's argument against the closed shop, or reproduce the menu. He could write a vivid scene about that luncheon, but it would derive not from what he saw and heard there but from the fictitious luncheon that was simmering in his mind when he went there. And it is certain that if William Faulkner happened to enter a shabby Southern drawing-room in the early stages of such an intrigue as the doom of his last chapter springs from, he would be wholly unaware of the incest or mass murder implicit in it. He would be insulated from it by the horror he was working up for his current novel. An inferior novelist might see the Rotary luncheon reasonably free of preconceptions or deduce a gathering horror from the behavior of the Southern chatelaine. But Mr. Lewis and Mr. Faulkner are good novelists; they have no capacity for observation, no energy to spare for intuition, and no practice at either.

Ask a novelist where he got the behavior of his characters in a given scene and you are likely to get one of two answers. One novelist will tell you that it rests on his prolonged study of human nature, here concentrated, purified, and focused on the necessities of his book. Another novelist will indignantly repudiate a suggestion that he has summarized a hundred case histories in this scene and will tell you that he "made it up." The second one is defining the act of artistic creation, and it will be safer to follow him.

When you or I in a warm reverie redress a grievance by squelching someone with the well-turned phrase we didn't have the wit to think of on the spot, when as we fall asleep we endow ourselves with the wealth or loveliness or daring that a heedless God neglected to give us, we are behaving like novelists. A novelist is a person who has a highly developed gift of phantasy and an ability to organize his phantasies in coherent sequences. He "makes up" stories; that is, his phantasy life is continuous, not episodic and fragmentary, and while he is composing novels, if not always, it takes priority over his sense of reality. You and I make up phantasies to redress our grievances, satisfy needs, and gratify impulses which it is inexpedient to express in action, and repair the omissions of the providence that has given us less than we deserve. So does a novelist; but whereas experience has taught us to pursue the activity as an off-hours pleasure only, a novelist has rejected that teaching. With him phantasy is not on a lower level than experience but on a higher one; it is not "less real" than what happens to him in the objective world but "more real." It is his conditioning connection with the objective world.

The characters and events in a novel have only a permissive existence for a reader, who accepts them most easily when they confirm the pattern or amplify the detail of his own phantasies, and who is always able to distinguish between the novelist's heroine and his own wife. But they have more validity to their creator; they are more immediate in time than the world of friendship and nutrition and fatigue in which his body haphazardly exists, and during the composition of the novel they are frequently superior to it. During that period they are the conduits by which realities reach him; they impart emotion to those realities instead of acquiring it from them. At a time when the beautiful Angelina is being agonized in the phantasies from which his novel flows, any agonies which the novelist's wife may suffer must enter into his awareness by way of Angelina's and be shaped by them. Any evidence of the collapse of capitalism which the novelist may encounter on his afternoon walks will be modified for his understanding by the pattern he is preparing for it in phantasy. Mr. Lewis will not see what is happening at the Rotary Club; that luncheon is an inferior thing, it exists on a lower level. He has been assembling a much more splendid Rotary inside him and it screens out the irrelevant actualities before his eyes.

Such phantasies are the basis of every novel. They are generated by the impact of the novelist's experience on his ego; they flow from what has happened to him in relation to his needs, urges, impulses, disappointments, fears, hopes, anxieties, and aspirations — to the sum of these from his infancy on. A novel is a psychological adaptation: a means whereby its author adjusts the world as he must feel about it to the world as he is forced to think about it. Necessarily therefore, it steams and ferments with its author's personal history. But usually the details of that history, except in their most trivial aspects, are quite beyond identification by a critic or inquisitive friend. The sophistication of a novelist consists of the ability to incorporate with his own emotions material which acquires life from them by induction and to fuse public and private elements into something new and different from both. The characters and events of a novel are not usually history but symbols, and the more mature a novelist is the more complex his symbolism will be.

You will not, that is, recover the novelist's quarrel with his best friend from the antipathy between Jack and Herbert in his latest novel, nor will you find his love affair with a movie actress chronicled in the career of Angelina, and no confession that an identifiable woman once treated him harshly is signified by the cruelties inflicted on Sophia. And Jack, the hero, is not the novelist as he wishes or imagines himself to be. Or rather, the novelist is indeed Jack but Jack is also an almost infinite number of other people who have affected the novelist's life and is furthermore compounded of needs and desires and compensations and penalties and dreads, some of them private to the author and others picked up elsewhere and welded in here because they are on the same wave-length. In the same way the craven Herbert is an act of revenge on various people who have injured the novelist, a defiance of some who have frightened him, and also a public confession of his own guilt. The secret villainies of the heart are here acknowledged and an incantation is made against their punishment. So with Angelina and Sophia. In both are vestiges of many actual women; and each of them is also a complex image of longing unfulfilled, desire unsatisfied, and revenge taken; and also they are a compulsive projection of the novelist himself. So with all the others, the little boy on page 60, the old family servitor, and the menacing crowd off-stage. When they walk and talk it is the novelist walking and talking, and also innumerable images projected from the swarm within him, deposits left on him by contact with many lives, and something straight from the compulsive core of fear and desire that throbs below his consciousness.

Everyone who reads novels must, however else he may classify them besides, divide them into a small group of very good ones and a large group of the mediocre or worse. There is a flagrant hint for us in the mediocre ones. In most run-of-the-mill novels the scenes that deal with childhood are better done, more convincing, more real and alive than the other parts. Novelists seem to find it easier to write about childhood than about maturity, as if their own adult life had proved less important than the enchanted years, or as if a compulsion lingering on from childhood were stronger than their adult will. Furthermore, the characters of a mediocre novel are sometimes preposterously simple in motive and behavior, as simple as a child thinks adults are. Or they seem to have a child's emotions when a grownup's are called for. Or they seem to be not warm, fallible, and contradictory human beings but just creatures in a fable, in a child's phantasy of virtue, heroism, villainy, danger, or destruction. What happens to them is as uncomplicated and as little related to what actually happens in this world as a child's image of what will happen to it if it expresses hatred of a parent.

In short, the peril of one who has an unusual gift of phantasy is that he may be emotionally fixed at the level of childhood, and a bad novel is commonly a form of regression toward infancy. A really good novelist must have many talents and their proportion may vary from person to person, but the common essential is this: that he must so far transcend his childhood as to impart to the phantasies from which his books are made the emotions proper to an adult. There is no such thing as a complete delivery from childhood — especially for an artist who, as all criticism recognizes, is invariably a person in whom the child he once was lives on concurrently with his mature self. The true generative force of phantasy derives from the years in which there is no distinction between the world of experience and that of imagination. So that, though a mature novelist's personal history cannot be recovered from his books, their pattern nevertheless reveals the pattern that was made basic during his childhood. No novelist ever has more than one story. Look at his collected works and you will find in all of them an assertion of the same magnificent simplicity: doom earned or doom avoided, desire fulfilled or unfulfilled, cruelty or tenderness triumphant, the world conquering or the world conquered, life stable or life flowing away. It was thus in dread or dream when the novelist was young and it will be thus in all his books. But the mature artist is one who can modulate and modify the dream — who can reconcile it with reality. An inferior novelist writes fables in compliance with a child's urges; a mature novelist has made those urges obey the teachings of experience.

In every novel the shapes of childhood will be walking, and part of its power for any reader will be the response of a child recognizing another child. But in a fine novel there is an additional power, that of meeting adults, children who have grown up to be men, who are no longer controlled by a child's fears and wishes, in whom dream has been shaped to conform to what really is. A fine novel is a victory for the reality-principle, for the faculty of control, for the human will.

It remains a vicarious triumph, since it is produced in print-er's ink. But art is the world of vicarious experience, and if only in that world are some of the achievements of maturity possible for the artist, it is only there that some of them are possible for the rest of us. None of us has ever completely si-lenced the little monster from whom he grew, and it is only in novels that we shall ever break all the chains that bind us to him. If a novel is sometimes the only place in which its writer can be altogether grown-up, it is also a place where a reader may put away childish things altogether and be what he will never be outside of fiction, a whole man.

Friday Afternoon at Country Day

WHEN NOT practising in these pages the Easy Chair conducts a general literary business elsewhere. It is so general that foul detractors have spoken of it as the Sears-Roebuck of contemporary letters, but at present it is overextended in one department, literary criticism. The Easy Chair has a morbid dislike of referring to itself as a critic, since criticism is the vaguest and most pointless of literary pursuits. It is one of those activities which, as Mr. Stuart Chase recently pointed out in *Harper's*, never deal in meanings at all, as meaning is understood in other occupations. When a scientist, a historian, a garage mechanic, an elevator boy, or a cook deals with a problem of his profession his thinking is constantly engaged with things. The things and the acts he performs in relation to them are what constitute meaning. But a literary critic, like a metaphysician, proceeds not from thing to idea to thing, but from idea to idea to idea. There is no way of checking, verifying, or disproving him. He has nothing to do with meaning. He just thinks.

Q. Is this liquid an acid or a base? *A.* Get out the proper reagents and make the appropriate tests, and everybody who does the same will come to the same conclusion.

Q. Is this book a good one or a bad one? *A.* Just sit there and think and you'll find out but nobody else will have to agree.

That is why the Easy Chair prefers to be called a historian and why, when referred to as a critic, it insists that the epithet be accompanied by a smile. . . . Well, as one or the other, the Easy Chair recently had an interesting experience. In a nostalgic moment it published some extracts from poems and speeches that our grandfathers thought were pretty fine. It did so with a certain apprehension lest readers enjoy them not with a proper antiquarian approval but with the spurious sophistication of the literary. As it turned out, however, the Easy Chair was the more snobbish. The selections it published brought in a big mail from the people who have to be thought of as enlightened, from whatever basis you assess enlightenment, and without exception they liked the stuff. They liked it not as antiquarians but as twentieth-century, post-war, post-depression, precatastrophe radical thinkers. They hadn't seen anything like those poems and speeches for a long time. They were glad to see them. They wanted more.

Such a phenomenon transfers you from literary criticism to what Teachers College (which is populated by literary critics) calls social significance. If Americans like the popular literature of grandfather's time, that is news. In criticism it looks like pretty bad literature, but in history all we can say is that it gets a vote large enough to be interpreted as a mandate. The Easy Chair does not pretend to say what the fact means or what its implications are or whither it may lead. But it recognizes a public obligation when it sees one.

All right. You are back in the 1870's. You are attending a Country Day School. That is, you have got past the reactionary stage of progressive education, which curiously believed that students ought to be collected in a bus and carried away from the barbarous Little Red Schoolhouse (the den of all educational vices) to a big, modern, consolidated school equipped with the best automatic, labor-saving gadgets. You have gone on to the more advanced stage of progressive education which believes that students ought to be collected from apartment houses and transported out to a Little Red Schoolhouse where they can look at plants and animals, help teacher scrub the blackboards in group co-operation, and carry firewood for the stove according to the basic principles of purposeful activity. . . . And it is Friday afternoon.

It is a socially conscious generation, shocked by inequalities in wealth that the corrupt system has been permitted to produce. Quite naturally, therefore, Friday afternoon hears many recitations from the treasury of proletarian literature.

> O! men with sisters dear!
>   O! men with mothers and wives!
> It is not linen you're wearing out,
>   But human creatures' lives!
> Stitch — stitch — stitch,
>   In poverty, hunger, and dirt,
> Sewing at once, with a double thread,
>   A SHROUD as well as a shirt!

The mutinous voice exults with that climax, on its way to others still more orotund, and the eighth-grade sans-culottes applaud. So from pre-factory sweatshops the program moves on to famine, absentee ownership, and the vices of economic royalty:

> There are rich and proud men there, mother,
>   With wondrous wealth to view,
> And the bread they fling to their dogs tonight,
>   Would give life to *me* and *you*.

That is from "Give Me Three Grains of Corn, Mother," a favorite poem for Friday afternoon. This was a generous people even before Granville Hicks, on his way to Damascus, discovered the poor. Its poetry was generous too, like that of to-day's sans-culottes, and had the same preference for tears.

> Under the lamplight, dead in the street,
>   Delicate, fair, and only twenty,
>   There she lies
>   Face to the skies,
>   Starved to death in a city of plenty.
> Spurned by all that is pure and sweet,
> Passed by busy and careless feet;
> Hundreds bent upon folly and pleasure,
> Hundreds with plenty of time and leisure —
> Leisure to speed Christ's mission below
>   To teach the erring and raise the lowly.
> Plenty to Charity's name to show
>   That life has something divine and holy.

Above this corpse the poem raises a vision of a home afar, out where the daisies and buttercups are — a home from which the dead maiden has wandered, where an aged couple are thinking of her now. Dead maiden, distant home among the buttercups, aged parents — the literature uses them frequently. There will be other maidens on Friday afternoon too, and rather more children and babies. Some of these will grow up pleasantly enough, barefoot boys with cheeks of tan, or little brown hands that drive home the cows from the pasture. But some of them will grow up only to fill a felon's grave, because of rum or evil counsel, and some will sleep beneath the starry banner somewhere along the James or the Rapidan. More still will die young. We are some years short of Little Boy Blue, whose neglected toys bring this particular theme to apotheosis, but there is a widespread mortality. Children die from poverty and disease, but oftener from heartbreak, and most often because their fathers drink or have to do their duty first of all.

> For Drecker, being great of soul, and true,
>   Held to his work, and did not aid his boy,
> Who in the deep, dark water sank from view.
>   Then from the father's life went forth all joy;
> But, as he fell back, pallid with his pain,
> Across the bridge, in safety, passed the train.

The Noble Worker, then, was not invented in 1933 as a receptacle for all of the Noble Savage tradition that Mr. Hemingway might not want, but flourished on Friday afternoon for generations. Drecker let his son drown to save the lives of the passengers, and Jim Bludso's ghost went up alone in the smoke of the *Prairie Belle*. There was another fire on another steamer, the *Ocean Queen*, which plied Lake Erie's waters, and John Maynard also perished to save first-cabin lives.

> But where is he, that helmsman bold?
>   The captain saw him reel —
> His nerveless hands released their task,
>   He sunk beside the wheel.
> The wave received his lifeless corpse
>   Blackened with smoke and fire.
> God rest him! Hero never had
>   A nobler funeral pyre!

All this poetry is charged with social message, but Friday has its pure estheticism also, a poetry that does not mean primarily, but is.

> O lonely tomb in Moab's land!
>   O dark Beth-peor's hill!
> Speak to these curious hearts of ours,
>   And teach them to be still.

The rafters give back an exquisite rotundity of sound, and the young esthetes are not interested in Moses but in the very things that will seem so fine and secret when T. S. Eliot reveals them to the grandchildren later on. There are many echo poems, J. T. Trowbridge's boy calling the cows, somebody else's vendor crying "Charco', charco'" — street cries, church hymns, field shouts, pure ecstasy of sound. "Toll, toll, toll," Mrs. Sigourney admonishes the ship's bell, "O'er breeze and billow free," and it isn't the shipwreck that the schoolroom loves, but just the vowels. Country Day may find tragedy in "My Son's Wife Elizabeth," but forgets it in admiration of pure poetry:

> "Cusha! Cusha! Cusha!" calling,
> For the dews will soone be falling;
> Leave your meadow grasses mellow,
>   Mellow, mellow;
> Quit your cowslips, cowslips yellow;
> Come uppe, Whitefoot, come uppe, Lightfoot,
> Quit the stalks of parsley hollow,
>   Hollow, hollow . . .

That was high tide on the coast of Lincolnshire, and high tide in the emotions of Friday afternoon.

History ought to mention the dying drunkards, the tyrants of the pagan past, the philosophers who climbed above the plain and saw earth's grandeurs melt away, the folk heroes of the forest and mountains, the classic heroes from Greece and Rome, the heroes who made way for liberty and died, the child who held his finger in the leaking dike, and scores of others. But the Easy Chair has space for only one more item of Friday afternoon — a late item on the program, with shadows on the snow turning from blue to purple, and the voices of Country Day turning from poetry and pleasure to prose and exhortation.

"Proud City! thou art doomed! the curse of Jove, a living, lasting curse is on thee! The hungry waves shall lick the golden gates of thy rich palaces, and every brook run crimson to the sea." The captured general Regulus has a striking fascination, and the eighth grade loves to hear him say farewell to family and Senate and defy the Carthaginians as he nobly dies for the state. He sounds pretty fascistic, and that would be an unlovely omen in Country Day except for an even greater hero, the slave who had only his chains to lose, lost them, and led the risen *proletarii* against their oppressors. The girls liked "Cusha! Cusha!" on Friday, but the ideal and idol of the boys was a figure of red revolution.

If ye are beasts, then stand here like fat oxen, waiting for the butcher's knife! If ye are men, follow me! Strike down yon guard, gain the mountain passes, and then do bloody work, as did your sires at old Thermopylae! Is Sparta dead? Is the old Grecian spirit frozen in your veins, that you do crouch and cower like a belabored hound beneath his master's lash? O, comrades! warriors! Thracians! if we must fight, let us fight for ourselves! If we must slaughter, let us slaughter our oppressors! If we must die, let it be under the clear sky, by the bright waters, in noble, honorable battle!

So runs one peroration, the slave inciting his fellow slaves, who have nothing to lose but their chains. A moment later, another orator begins to work up to a still finer climax, when the chains are gone forever and imperial Rome sends envoys to treat with the triumphant rebel:

Look on that narrow stream, a silver thread, high on the mountain's side! Slenderly it winds but soon is swelled by others meeting it, until a torrent, terrible and strong, it sweeps to the abyss, where all is ruin. So Spartacus comes on! So swell *his* forces — small and despised at first, but now resistless! On, on to Rome we come! The gladiators come! Let Opulence tremble in all his palaces! Let Oppression shudder to think the oppressed may have their turn. Let Cruelty turn pale at thought of redder hands than his! . . . Now begone! Prepare the Eternal City for *our* games!

Twilight fills the room at Country Day. Opulence trembles in all his palaces, the past rises before us as in a dream, like a plumed knight James G. Blaine marches down the halls of the American Congress and throws his shining lance full and fair against the brazen foreheads of the defamers of his country and the maligners of his honor. . . . The aged minister unrolls that faded flag; it is a blue banner gleaming with thirteen stars. He unrolls that parchment; it is a colonel's commission in the Continental army addressed to BENEDICT ARNOLD! And there, in that rude hut, while the deathwatch throbbed like a heart in the shattered wall: there, unknown, unwept, in all the bitterness of desolation, lay the corse of the patriot and the traitor — and that arm, yonder, beneath the snow-white mountains, in the deep silence of the river of the dead, first raised into light the Banner of the Stars. . . . And I said I would rather have been a French peasant and worn wooden shoes. I would rather have been that poor peasant with my loving wife by my side, knitting as the day died out of the sky — with my children upon my knees and their arms about me — I would rather have been that man and gone down to the tongueless silence of the dreamless dust, than to have been that imperial impersonation of force and murder known as Napoleon the Great. . . . But what do we see? We see a world at peace, adorned with every form of art, with music's myriad voices thrilled, while lips are rich with words of love and truth; a world in which no exile sighs, no prisoner mourns; a world on which the gibbet's shadow does not fall; a world where labor reaps its full reward; and over all, in the great dome, shines the eternal star of human hope.

If the passage stirs no memory in you, you have had too meager an inheritance — and maybe you had better not be too sure in your opinions about the Americans. On the other hand, if the passage gives you a vague feeling that you read it all just a day or two ago, don't suppress the feeling. You did, over and over. You'll read it all again too before long.

Well, what? Well, this isn't an acid or a base. It is literature. You think it sounds silly? Brethren, we had better not be fastidious about silliness if we are going to deal with literature. The tears flow easily? No more easily than now. In 1870 it was the death-wish that got the most applause, whereas to-day it is the castration complex; but both are good for a heavy dew. Besides, are we forbidden to weep over the dying or the poor unless we first consult a dogma of criticism or an ideology? Then, in a word, the literature is sentimental? You seem to be dreadfully uninformed about the literature of our day.

Friday afternoon at Country Day was just a difference in phase, not in substance. From history's watchtower the phases look astonishingly alike, except that the boys and girls in 1870 may have had a little better education in literature. At any rate, they took in literature by way of the ear as well as the eye. Reading was something more than skill at flash-cards, and poetry had to exist in a dimension it has since forfeited. Liberal thought may suppose that our culture has enormously improved with the disappearance of oratory like the vision of the future quoted above. But that pure judgment would have to be passed in an area not served by the radio. And if we have to decide whether this is an acid or a base — well, you and I are doubtless superior persons. We have a very low toleration of popular literature, now and forever. We would rather perish than enjoy "By Nebo's lonely mountain" or "High Tide on the Coast of Lincolnshire." Righteousness is our garment and we never sneak a look at O. O. McIntyre or the confession magazines.

FROM THE *Saturday Review,* OCTOBER 9, 1937

Writing for Money

THERE are two classes of writers who do not write for the *Saturday Evening Post:* those who have independent means or make satisfactory incomes from their other writing, and those who can't make the grade. Many of the former and practically all of the latter try to write for the *Post.* It is edited by almost morbidly discreet men, but if you catch one in a confidential moment you will hear some fascinating tales. You will also get a pretty comprehensive list of our leading novelists, and of the short-story writers that excite Mr. Edward J. O'Brien's emotions, who more or less regularly try to sell something to the *Post.* Few of their offerings sell. The *Post* is eager to get good stories and would be glad to publish the work of those who denounce it most vehemently in the little magazines — if it only were publishable. It is commonly unpublishable for a simple reason: the leading novelists and Mr. O'Brien's arty souls condescend both to the audience and to the literary medium. They try to "toss off a story for the *Post*" and they assume that to be phony is to be popular. So the editors send back the tossed-off story, an editorial on literary prostitution promptly appears in a literary forum, and the aspiring young are warned by the rejected that there is something despicable in writing for money.

"Writing for money" has come to mean writing fiction for the "slicks," for magazines which have circulations of a million or more and so can pay high for contributions. That specialization of meaning gratifies the connoisseur of literary ideas. You are, let us say, Mr. Robert Sherwood. You shake together some noble and sentimental claptrap, some 3.2 per cent ethical ideas, and some of the sure-fire melodrama that war handily provides, and, with the expert technique that is the first requirement for a *Post* writer, you shape the blend into *Idiot's Delight*, which promptly makes you a fortune. Just as promptly the truly literary will decide that you are a good deal of an artist. But Mr. Hergesheimer's *Quiet Cities* and Mr. Beer's stories about Mrs. Egg, which had a much higher intellectual quotient and much more genuine emotions, and which fell far short of making a fortune, were "writing for money" and so had no claim on the admiration of the literary. Moral for the aspiring young: to live on cake without consuming your principal, write for the stage.

The aspiring no less than the humble must grapple with economic problems when writing fiction. If a novelist writes one sellout, an *Anthony Adverse* or a *Gone With the Wind*, he need have no further financial worries as long as he lives. If he can count on publishing a best seller, say a *Drums Along the Mohawk*, every two or three years, he may likewise live on cake and support his distant relatives. No one can count on writing a sellout, however, and no serious novelist can count on regularly writing best sellers. Far otherwise. An average first novel earns between three and five hundred dollars in royalties; it is an unusually successful one that earns up to a thousand. Usually, a second novel makes rather less than the first but, if the author's skill and reputation progress satisfactorily, a third one may earn as much as fifteen hundred dollars. A successful fourth novel may make twenty-five hundred, and from then on, so long as the novelist's skill holds and he gets all possible breaks, he may count on five thousand dollars or more from every novel he publishes.

This is a rose-colored summary, of course, and applies only to exceptional careers. Very few novels make as much as ten thousand dollars in royalties alone, and dozens of well-known novelists, including many of the best, average less than twenty-five hundred. It takes from six months to two years to write a novel, and neither the Guggenheim Foundation nor admiring relatives will continue their subsidies forever. The income of a novelist will not ordinarily enable him to maintain a home and rear a family. Till 1948, therefore, when the literary left will bring Utopia in, he must either get a job and write novels in his spare time, or devote his spare time to writing for the slicks.

A slick serial can be written in from one to three months, and will sell for from five to fifty thousand dollars or even more. A slick short story can be written in from three days to a month, and will bring from five hundred to two thousand dollars or even more. Once established, a slick writer can easily make ten thousand dollars a year in his spare time — I know of one who averaged that much while carrying a full-time schedule as a college teacher and conducting another full-time career as well. The general practitioner who writes only the kind of stories that most amuse him and devotes himself to the more adult and intelligent parts of the field is limited to a maximum of about twenty thousand a year. The merchandisers, writers who produce a standard brand of trade goods which the customers ask for by name, range from twenty to fifty thousand dollars a year, and there are a good many of them. To make more than that you have to be a very special kind of writer, but if you are that kind the ceiling is very high. I have no statistics but I imagine that there must be twenty slick writers who make more than fifty thousand a year and at least a half-dozen who can count on more than a hundred thousand dollars year after year from their magazine sales alone. Though not on a parity with the income of even a middle-flight movie actor, that is respectable money.

What the moral implications of these facts are, I do not know. The professional implications, however, arise from a single fact: that writing for the slicks is a branch of the amusement business. People read the magazines primarily for entertainment. There are other important reasons, too — they read to have their ideas confirmed and their emotions ratified, to have their phantasy life stimulated, and to increase their knowledge of the minor sanctions and rituals of society — but first of all they want to be amused. It is a harmless desire.

It necessarily follows that, though they may like to be threatened or thrilled, they do not like to be scared; that, though they may enjoy a seasoning of horror, they must not be appalled or disgusted; that, though they may play with ideas, they will not wrestle with them. Satire flourishes in the slicks, but it is satire of manners. Few themes or subjects are tabooed but every subject must be treated in such a way that basic fears, disgusts, and prejudices are not roused. The "unhappy ending," the sole criterion of art when the *Dial* still lived, is a commonplace in the slicks but genuine tragedy would be as out of place there as a chorus from *Antigone* interpolated between innings at a baseball game. People do not read the slicks to encounter the brutalities, the profundities, or the complexities of experience. That fact, not the timidity or hypocrisy of editors, determines the nature of magazine fiction.

The treatment is everything. Thus it was once believed by *Post* writers that Mr. Lorimer's one unshakable taboo was miscegenation, but Mr. Charles Brackett succeeded in violating it. His story was laid in France (in general, the greatest risks had better be taken on alien soil or in earlier times) and the color in the hero's ancestry was an ambiguity that the heedless would not perceive. Homosexuality can exist in the slicks only as an indirect allusion. Illicit love must be carefully handled. It must be explained by an overwhelming weight of sympathetic circumstance, it must be proved sincere by tribulation, or it must be proved empty and unprofitable in the end — and it must be subordinated to the element of "story," of rapid action developing out of situation. Fornication may not occur in the immediate scene, and the safest usage is indicated by a remark attributed to Mr. Lorimer, that no magazine could be held responsible for what happened between installments. Violence of all kinds must be handled with the same care. So long as it enhances the element of story, so long as it is used merely to heighten a more permissible effect, it is not forbidden. There are stories which deal with murder, with accident and catastrophe, with lynching, but they use such subjects in support of themes or situations which appeal to the reader's sympathies. Similarly, personal failure, suffering, and death are common enough in the slicks but the process which employs them is aimed at confirming the reader's ideas or stirring in him phantasies much more agreeable.

In short the magazine story does not and cannot explore the profundities of human experience, probe psychological intricacies, or describe life brutally or cynically. It is frequently thoughtful, pessimistic, or satirical, it is sometimes extremely unflattering to human nature and human belief, but it must be so in pursuit of an agreeable end or in vindication of a more optimistic ideal. It is only rarely intellectual, and its ideas are seldom weighty. It works with simple emotions and, except for heroism and fortitude and honesty and similar primary virtues, it works with them superficially. And it uses any theme primarily as material for the creation and resolution of a situation. "In this office," an editor once remarked, "a story is defined as a narrative in which something happens." That is the complete definition of the slick story, and when it is understood everything else is clear. The slick writer is a story writer.

Such limiting conditions make for conventionality — and therefore put a premium on novelty, novelty of character, of situation, of locale, or presentation. The story that will always sell is the story of what the editors call "young love" (the story of personal risk in a good cause is probably second, the one which gives an inside view of some unfamiliar but interesting occupation probably third, and "young married stuff" fourth) — but if boy meets girl in some place or gets girl in some circumstance hitherto unemployed, it will sell faster and for higher pay. The slicks have an alert and topical news sense. Last week a story appeared which utilized the Duke University experiments in "extra-sensory perception" [whose first results had been publicly announced only a couple of months before] and that immediacy illustrates the effort for new things. There has been a "young love" story in a bathysphere and you may confidently expect one in an iron lung. There have been stories flagrantly based on Lindbergh's Atlantic flight and on the kidnaping of his son, stories of Everest expeditions, of collapse on the tennis court, of identifiable bankruptcies and frauds, of every eight-column headline. The slicks like formula stories and they like stories which escape from formula, but most steadily they like stories in which the easily recognizable or the long familiar is given a setting and a twist it never had before.

Nevertheless, though the greater part of slick fiction is superficial and conventional, the best of it has many virtues. Not all human emotion is complex or profound and not all experience is frightening or disgusting. At its highest level, the slick story is gay, ironical, sophisticated, adventurous, immensely entertaining or exciting. It has a shrewdness of its own and it is the vehicle of some of the sharpest observation of the contemporary scene, especially contemporary manners and fashions, that is to be found in our fiction. Its realism, though light and shallow, is frequently quite as good as any in the contemporary novel. You will not encounter realism about homosexuality, let us say, or strikebreaking or adultery, but you will find superb realism about women at matinees or literary clubs or the A. & P., men in the locker room or the bar or the commuters' car, married people worrying about expenses or the children's diseases, adolescents adjusting themselves to the high-school world. In many of the trades and businesses, in many of the common activities and minor relationships of life, and especially in fashions of behavior and belief and amusements, the best slick fiction is frequently better than any except the very best novels. The historian is going to recover the surface of American life — at least of middle-class life — much more fully and with less distortion from the slicks than from the novel of our day. The slicks render the surface more honestly, more accurately, and with greater respect. The slick writer, unlike the novelist, is penalized if he loads his dice.

Unlike the novelist, also, he is forced to master his medium. Serious fiction would be greatly improved if every novelist could be required to serve an apprenticeship as rigorous as the slick writer's. There are occasional meteors who make the *Post* with their first story and have no trouble thereafter, but most slick writers travel a long and laborious way. An experienced writer of novels (or of the boneless stuff that *Story* prints) can learn to write slick stories after a year or so of assiduous practice, and ought to be able to sell ninety per cent of his work after three years. But writing for the slicks is a skilled craft which must be studied seriously, and there is no way of shortening the learning process.

It is a craft which requires exactness, compression, flexibility of intelligence, and versatility of style. The writer must do his job under the tyranny of space limitations, and he must be crystal clear. He must learn to do without inessentials and he must think things through — he can afford neither the verbosity nor the vagueness that sometimes creates reputations in the novel. He must practise an economy of means that would seem parsimony to the most conscientious novelist. He must master form — the effects of the slick story result from a technique as intricate and interdependent as that of the sonnet. And he is held to his job as, in the circumstances of our publishing system, no novelist is held to his. If a given scene can be done in three hundred words, a novelist may fumble it through three thousand — or may let the first, sloppy approximation slide into the book. Very few publishers, none if he is an important novelist, will discipline him. There is another publisher around the corner — and the difference doesn't show in a novel of a hundred thousand words, the reader may skip the passage if he wants to, and if fifty thousand people won't buy the book, why, five thousand will. But in the slick story, that job must be done in three hundred words. If it isn't, there will be no sale at all. And there can be no contradictions, no opaque places where the writer isn't quite sure but maybe the reader will be, and no debauches of beautiful but irrelevant rhetoric. If book publishers held novelists to standards of workmanship as high as those uniformly enforced by editors of the slicks, fewer novels would be published and fewer novels would be flops.

The writer who thinks he will just toss off a story for the *Post* gets it back because his craftsmanship is bad. He is usually too contemptuous to study the form he is trying to work in, and may go on for years sending in misconceived and flabby stuff and confirming his belief that the editors are enemies of art. But the writer who masters the craft has a dependable profession which is but little subject to the fluctuations that affect both business and art. His professional risks are obsolescence and formula. Fashions in amusement are short-lived, and the slick writer must not be superior to the popular taste by which he supports himself. Formula, the mechanical solution of mechanically composed situations, is not as common in the slicks as it is in the anthologies and the little magazines, but the possibility of writing it is always present. Sure-fire stuff will succeed for a while and is a great labor-saver, but it soon makes a writer incapable of anything else, and the impersonal editors discard him for writers who are more ingenious and more versatile.

There is no conflict between writing for the slicks and writing serious fiction. True, any time spent writing a slick story is time which cannot be spent writing a psychological novel, but so is time spent earning a living in any other way. The slick writer is not debasing himself or prostituting his art. He cannot expend his profundity, forthrightness, and subtlety in magazine stories, but working in an office, writing for a newspaper, or correcting freshman themes sets the same limitation on him. Within the areas of experience which the slick story touches, he can utilize all the shrewdness, humor, observation, intelligence, and skill that he possesses. He will enjoy himself more and exhaust himself less than he would in an office job, and he will have more time for the work that most interests him.

Furthermore, he will gain a good deal. He will learn economy, clearness, compression, and polish; and he will learn a lot about sheer style. Serious fiction in America owes the slicks a sizable debt for having made better writers of a considerable number of novelists. And finally, the man who is making a comfortable living from the magazines will not feel a pressure that degrades some of our most ambitious fiction. His serious novels do not have to be aimed at the box office: he is free to write them as he pleases.

But though the writer of serious fiction may easily learn to make good money from the slicks, he cannot achieve the largest incomes I mentioned earlier. The big money comes from serials, and the biggest money from serials in the women's magazines. Prices of thirty thousand dollars and above are confined almost exclusively to those magazines, and they are paid for a particular kind of fiction. Here the slick story ceases to be merely entertainment. It becomes a confirmation of the myths, ideas, beliefs, and philosophy of life of the popular audience.

No one who has not got that philosophy can borrow or counterfeit it. The slick writers of the highest bracket (they are practically all women) believe firmly in the moral overtones of their stuff, which are what give it cash value. They believe that courage and loyalty are enough, that to struggle hopefully is better than to arrive, that you will nevertheless arrive if you struggle hopefully, that natural goodness wins in the end, that truth crushed to earth will rise again and very profitably, that virtue triumphs after temptation and tribulation, that human nature is warmed and illuminated by a spark of the divine. They devote the formidable skill of the slick writer to vindicating such sentiments, and since the popular audience shares the sentiments and desperately wants them vindicated, they cash in. It is idle to quarrel with or express superiority to these simplicities. In all ages they are what the popular audience has most wanted from literature and what it has most rewarded. The women's magazines, and the slicks in general, merely canalize the popular taste.

No labor, ingenuity, or conscientiousness will enable a writer to produce this kind of fiction unless he naturally possesses the sentiments out of which it is made. If he has them he will not, I take it, be a writer of serious fiction, and if he lacks them he must adapt himself to the penury of from ten to twenty thousand dollars a year. Don Marquis said it once and for all, years ago, in "Preface to the Novels of Harold Bell Wright." "It is," Don said, "it is Moral Worth that gets the Mazuma. And it can't be faked."

III

AN HOUR BEFORE DEADLINE

Lycanthropy

~~~~~~

TIGER, So FAR none of Ernest Hemingway's characters has
TIGER! had any more consciousness than a jaguar. They are
physiological systems organized around abdomens, suprarenal
glands, and genitals. They are sacs of basic instinct. Their cere-
brums have highly developed motor areas but are elsewhere
atrophied or vestigial. Their speech is rudimentary, they have
no capacity for analytical or reflective thought, they have no
beliefs, no moral concepts, no ideas. Living on an instinctual
level, they have no complexities of personality, emotion, or experience.

Working exclusively with such people, Mr. Hemingway has
created the most memorable prize fighters, bullfighters, literary hangers-on, fishermen, duck shooters, and thugs that
American literature has ever seen. With Frederic Henry, a
man without consciousness caught up in a catastrophic mob-
panic, and Catherine Barkley, a woman who lives in completely
unconscious obedience to instinct, he has composed a novel
that will last as long as any in its generation. No one else writ-

ing in America to-day can give a scene the reality that Mr. Hemingway gives it, or can equal his dialogue, which reaches the reader as living speech.

That is an achievement on which any writer who ever lived might well rest, but Mr. Hemingway seems uneasy about it. He has grown, as our reviewer says, increasingly belligerent about personalities more complex than those he creates, about ideas, about every kind of experience that is not localized in or near the viscera. But if his characters are incapable of ideas, Mr. Hemingway is not. Their mindlessness is itself the assertion of an idea. It is one of Mr. Hemingway's root ideas and has come to dominate his work. Every so often it should be taken out and scrutinized.

Since the thinking of the Hemingway characters has been confined to a form of omphalic irritation, they have not usually had any social awareness. The social significance of *To Have and Have Not* is also negligible. The dice which Mr. Hemingway is rolling are so openly and flagrantly loaded that he cannot mean us to think of his sterile millionaires and his gonadotropic "conchs" in economic terms. The social assertions and findings are so naïve, fragmentary, and casual that they cannot be offered as criticism of the established order: beside them, the simplest of the blue-jeans-and-solidarity Cinderella stories that the *New Masses* was praising three or four years ago would seem profound. The significance of the title is not sociological: it is one with the significance of Jake's wound in *The Sun Also Rises* and with the symbolism of the plaster cast in which the hero of *A Farewell to Arms* had to make love. The millionaires and the literary lice are not the "haves" — they are the "have-nots." The "haves" are the conchs, and particularly Harry Morgan. Just what it is that Harry Morgan has and his oppressors lack we are told specifically and repeatedly. Mr. Hemingway has given us the supporting argument before.

It is curious where that argument takes you — where it has

taken Mr. Hemingway. "Since he was a boy," one of his com-
panions says of Harry Morgan, "he never had no pity for nobody. But he never had no pity for himself either." Quite
clearly, for Mr. Hemingway the second half of that antithesis
is a complete justification of the first half. If you do not pity
yourself you need not pity anyone, and conversely you must
not pity yourself lest you grow weak by pitying someone else.
Yet one wonders whether a man is completely vindicated and
sufficiently praised when it is said of him that he does not pity
himself. One wonders if refusal to pity himself is enough to
make Harry Morgan so admirable as Mr. Hemingway con-
siders him. He breaks faith with and murders the Chinaman
who employs him; after rumrunning and miscellaneous violence, he becomes an accessory to bank robbery and more
murder; and he finishes up with a quadruple murder. But floods
of adrenalin are always surging into his blood stream, and,
when he is wounded, both his central and his sympathetic nervous systems are polarized in support of his will to live. Mr.
Hemingway is in the position of saying that nothing else
matters.

"He never had no pity for nobody. But he never had no pity
for himself either." It is not by chance that that analysis summons up an image of a trapped animal escaping by gnawing
off its foot. "She watched him go out of the house, tall, wide-
shouldered, flat-backed, his hips narrow, moving, still, she
thought, like some kind of animal, easy and swift and not old
yet." Also, "Him, like he was, snotty and strong and quick,
and like some kind of expensive animal." We have reached
the end of a path that Mr. Hemingway has been traveling for
a long time. The highest praise he can give a man is to say that
he is like an animal.

You see, it is only the animals who never deny life by forsaking the level of pure instinct. They are clean, honest, unpitying. They live in the reality of blood-consciousness, im-
mersed in primary and direct experience: hunger, thirst, desire,

alertness, wariness, aggressiveness. When they couple they do not weave a dishonest poetry over the clean delight of physiological function. When they kill, they kill without guilt, without remorse, without rationalization. They do not pose; they do not talk nobly; they do not live in a fog of thought, in the diseased secretion of the mind that betrays and enfeebles man. They do not kid themselves with ideas; they do not delude themselves with reason or reverie; instead, they are clean, sure, and very strong. They pity neither themselves nor other animals. They live instinctively, they defend themselves to the death, and every mammal pleases but only man is vile. What gave the death of the bull its tragic beauty was the fact that it perished at the moment of total aggressiveness, charging at its mortal enemy with all the physiology of its animal nature concentrated in the instinctive, self-justifying act of destruction. And now, compared with the human world which gives the sterile dominion over the potent, how beautiful is the long curve of the shark diving for gouts of blood.

Every man to his preference. Mr. Hemingway is certainly entitled to fall in love with sharks if he wants to, and our literature is the richer for his admiration. There has been, of course, much anthropophobia in modern literature. If the admirers of D. H. Lawrence, for instance, have not consciously loved alligators, they are at least accustomed to praise the faculties of alligators that may be discerned in man. But it is hard to see just how man himself may profitably employ the idea and just what reference either the alligator or the bull has to the problems man is working with in the modern world. And it will be interesting to see how the literary left, which temporarily regards Mr. Hemingway as an ally, will adapt his conclusions when adopting them. The cult of blood-consciousness and holy violence, as well as the clean beauty of the shark, has so far been the property of their political opponents.

It would be even more interesting to find out what Mr.

Hemingway thinks of Mr. Robinson Jeffers. Utilizing the diseased secretion of thought to the utmost, Mr. Jeffers has also reached the conclusion that the animals are superior to man, but he finds the waving grasses still more admirable. Unpitying alligator or undeluded chlorophyll — which shall we prefer, which shall be the measure of things?

RATS, LICE,   NEVERTHELESS, Mr. Robinson Jeffers has
AND POETRY   not fully resolved the conflict. From where he perches with an old she-eagle on a cliff far above the darkling plain, struggle and flight seem just the same to him, and whether it is men or lice who struggle does not matter much except that on the whole lice are the more virtuous. What he sees from his pinnacle is all of one piece, and the conclusions he draws from it are sharp and clear. But once an eon the rock trembles ever so gently, just enough to blur the edge of his conclusions with a faint doubt, like breath existing for a moment on a mirror, and the conflict rises up again.

When it doesn't rise up, everything seen by the aged eagle (but that was another poet) is steel-cut and cold, for the high places bring vision. The beasts are not contemptible: man is contemptible. If life had perished utterly, earth and heaven would have been perfectly lovely. But it hasn't perished and so the cosmos is not abandoned to the inhuman nobility of inhuman things. The best that one can do is to avoid men, live with more kindly wolves and luckier ravens, and wait for the end of things. The end is coming, but not soon enough. So here we crawl and swarm in a purulence of black desire and red blood. Tyrants are ignoble and their victims contemptible. (To know this is to be a poet, and who says that literary people are ignoble and contemptible?) A rich and vulgar and bewildered civilization is dying at the core. But not dying quite fast enough, and so man dreams of his greatest joy, of the supreme gift that his fellows like drunken Jesuses fling at each other. Too proud to face his wish for death before the crowd, he invents war to confer it on him. Mr. Jeffers prefers the kindly wolf.

Yet sometimes the mirror fogs a little. For a moment the scene will have a beauty that may not be marsh gases burning over putrefaction. There will be an instant of integrity, of wholeness. Now the high place knows, of course, that hope, courage, belief, will, intelligence, or anything like that is part of the gangrenous or erysipeloid corruption, but the instant of integrity or wholeness may be something else. And it occurs in the *lupus vulgaris* that is man. It is hard, in fact impossible, to harmonize with the way the darkling plain looks from the eagle's nest. So the rock trembles and Mr. Jeffers is less than sure.

At least twice in his new book Mr. Jeffers analyzes this conflict for our sake, but another diagnostician should be called in consultation. All such examinations eventually get back to first principles, and it will save space to begin with them. Chesterton once had a parable about conflicting political views on the best way of lighting a city street. A monk who suggested that they begin by determining the nature of light was mobbed by people who wanted action, and in the melee the lamppost was wrecked. But presently the politicians found themselves required to determine the nature of light before they could do anything, only now the discussion had to be conducted in the dark.

It is amazing that only the rudiments of psychoanalytical thought make headway in American literature. Writers behave as if the principle of infantilism could be properly expressed only in infantile terms. What Mr. Eugene O'Neill makes of the Oedipus Complex is about what a Hollywood director would make of Einstein's time-space in a routine for Fred Astaire. Mr. Jeffers's use of it has a million more ergs than Mr. O'Neill's but it remains rudimentary and, what is more important, it ends up with Mr. Jeffers sick and appalled. He begins with the sound principle: Know Thyself. But he comes out with a neurotic principle: Therefore Kill Thyself. So he joins hands with a multitude of modern writers to whom both common sense and psychoanalysis would apply the simple judgment of Bernard Shaw, that the fate of the man who sees life as it is but thinks about it romantically is despair, and such despair isn't worth bothering about.

So men want to poison their fathers with KCN and women want to possess their sons, do they? So the cancerous tissue of the brain quickens with this energy of incest and parricide, does it? Then the hell with men, women, and brains — our guilt is more than we can bear, the race stinks of pus and is less decent than the snakes, and the world will be but an open sewer till the ultimate wandering star has burned it up, cleansed it of life, and freed it to the dominion of the great, beautiful ferns.

But common sense and psychoanalysis point out that men do not poison their fathers, that they neither possess their mothers nor are possessed by them. The cancerous energy so works in them that they grow up to be free adults and to live happily with their wives. The same energy works out in the various ways that distinguish man from the snakes, and common sense sees, if poetry fails to, that there is some credit balance in man's favor.

This familiar dilemma seems to be confined to literature. You work hard to achieve what you are sure is a noble thing, the tragic sense of life. Then, having achieved it, you belly-ache because it isn't fun. You still think it might be, though, if only it could get noble enough. So when, from the high place, you see something that looks like a crucifixion, you determine to accept it in the exalted reconciliation of tragedy if the figure on the cross turns out to be an angel. But it turns out to be just a man, so it must be worse than a man, it must be a rat. And crucifixion is too good for it.

Much of the modern world's despair springs from a belief

that man ought to be an angel and therefore must be treated
as a rat because he isn't. From noble minds loving the theoretical people and being disgusted by the actual mob. From the intellectual's theorem that something must certainly be done
about the rat in man, and his assent to the practical idealist's
ways of doing something about it. Hitler, Stalin, and Mus-
solini know how to increase the saturation of angelic qualities
in man's soul, and no nonsense about it. Poets who agree with
them about the rat become preposterous when they object to
the measures employed to bring the angel in.

If you look carefully at the crucifixion, however, you will
observe that it did not begin in August, 1914, November, 1918,
or October, 1929. If there has been a time when life was other
than precarious or when mankind was immune from danger,
agony, cruelty, or disaster, it must be sought in prehistory
only. The dictators promise us that just around the corner is
an era when those immunities will be attained, if first we root
out the rat in man by pruning him of liberty and individuality
and washing him in enough blood. Literature is, of course,
perfectly free to agree with them on the ground that man
isn't an angel but ought to be.

On the other hand, it is also free to stop sniffling about pin-
feathers and to decide that crucifixion is preferable to either
massacre or suicide. The best armament against disaster is
reconciliation with man as he really is. It is quite true that
neither men nor rats smell as sweet as angels are said to and
that men have not solved the problems of living together in
society. But another differentiation is that men try to solve
them. Though crucified, they will go on trying to, independ-
ently of the scorn or approval of literary persons.

Literature is very odd, brethren: humanitarianism consists
of finding humanity contemptible. Oh, and about lice and the
great ferns: they can't read.

Rule or Ruin

DEATH OF THE
SENTENCE
IN THE current *Atlantic Monthly*, Mr. Wilson Follett unmasks the strategy of the editor of this magazine and so forces the steering committee of the literary left to change its plans. Advantageously placed on this reactionary periodical, we have been masquerading as an enemy of enlightenment and so have wormed our way into the confidence and secrets of the Tories. We have been organizing our position so that, when the great hour came, we could turn capitalism's own guns on the poor dupes that had trusted us. Mr. Follett has stopped that for good: he has exposed us as a revolutionist. Mr. Edwin Seaver, though he is not privy to the steering committee's intrigues, divined the same truth last June, when we incautiously permitted our agent to praise the speech that Mr. Earl Browder made at the Writers' Congress.

Mr. Follett accuses us of trying to destroy the English sentence and queasily admits that our attempt has pretty well succeeded. He selects us as representative of the Time Spirit, of which he is far from fond, and uses some of our writing to show how the sentence, as the centuries of mankind knew it, has disintegrated during the last generation. Precisely as scientists are trying to break down the atom and have chosen detonation as the most promising way, so contemporary writers are trying to explode the sentence so that none of its traditional (and logically indispensable) syntax will be left. The writers have had more success than the scientists, for on all levels from James Joyce to the *Daily Mirror*, the printed page is strewn with dismembered fragments of old-issue sentences. . . . An unhappy coincidence has us asserting, in the current issue of *Harper's*, that if the Utah schools taught us nothing else at least they gave us a sound knowledge of grammar.

Mr. Follett's brilliant article should be read by everyone who is interested in writing. It says much that needs saying and that cannot be said too often or too forcibly. Mr. Follett may be shocked by the admission, but we agree with him. We agree, that is, with some of his contentions. For, though he seems to be talking about only one thing, he is really talking about two things or more than two. We go all the way with him when he attacks slovenly writing, the kind of writing that results from careless and slipshod thinking; our sword and pen are at the service of his crusade. But when he attacks in the same terms the careful, calculated writing which departs from conventional syntax because it must depart from it in order to achieve its ends — we are constrained to denounce him as an obscurantist, a heresiarch, and a dangerous enemy of the good, the true, and the beautiful.

When it comes to the clear expression of exact meaning, we are more royalist than Mr. Follett. When thought is organizable in sentences we stand for its being so organized. We will support his efforts, and anyone else's, to make the English sentence say exactly what it means, as simply, as directly, as clearly, and as grammatically as possible. The sloppy, ambiguous, wretchedly carpentered sentences which he arranges according to an ascending scale of horror are fully as offensive to us as to him, and we deplore quite as much as he the ignorance and carelessness of writers and the slackness of editorial standards that allow them to get into print. The horrible example which he quotes from the *Saturday Review* caused us more pain than he can possibly feel about it.

But the organization of thought in sentences in order to convey an exact meaning inescapably is one thing, and the representation of thinking and feeling in fiction is sometimes an entirely different thing. If a novelist were always to organize the thinking of his characters in complete sentences he would sometimes gravely misrepresent it, and in misrepresenting it he would create the very kind of ambiguity that Mr. Follett denounces. The sentence which he quotes from our novel is part of a passage (thirteen pages out of four hundred and seventy-one) which presents the reverie of a character at a time of intense emotional stress. It borrows a method from Joyce and is written in accordance with what the psychologists call free association. It presents a state of mind in which thought and feeling are not formulated in sentences. If it had been forced into sentences in the novel, its reality would have been destroyed. This passage is at one extreme; most of the book is at the other extreme, and consists of completely formulated thought expressed in rigorously grammatical sentences. In between the extremes there are various other stages of subjectivity, in which the sentences are formulated to the same degree that the thought and emotion they represent are formulated. What is wrong with that?

Mr. Follett says that it is anarchy and finds that the villain behind it is the subconscious mind. But it is certainly a novelist's right to deal with the unconscious if he wants to. When he undertakes to represent its effluence into consciousness he cannot organize thought into formal sentences, for the essence of such thinking is its lack of organization. When, in such contexts, he writes in the way that Mr. Follett deplores, he is completely harmonious with the spirit of the English language and the logic of prose. He is not an anarchist but a purist.

Mr. Follett does not accept that fact, and we can go only part way with him in the rest of his article. Grammar was made for man, not man for grammar; in fact, grammar is made by man. The traditions of syntax are not part of the physical foundations of the universe; they are merely empirical statements of principles which commonly facilitate clear communications. We must not so venerate the statement as to forget its objective. Even the most pedantic treatises of a century ago took account of ellipsis and elision, and sanctioned idiomatic constructions which seemed to violate the formal rules. To-day, Professor Curme defines a sentence as "an expression of a thought or feeling by means of a word or words used in such form and manner as to convey the meaning intended." "To convey the meaning intended" — the reader's complete understanding of the writer's meaning, unhampered by esthetic shock, is everything. A sign outside our window says "Tarrytown eight miles"; another one says "STOP! Children Crossing"; and, at the moment, a neighbor trips over a lawn mower and says "Damn!" Only the last of those sentences observes the traditional syntactical form, but it would be foolish to call them poor English or to deny that they are completely clear. Sir Thomas Browne would not have written the first two in that way, but how else would Mr. Follett write them?

Syntax, like all the rest of grammar, has changed a good deal since *Religio Medici.* While the language remains healthy, it will go on changing. But Mr. Follett must surely know that the best English prose to-day which sets out to convey exact ideas is as clear and as rigorous as any ever written. It is such prose that he should compare with earlier prose intended to accomplish the same end — he should not denounce a wholly different kind of prose because it does not do what it does not try to do.

Later on we will continue this argument, for we have still much to say on behalf of contemporary writing. But first we may have to clear the board of other critics of our style. A number of correspondents have objected to our vocabulary and our idioms. They say, in effect, that though we may write swell we don't write elegant. We will destroy them in the public interest and then come back and defend the modern style.

GRAMMARIAN'S YEARS ago when the world was fra-
FUNERAL grant and we were an instructor in English at a distant university we published our first novel. Only microscopy could determine whether the world at large or our colleagues in the good life had the smaller interest in that event, though future historians will use it to date the renascence of American literature, but we were already too old in sorrow to expect anything from either the world or the faculty. But after the novel had been out for a couple of months the one great scholar of the university summoned us to his office and began to praise our style. We wrote well, he said, we wrote beautifully, we wrote with an exquisite feeling for the subtlety, the splendor, and the power of the English tongue. "Why," Professor Curme said, his eyes in a fine frenzy rolling, "I have counted them and there are no less than eight split infinitives in your book!"

Since we play only by ear we cannot honestly say that we split those infinitives with an engineer's precision and a poet's joy, but from that day on no denunciation of our inelegance has troubled us much. We continue to split infinitives when they sound best split, though usually we are not aware of having split one till the letters begin to come in. We could refer our disparagers to the elegant Mr. Fowler who, in *Modern English Usage*, declares that it is better to split an infinitive

than to be either awkward or ambiguous. But we like to refer them to Professor Curme, who puts the matter more to
our taste. "The much censured split infinitive," he says, "is
an improvement of English expression. It first appeared in the
fourteenth century and has since been gradually gaining favor
as it has been better understood. At present it is widely used
by our best writers, who feel its advantages. It is avoided by
many, especially our minor writers, who here follow the instructions of their schoolteachers." That's telling them.

Mr. Wilson Follett, whose article on logic and the sentence
we were discussing last week, weakens his case when he says
that a lot of people write to him whenever he uses a preposition to end a sentence with. He claims those people as allies
in his crusade for good writing, but a little more reflection
would lead him to disown them. We once heard Mr. Charles
Townsend Copeland read aloud from a best seller in the presence of its author. He came to a sentence which ran something like this: "She pulled her skirt down and pulled up her
stockings." Copey stopped reading, pushed his glasses high
on his forehead, and moaned, "Walter, why didn't you say,
'She pulled her skirt down and her stockings up'?" Walter
righteously answered, "Why, Copey, I wouldn't end a sentence with a preposition." We felt then that Walter, though
he was following the instructions of his schoolteachers, had
a lot to learn about prepositions and about style. So have the
people who write to Mr. Follett — and to us.

There is a flaw in the syntax of the sentence that ends the
paragraph above. Mr. Follett will probably not object to it
but a lot of our correspondents must. And, doubtless, many
will. Mr. Follett will probably object to that last sentence.
Our correspondents will say that it is an independent clause
which properly belongs with the sentence preceding it, but
he will say that it has no proper subject and that the predicate
is not complete. We say, however, that it is sanctioned by
the strictest grammarians because both the subject and the

rest of the predicate are "understood," and, forsaking the defensive, we assert that the sentence is O.K. [perfectly all right, to you] because whether or not the grammarians sanction it, it is immediately clear to everyone who reads it. Which is all that good sense requires. With *that* sentence Mr. Follett rolls in agony on the floor and a thousand quills are sharpening across America to confirm his judgment that anyone who would write it must be an anarchist.

Our correspondents who follow the instructions of their schoolteachers too conscientiously end by preferring correct grammar to clear, idiomatic, and graceful writing. This is especially true of those who insist that every pronoun must have a specific antecedent and that the elided parts of verbs must be filled out when the tense forms differ. Thus the rules require the first word of our last sentence to be followed by a noun which makes its reference specific. But the sentence is quite as clear as [it would be] if it began "this statement," "this observation," or, as the pedantic horribly write it, "this situation." No one can possibly mistake the reference of "this" [;] so the sentence as first written satisfies all the demands that logic can make of it and avoids the awkwardness that follows when you insert the noun. The awkwardness would be slight here but in some cases it is considerable, and in those cases sound judgment will prefer elision to correctness. Good writers always have preferred it and always will.

Grammar says, and our censorious correspondents say, that the last sentence above is also faulty. The "understood" portion of the last verb, you see, would have to differ in form from the preceding "expressed" verb. The sentence as written implies ". . . and always will preferred it," which [qy.: antecedent?] would be nonsense. Of course it would [be (nonsense)]. But the sentence as written is not nonsense. No one could possibly misunderstand it. Since it cannot be misunderstood and since it is less pompous than the grammatical sentence, it is the better of the two. Be clear, be simple, be graceful, and let who will be right.

Most of our correspondents, however, object not to our grammar but to our vulgarity. The "lousy" we heaved into this chaste page three weeks ago is still bringing in letters, and the occasional "hells" which the managing editor inserts to liven our copy are a benefaction to the postal revenues. We are reproached for saying "isn't," we are disfellowshipped for saying "different than" and "one . . . he," we are proscribed for saying "hooey," and we are damned for saying "damn." Our conventional mind would find its natural expression in the flatulent and polysyllabic rhetoric of a Professor of Education lecturing on methods of teaching style, and if we consulted our own preference our writing would always wear spats. But we have ideals and they force us to write inelegantly in the cause of good English. Every "oh, nuts" we print sends us to bed with a migraine and costs us the price of two penitential doves. But if we can serve belles-lettres by abasing ourself, pain and expense do not matter.

The man who must put on spats before he can talk with a friend is goofy. Good writing is where you find it, whether in *Variety's* headlines or in the reports of the Coast and Geodetic Survey. Good writing is the adaptation of style to the mood, the meaning, and the audience. Good writing is, especially, the use of words which have the emotional overtone proper to the context. "Lousy" was good enough for Shakespeare and it's good enough for a Professor of Education. If the Professor means "lousy" and refrains from writing it, he is the kind of person who would say "lady dog" and there is no place for him in hell, heaven, or the *Saturday Review*. We propose to go on using the language of literate speech, to go on saying what we mean and to go on betraying our ideals in defense of the living English tongue. Ever hear of poetic license, gents? Don't get the idea that it is something issued by the Department of Public Safety and Pedagogics.

Crackle on the Left

THE WRITERS' CONGRESS   WE HAVE received from the League of American Writers a call to attend the National Congress of American Writers to be held in this city over the first week-end of June. It is signed by twenty-two writers. For some of them we have the highest respect both as thinkers and as literary craftsmen; some of them strike us as considerably better at phrase-making than at thinking; some of them a perverted mind prohibits us from considering anything but lollipops. We are going to see that the *Saturday Review* has a representative at the Congress, a convinced spirit who has more youth and more belief than we can ever have again, but we intend to stay away. If we played golf we should be scrupulous, as a writer, to get in at least thirty-six holes on each of the three days.

We are passing up this convention of literary people from habit, from constitutional distaste, from a phobia of being bored, and from a variety of other motives. It is not that the purposes of the twenty-two writers seem to us anything but admirable. Well, some of them do seem meaningless, such as "to defend the political and social institutions that make for peace and encourage a healthy culture," which, in order to acquire meaning, would need more definition than it will get at the Congress. Some of them seem a little fantastic, as "to provide a center for the cultural activities of American writers in general, and a link between writers now separated by age or place of residence" — what are the cultural activities of writers except writing, and what would a center be? — are you proposing an edifice like a Y.M.C.A. or a foundation of goodwill like the Drama League? — and what do you propose to have the writers do when they get into such a center? Some of them are pretty loose and vague, as "to effect an alliance for cultural defense between American writers and all progressive forces in the nation" — some of the forces that seem progressive to us would cause pain to some of the boys, and we doubt that, even if they agree on the forces, they will find any way of effecting an alliance except more conventions.

We are certainly sympathetic with some of the purposes, especially that of defending freedom of thought and expression. But again a constitutional defect makes us differ from the delegates. We believe in getting out and raising hell when freedom of thought and expression is threatened, but passing resolutions has never interested us much. The delegates will get up and say splendid things, they will adopt some resounding resolutions which will use perfectly beautiful words to express the most admirable sentiments, and then they will come out to the street in a glow of righteous achievement and be a little surprised that the traffic could go on while people were being so stark. But freedom of thought and expression will be just where it was before the committee phrased the resolutions.

Conventions are just gatherings where people have a good time and the resolutions they pass are merely intended to show that the delegates' hearts are in the right place. The published works of some of the signers of this call are charged with scorn of the conventions held by the D.A.R., the Boy Scouts, and the Amalgamated Association of Embalmers. Those conventions are supposed by the literary to be tawdry and vulgar, but the only difference we can see is that the writers and the embalmers have different ideas about what constitutes a good time. And we don't need the resolutions for we already know where their hearts are, and we know too that no writer's heart is going to be changed at the Congress, any more than a Daughter of the American Revolution's is. The signers say that their ideas do not "have to be accepted on pain of intellectual excommunication." We'll take a bet on that.

We may instruct our representative to risk excommunication in the interest of experiment, and have him invite the delegates to bring one set of their ideas into conformity with another set. Our emotions — and our representative's — have been on the side of the Spanish government from the beginning; we, and he, have supported its cause with some money and some advice to more active sympathizers. But we should like the Congress to dissipate a paradox that troubles us. We are all on the side of the government because it is the elected government, because the attack on it is an attack on civilization made by the powers of barbarism, because its fight is the fight of democracy against the militarized state, because it stands for law as against force. But that is why we were on the side of England and France twenty years ago. Barbarism and military despotism were attacking civilization then, and democracy had to crush them in the name of law and reason and the hope of a better future. Then it strangely turned out that nothing of the sort had happened, that we had been misled by a skillful propaganda conducted by masters of the art; we were just credulous fools who pulled England's chestnuts out of the fire for her. And so on — consult the books of some of the delegates. So suppose our representative gets up in Congress and asks whether the American sheep are baa-ing the way skillful propaganda directs them to, or whether the earlier

situation has perhaps been misconstrued. Will he get any re-
cantations? Will he be informed that it isn't propaganda when
it's on the right side? Or will he be thrown out on his ear?

We don't, that is, believe these protestations about truth-
seeking and the open mind. Our guess is that the delegates
will go to the convention in full possession of the truth. They
are sure of the future as ever Joseph Smith or Alexander
Dowie was, both of whom had a corner on truth. Listen to
them prophesy: "Fascism will be encouraged and financed
as an effective means of 'keeping labor in its place.' Even war
will be used — it has been so used already — as the best way
of breaking strikes." Thanks, we hold to the unfixed universe
and a future with some unknowns in it.

That, probably, is what has most weight in our abstinence
from conventions: the boys think of such a gathering as a
dignified assemblage giving strength and unity to those who
compose it and recessing in the end with a great deal done —
and we don't. We like writers, but we like them writing, not
making speeches and adopting resolutions. We haven't the
slightest doubt that they will have their sentiments confirmed
by the Congress and will come away from it thinking highly
of one another, but we doubt that anything else will be accomplished. We can't help thinking of the assemblage as composed of the people who compose it. We've read their books
and we have the most diverse opinions of them. Some of them
are pretty formidable, but some of them are pretty frail. We
know what they think; we could even put on the prophet's
mantle and predict what they are going to say; we could certainly write in advance the resolutions they are going to adopt.
Beyond that we have no belief in this Congress, and only one
interest. That interest is pragmatic: will a committee report on
the achievements of the last Congress and how they have been
added upon in the interim, and what will the report say?

INVITATION TO WRITING in the *Atlantic Monthly,*
THE WALTZ   Mr. Wilson Follett has thoroughly
confused us about the meaning of a proverbial phrase, "the
devil to pay and no pitch hot," but to our best belief it describes a situation that has arisen among the orators on the
left flank. It seems that the proprietors of the Writers' Congress intended not to invite us to attend. Just how pointed
that intention was we do not know; they may have meant to
ignore us on a high moral plane or they may have meant to
humiliate us with a social snub. But someone sold them out and
sent us an invitation all drawn up in proper form, including
the "R.S.V.P." of the strictest bourgeois tradition and offering us an opportunity to sign the Call. If we had taken ad-
vantage of that opportunity the government of the literary left
would have fallen before a vote of no confidence, but fortunately we didn't. We merely announced, on this page, that we
weren't going to attend the Congress.

That was bad enough. The editors of the *New Masses,* a
periodical so reminiscent of the Ogden High School *Classicum*
of 1912 that we were probably its Exchange Editor at fifteen,
were shocked. If we had been invited, then some revisionist
had transgressed the principles which Emily Post has codified
once and for all. They interviewed the sponsors of the Congress, who informed them that they certainly had not invited
us. Thereupon the editors of the *New Masses* observed the
purest literary tradition, as from time to time we have de-
scribed it here. Instead of digging out the facts, however
scandalous, and being realistically governed by them, they
adopted a comforting theory about them. The implications
of our being invited were uncomfortable and perhaps even
frightening. Therefore we could not have been invited. So
the boys took a firm stand on Mrs. Post and called us pre-
sumptuous and ungracious.

In emergencies like this it is craven folly to adopt the literary explanation merely because it is the most comfortable

one. The appalling fact is that we did receive through the U. S. Mail an invitation which was addressed to us by name and which looks genuine. Someone may have forged it, of course, but if so the situation is every bit as disquieting. Genuine or forged, someone sent it to us, and it is the inescapable duty of the *New Masses* to find out who he is. We shall be glad to sink all factional differences in the greater effort and to co-operate with the boys in their investigation, only asking them to face without flinching whatever facts may be brought to light. So far we can see only three working hypotheses, all of them distressing and two of them dreadful.

The least disturbing hypothesis is that some evangelist among them still hopes to convert us and mailed the invitation in a mood of pure prayer. Mr. Granville Hicks, who was recently explaining to us that there is no difference between the literary interests of Proust and those of Albert Halper, is an enthusiastic and prayerful soul, and it may have been he or someone near to him. If it was, we can only say that we intended no rudeness and that if he will sign the next one we will reply in a way which Mrs. Post cannot possibly condemn. The task of his colleagues is simple and not too painful: they have only to explain dialectics to him.

But with the other two hypotheses we approach darkness and doom. It may be that an agent of the black reaction has got into the councils of the righteous and is boring from within, intending to discredit the Congress by inviting us to it and perhaps even getting us to attend. At this moment someone who has been admitted to the inner shrine, one who shares all the secrets and takes part in all the deliberations, may be a labor spy and an *agent provocateur* in a fascist plot. Only our transparent honesty in declining the invitation has betrayed his activity. But there is an even worse possibility. This unknown may not be an agent of the opposition: he may be one of the faithful who has backslidden and become a counterrevolutionary, which, as everyone knows, is far worse. Instead of originating in a fascist plot, our invitation may be part of a Trotskyist plot.

In either case, the editors of the *New Masses* are running a foolish and vainglorious risk by contenting themselves with denunciations of us. While they enervate themselves in the pursuit of adjectives, a spy or a traitor is in their midst. One of the most trusted among them is false as hell itself, and the very walls have ears. While they lingered in a literary lotos-land we were invited to this Congress, and while they sit still and call us ungracious we may be invited to the next one. Only the sternest measures will suffice; the boys have got to stop talking and begin to act, which is, you will remember, what we advised them to do a couple of weeks ago. We shall await with the liveliest interest word that the *New Masses* has begun a purge. If we can help, simply let us know.

The rest of what the boys say amply supports what we said, and confirms our prediction so well that, much as we have denounced literary prophets, we are tempted to set up as one. A line in the Call caught our eye: "We are not advancing these ideas as fixed theories that have to be accepted on pain of intellectual excommunication." Our observation indicated that that was hooey and we asserted that the boys didn't mean it. In the interest of experiment we suggest a tentative theory to be "discussed among writers as freely and widely as possible," and predicted that anyone who voiced it at the Congress would get thrown out on his ear. The boys didn't even wait for the Congress but threw us out on our ear two weeks before it was to convene. They call us cynical because we don't play golf but the truth is that we are practically as hopeful as they are, and so, still in the interest of experiment, we come to bat with another suggestion. Is our invitation still good, in spite of its reaching us through a deplorable misunderstanding? If it is, we move, Mr. Chairman, or if it isn't we instruct our representative to move, that the words "and communism" be inserted after the word "fascism" at the appropriate place in every resolution adopted by the Congress. Heads stands for pain of intellectual excommunication and tails for discussion as free and wide as possible. Which do you call?

The boys seem to have been pretty emotional when they read our editorial and so they didn't see just what we were saying. We said that we respected some of the writers who signed the Call but thought some of the others lollipops. We may have had some low hope of being called upon to name names, but the *New Masses* brandishes some names at us which, it is well known, we have respected a lot more consistently than the *New Masses* has. They call us conservative and we certainly are slower than they are to change our literary admirations when someone in authority says to change them. But we wish especially that the *New Masses* would read what we said about literary conventions in relation to effectiveness, and would then proceed to show us up. We aren't cynical, boys, instruments of the most delicate precision are necessary to reveal the small fraction of a degree by which we fall short of you in hopefulness. But we cannot see that these fraternity meetings ever accomplish anything beyond the production of self-esteem and the generation of carbon dioxide. You are eloquent and moving in expressing your belief that we are wrong but there is a better way to prove your case. Have this Congress accomplish something. Be sure to let us know what it is.

Costume Piece

THE BONNIE BLUE FLAG   MARSE ROBERT was a great general, but the Cause lost in the end. Defeat corrodes the heart even unto the third and fourth generation, and there have come to be those trumpets blowing yellowly in copper light that trouble the reveries of Mr. Faulkner (who has served the Cause in a good many pages of nostalgic prose). The night brings meditation and, dreaming, one may almost rearrange. It cannot be altogether as a tenet of agrarianism that the unreconstructed poets of Nashville have raised Nathan Bedford Forrest above Jeb Stuart, above Jackson even, till he sits at Lee's right hand: in that apotheosis must tremble the whisper of a great Perhaps . . . Perhaps . . . Almost . . . four hours in Hampton Roads . . . a shot in the spring dusk at Chancellorsville . . . spindrift blown back where the high tide broke on Cemetery Ridge. A passionate *if!* sleeps uneasily in the grandsons' blood and though they cannot win Marse Robert's war, they can draw their breath in pain to tell its story.

And, if one may be forgiven, how! There was the siege of

Vicksburg in *So Red the Rose*. There was Shiloh in *The Longest Night*, the campaign for Atlanta in *Gone With the Wind*, Chickamauga in *None Shall Look Back*. In a few weeks there will be the siege of Richmond in *Bugles Blow No More*. Beyond that is the unguessed future; heaven knows how many publishers have held a wet finger to windward, how many novelists, maps pinned to the study walls and *A Diary from Dixie* open on the desk, are swept up in the panic that follows Grierson's Raid. Many climaxes are still untouched — Vanderbilt's preference for the War in the West having kept fiction inattentive to the Peninsular campaigns, the Shenandoah Valley, the Confederate navy, even the two great invasions.

Surely trumpets may blow yellowly for Jeb Stuart riding round the Federal lines singing madrigals and wearing roses at his saberknot (he has so far been left to the Yankee Hergesheimer), for that tragic moment when a patrol of Averell's found the copy of Lee's marching orders, for that line of winter huts along the Rappahannock. Surely the Army of Northern Virginia will win once more the perfect battles that have enraptured strategists for seventy years. Surely fiction will find use for the Right Reverend Lieutenant General Leonidas Polk, for that Bayard of the second degree John Gordon, for that burlier Forrest, Uncle Dick Ewell, the woodcock, whose frontiersman's oaths and table manners corrupted by the Apache campaigns frighten the admiration of ladies, who has to be strapped in his saddle since he lost a leg at Groveton, who in moments of well-being cocks his head to one side and utters shrill bursts of song and chatter in the amiable delusion that he is a bird.

They are not yet in fiction but they will be. The South lost the war but is in a fair way to win the renaissance. For fifty years following 1865 there was little war fiction worth the paper it was printed on, except as the nightmares of Ambrose Bierce and the fantasies of Stephen Crane required a local habitation. Then the production of spy and parted-lover novels subsided and it slowly became possible for fiction to raise up at long intervals such a fine and lonely monument as Mr. Boyd's *Marching On* or Miss Scott's *The Wave*. But now suddenly, after seventy years, all Dixie is in flower. The sophomores among us can remember when Southern literature was just Miss Glasgow and Mr. Cabell; the elders recall when Illinois, succeeding Indiana, was fiction's truest home; the patriarchs go back to the time when Mr. Mencken ventured out in the footsteps of Frederick Law Olmsted and returned with "The Sahara of the Bozart." In fact Mr. Mencken may have begotten the renaissance. He marched three times round the walls blowing on a ram's horn, and now all our novelists are Southerners. And they all write about the War. "Truth crushed to earth shall rise again," says South Carolina's memorial window in Blandford Meeting House, quoting words which a damn Yankee wrote, and these days truth rises in thousands of pages, the Rebel yell exults across Parnassus, and the Yankee lines are still.

Or maybe they aren't. Reinforcements may even now be on the way to support Mr. MacKinlay Kantor, and in fact there is rumor of a formidable counterattack already preparing, one of the high command of Northern fiction leading it in person. History may repeat itself in fiction even more literally than we are yet aware. In the War the South carried everything for the first two years, but once the North's enormous reserves in manpower got organized they soon prevailed. It may be that fiction to-day is only at Chancellorsville and that Gettysburg is to come, and then Grant in the Wilderness, and at last Sheridan's cavalry screen moving aside to reveal the encirclement at Appomattox.

Fiction's rediscovery of the principal occurrence in American history has produced much good reading and will doubtless produce much more. That is a clear gain, and the increased national awareness that it attests is gratifying. Nevertheless, as the books multiply and it has become necessary to introduce the wood-pulp industry in the South to keep up with them, increasingly there come moments when one does not care to read a Civil War novel. The public still supports the gigantic war effort, but let the publishers take note of those ominous moments. There may soon be draft riots in New York and mobs storming the warehouses in Richmond. In sheer surfeit we may demand an armistice, and some day a bright, new, thousand-page treatise on how plumes trailed in the dust after Bragg blundered may be greeted by a bored populace shouting: Let us have peace.

HORIZON LAND In 1867 a herd of Texas cattle was driven northward to meet the railroad at Abilene, Kansas, and the Long Trail was thus established. In 1874 barbed wire was invented and the open range began to be fenced in. In 1885 drought and tightening credit brought the price of steers down from $35 to $8, ruining the barons, and the cattle business began to take the shape it has to-day. By 1895 the social system which Walter Webb calls "the cattle kingdom" had altogether disappeared. A boy old enough to drive a chuck wagon with the first herd of longhorns entrained at Abilene could have seen the rise and fall of the kingdom and still have been no more than middle-aged when it lapsed into legend.

Before 1900 the cowboy had emerged as the final inheritor of the Western romance whose successive images had been the long hunter, the trail breaker, the voyageur, the bear hunter, the mountain man, the gold washer, the scout, and the lieutenant of cavalry. His idiom had already been fixed by a competent journalism when Stephen Crane tried to make literature of it for the first time. In 1902, when Mr. Owen Wister assembled a novel out of some short stories and called it *The Virginian*, a flood began to rise that has never since abated. The cattle trade is the only American business which has evoked a literature, a mythology, and graphic symbolism of its own. And all of them refer to a period of less than thirty years. Time need not be spent exploring reasons. The cattle business was localized in a part of the country toward which the national phantasy has always turned, it had the movement of masses under a wide sky, its common routine was both picturesque and dangerous, all its ways and folkways were tinged with strangeness. The cowboy was a free man, an individualist, an equalitarian; his necessary clothes were romantic and his necessary behavior was daring; he was an equestrian, a mounted man, and from professional necessity he carried his law, his security, and the defense of his beliefs on his thigh.

The humblest level of this literature is the cowboy story, which has produced thousands of novels and has appeared in all magazines from the *Atlantic* down to the pulps which specialize in it. Above this level you come to a kind of poetry, very bad as poetry but unpretentious and honest, expressive of the nostalgia of a frontier nation that has lost its frontier. Above that is another poetry, the balladry of the cowboy himself, usually lachrymose or obscene but as genuine a folk poetry as any America has produced, now engaging the interest of antiquarians. The next step brings you to a bulk of reminiscences, memoirs, biographies and autobiographies, expositions and descriptions, records, collections of legends and anecdotes that embody the actual experience of the cattle kingdom and are indispensable to history but only occasionally, as in the work of Andy Adams and Ross Santee, attain the stature of literature. Above this should be a stratum of imaginative interpretation, of art, but one name hardly makes a stratum and the literature of the cattle kingdom produced only one artist, Eugene Manlove Rhodes.

The cowboy story is a set of conventions and clichés which originally may have had some relation to the life it pretends to depict but speedily lost it in obedience to the phantasies of the eastern consumer. It was Mr. Rhodes's misfortune, because his novels also dealt with cowboys and herds of cattle and the life of the open range, to be grouped with these conventions and so to be dismissed. But there was this difference: his work was true to the life of the cattle kingdom, he was an artist in prose, and he portrayed both the reality and the romance of that brief era with a fidelity that only a few have ever tried to maintain and only he succeeded in maintaining. For a quarter of a century now there has existed a small, enthusiastic group of admirers of Gene Rhodes. It seems likely that they will increase as time's critical process goes on, and that he will eventually be confirmed in his rightful place, as a distinguished novelist whose material happily chanced to be the cattle kingdom. His books are its only important contribution to American literature.

Those books are, of course, a primitive literature — primitive not in technique, for he was a craftsman of the first order, and one more cause of the public's indifference to him is the intricacy of his tale-telling, but in emotional content. They deal with such simplicities as courage, endurance, steadiness of nerve and purpose, loyalty, honesty, and honor — the necessary survival virtues of the kingdom. There is a primitive separation between such virtues and their opposites which permits no half-lights and no psychological subtleties — and that too follows from the conditions of a life lived out of reach of the restraints of society, a life which had to recognize its evil at sight and to get its villains identified and out of the way just as promptly. They are primitive also in that women characters are infrequent and all but inconceivably lovely and virtuous when present — another fidelity, since that is the way the kingdom thought of its women. The books are violent as well, but they are not melodramatic: they merely embody the reality of the time and place, and there were plenty of men, some of them in high places, who wanted to go gunning for Gene Rhodes on the simple ground that he wrote history and not fiction, disguising these objectors much too little. His books have, in short, many of the characteristics of a life singularly like the one he was reporting, the Scotch border, whose songs, significantly, his heroes commonly sing.

Those books, one is confident, will get more attention as time goes on. The historians have already discovered them and recognized their quality. Literary criticism will take note of them, if they are often enough called to its attention. All other fiction of the cattle kingdom is too humble and inept, if genuine, or else mere cliché, but this is literature. Word comes that a memoir of Gene Rhodes with a collection of his letters is in preparation and will be ready in a year or two. (What ever happened to the proposed collected edition of his books?) May it introduce to those who care about American literature an artist of importance, one of the very few who have appeared in any of our horizon lands, and the only one who has dealt with the most permanently glamorous of them, the cattle kingdom. For make no mistake about it: whether or not you have ever heard of Eugene Manlove Rhodes, he was a writer who must be taken into account.

CONTINENTAL DIVIDE   A SAGACIOUS publisher — if the use of that adjective does not add ambiguity to tautology — recently expressed a hunch that the next fashion in our fiction will be a shift toward the West. Pretty soon, he said, somebody is going to write a Western that will be deeper and more intelligent. When he does he will go to town, and in three months there will be a buffalo skull in every publisher's office. He would prophesy no farther but repeated his conviction that the April rains are over, the trail is drying out, and presently the white-tops will be yoking up.

There may be something in what he says, for the Civil War cannot last forever. The Vanderbilt movement will continue till its young men are graybeards, unless the Federal government adopts its platform and undertakes to supply a poet through the Bureau of Animal Husbandry to every community that will agree to plant flax and indigo, build a threshing floor, and re-establish the pearlash industry. But the Lost Cause fiction we were recently discussing here is bound to flag pretty soon, and even before that the public is likely to look elsewhere for the vitamins. The same forces that made Gettysburg common a good buy (*Nation* editors: should we refer to them as intensified nationalism or merely as a by-product of war buying?) will still operate, and since there are only a few subjects they can operate on, the West is indicated. Our publisher's belief that this will be a more intelligent Western fiction is supported by what happened with the Civil War. If you compare Caroline Gordon with Mary Johnston, or MacKinlay Kantor with Winston Churchill, you see exactly what he means.

It will probably not be a fiction of the cattle kingdom. Thirty years of cheap fiction about cowboys, rustlers, evil sheriffs, roundups, stampedes, six-guns, and branding irons have created an inertia which serious literature finds it hard to overcome. Having produced Eugene Manlove Rhodes, it needed another quarter of a century to produce Mr. Conrad Richter. Fiction is likely to move farther back and farther West, before 1860 and beyond the hundredth meridian.

It is astonishing how little modern fiction has dealt with the Westward expansion, which after all is the fundamental American experience. And such novels about pioneering as we have (except a very few sporadic ones) stop short exactly where the West begins — which is where the annual rainfall drops below twenty inches, or halfway across Nebraska. Our novelists took the pioneer as far as the Dark and Bloody Ground with great enthusiasm. With a diminished zest they went on to the Lincoln country and then spread up and down the Mississippi and its bayous. Only a handful have ever pushed a pirogue across those unvexed waters. Iowa has been satisfactorily settled, and Kansas has bled a little, but there serious fiction reaches trail's end, looking toward the high plains. The rest is so frivolous and fantastic that Mr. H. L. Davis and Mr. Harvey Fergusson have found the country as empty of white men as it was when Lewis and Clark got there.

Why should so shallow and conventional a novel as *The Covered Wagon* remain the best treatment of the far Western migration in our fiction? As a spectacle, a saga, or a premonition of the modern America, the prairie schooner offers quite as good material as the downfall of the plantation system. Why should the building of the transcontinental railroads, a subject rather richer for sociological fiction than a strike of the garment workers, be represented by nothing except Mr. Zane Grey's preposterous *U. P. Trail* and a sentimental romance in *Collier's?* Is Spanish California to be abandoned to the *Cosmopolitan*, and is it believed that Bret Harte exhausted the possibilities of the gold rush? Is the settlement of the interior West to give us only novels about the beet pickers, and is fiction finished with the mineral frontier when it has several times informed us that the empire builders had bad table manners and their children are weaklings? Finally, can no novel better than *The Lions of the Lord* be written about one of the most fascinating episodes in American history, the hegira of the Mormons?

This generation has developed a new kind of historical fiction. Stock figures have dropped out, romantic fantasy is at a minimum, the enlisted man rather than the major general is the hero of the war novel, the novel of pioneering is devoted to the life of the pioneers rather than the oratorical crises of national destiny. The form retains spectacle and panorama, but is realistic, hard-bitten, and unrhetorical. Fiction of the West skipped the very field that this kind of fiction can best occupy. It began on the level of the mythological and then, with a premature sophistication, straightway began to import the novel of the middle-Minnesota period in which soup dribbles down the paralyzed side of grandma's face. There has been very little fiction about the real energies of the West or about its rich, violent, and very moving past. The field is practically untouched, the logical way into it is by means of novels like those currently written about the Civil War, and our publisher may be right in believing that fiction is ready to move out and locate.

Mr. Thomas Hornsby Ferril's trenchant article which recently appeared in these columns explained one serious danger that such a literature faces. An emotionalism that sees human figures as dwarfed by the gigantic scale of the natural environment ends in sentimentality. Other sentimentalities lurk in the sagebrush and the mesquite, notably the one that has the New Mexico coteries praying to the thunderbird. It may be taken for granted that anyone who thinks of Indians as the Amerinds is not going to add much to our literature. Preciosities about the mystical awareness that neolithic savages are supposed to have, and how the rain dance and the worship of the corn spirit (in rhythms much too subtle for coarse people like you to understand) show exactly where American life took a tragic turning — are going to remain preciosities. Mr. Harvey Fergusson has shown how to write intelligently about the Western Indians: fiction that wears a squash blossom in its hair or talks about the plumed serpent is just silly.

The odd development of coterie art, in fact, is a serious threat to Western literature. Twenty years ago there wasn't a coterie between the hundredth meridian and the crest of the Sierras, now there is one at every college and most flag stops. They produce little literature and what they produce is very bad, but they generate an enormous mass of critical theory and, like all coteries, they war energetically on one another. The art of literature is largely that of anathematizing people for being regionalists when they should be sectionalists, localists, Congressional districtists, and on down to county lines. They are currently reworking the early clichés of Greenwich Village with an air of original discovery, beginning to experiment with the manifestoes and methods current on the Left Bank thirty years ago, and writing, when they write at all, the most appalling balderdash. In a passionate dogmatism they wholly omit to look at how people live in the West. If we are to have some serious Western fiction, it will have to begin by repairing the omission. The Western novelist must tear up his coterie card, immerse himself in the life around him, and write about what he sees in terms of what it seems like to him and not in terms of what the dogmas of his little group or favorite English prof make it out to be.

On Notions

∼∼∼∼∼∼∼∼∼∼∼∼∼∼∼∼∼∼∼∼∼

NYMPH   APPLE blossoms break out across the countryside, the hylas have spoken for the third straight night, the whippoorwills complain from hill to hill, and the young gentleman from New Haven, Cambridge, Princeton, and the lesser elms is in town for a day to choose among his opportunities. If an oblique question in his eye tarnishes his nonchalance when he gets to this office, one learns that it has to do with a marked copy of the *Advocate*, the *Lit*, or the *Nassau Lit* which he sent us last December. He explains that if he dealt with the *Saturday Review* severely in that editorial, it was because only for the *Saturday Review* can he feel any hope at all. We can be plucked from the burning, but for our competitors, all of them, there is left only a folding of the hands for sleep.

He lectures. To begin with, we should double our size: literary leadership cannot be exercised in less than sixty pages. Reviews must be longer; we must give reviewers space to bring the eternities in. But first a more fundamental reform must be made; he finds our reviewers without exception stodgy, uneducated, and timorous, and he would sweep them all out clean. Literary articles are, of course, an essential, but we should publish better ones than we do and we should run at least three a week. A number of new departments must be established at once, one to keep in touch with the college magazines, one to appraise the coteries, one devoted to the art of the unconscious mind. Four pages of poetry would be about right, but nothing can be expected from any living poets except the very youngest and we must publish only those who have gone beyond Day Lewis. Our advertisers must be rigorously censored and as soon as possible it will be well to dispense with advertising altogether.

After another cigarette he discusses his relationship to all this. He will be in New York next September and it will take him some months to establish himself. His novel (inquiry reveals that it is to combine the methods of *Men of Good Will* and *Work in Progress*) may not sell more than seven or eight thousand, and he can expect little remuneration for his poetry. Frankly, he must for a time support himself by writing articles for such magazines as *Harper's* . . . and running one of our departments would not trespass on his novel and he will be able to review three or four books a week.

The intrepidity and the informed knowledge that our reviewers lack are thus offered to us. He willingly answers questions. Thus, it would be a service to literature and a kindness to Mr. Hemingway if the Hemingway myth were to be done away with now, once and for all. The Thomas Mann cult is a vast reservoir of sentimentality, and in these desperate days it is our duty to root out the sentimental. Mr. MacLeish has too long impeded the progress of poetry and, for his part, our young man would be willing to slay Mr. MacLeish. Dos Passos? — a bungler. Lewis? — a best seller. Robert Frost? — a Victorian. The only form of fiction competent for the new order is the group novel, and poetry must be stamped from steel like the machines it must deal with. Where then shall we look for the meritorious? — a grave, sad smile, an explanation that, candidly, there is none now, but the newness is about ready to begin. So he leaves, but first he acknowledges that, though primarily interested in poetry and fiction, he knows something about economics, history, metaphysics, the fine arts, and psychology. If something like Spengler comes in, for instance, or when Dr. Freud publishes another book. . . .

Thus the nymph or pre-adult stage of the literary person. He and the hylas trouble the heart these spring days, stirring a fragrance of other springs. There is nothing you can tell him for you cannot speak on any wave-length he can tune to. Intrepidity of thought, oh, yes, Lord! but like cleverness it is a dime a dozen, and what we are in the market for is a costlier and rarer thing: skill in the fingers and judgment that has tanned in a lowlier pickle than the *Advocate* or the *Lit.* You cannot make that carry through to him, and you cannot tell him that writers are made not by appointment but by election. You cannot tell him that of ten like him there will be only one left by September, of fifty but one left two years from now, and of a hundred hardly one whose blend of Joyce and Romains will ever see print. You cannot make clear that of the survived one-hundredths something less than half will ever make moderately good reading.

What is inconceivable to him is the bitter fact of apprenticeship. Except when he is an accident, the biological aberration so rare that it seems monstrous, he will not be able to write readable prose till he is thirty or have anything to say in it till he is thirty-five. After ten years of writing sentences for some hours a day he may be able to construct them well enough so that only one rewriting will do, so that they say what he means them to and give the reader a small dividend of pleasure as well. After publishing a half-dozen books that sell between five hundred and fifteen hundred copies, he may have learned enough craftsmanship so that he can plausibly count on the next one's selling seven or eight thousand if luck is on his side.

By the time he has acquired skill he should also have lost his certainties and so have become eligible for reviewing. The trouble with the young reviewer is ignorance of how a thing is done, for which there is no help but the experience of doing it, and a habit of final judgment. He has the ruthlessness of the untested and his college press condemns the best work of the day with a finality that the Miltonic deity refrained from after the wars in heaven. He worships the principle, he has no pity for the workman. College has given him a sackful of principles but he has written no books. He knows what a writer ought to have done and how he ought to have done it, but he has no conception of the possible and allows nothing for the grain and cell structure of the medium, the viscosity of the material, or the limitations of the tools. He has been schooled in abstractions deduced from traditional classics on the one hand and from the preciosities of the most advanced art of the moment on the other, and he has never learned that books are written as needs must. He has the intolerance common to all idolators of the ideal; he has not had to forgo perfection in order to write a book. He has — sometimes — read widely but he has not read deeply; he has written cleverly and intrepidly but he has never faced the need of writing well.

There is no definition of skill: it is, simply, something that comes after many repetitions of an act for which you have some natural ability. Still less is there a definition of judgment: it is something that comes, rather later than skill, from intelligently associating the specific instance with what you have intelligently learned from and about a good many other specific instances. Skill and judgment do not come in matched sets, and they are not born of a miracle. A benign fortune may have endowed the young literary person with everything else that makes for excellence, but he must get these for himself. He has made the first step when he realizes that they do not come easily, but it is the first step that ninety and nine never take. Writing, they have always thought, is easy, for they have always written easily. Why not? — they are gifted, they have a natural ease, a natural brilliance. So the ninety and nine drift off into circumstance and other inspirations — "I am willing," one of them writes, "even to do office work." The hundredth has made his start when he has at last recognized that it is harder than he thinks.

WHAT OF THE NIGHT? For some years now a college professor in one of the Southern states has been periodically sending out a form letter asking, What of the Night? Like everyone he is frightened by the signs in the heavens and he wonders if we other peerers into darkness discern anything that makes us think the light is coming. Like everyone he will, when enough of us have answered him, write a book. We have always thrown his letter away, along with the letters asking us to buy shirts, add our signature to the eight hundred and sixteen literary autographs amassed by a twelve-year-old boy in Wilkes-Barre, and supply brief biographies of fifty leading authors so that a high-school girl in Dayton can write a theme. Belatedly, we realize that we have been acting churlishly. Some day we may want to write a book, too.

"Do you see any sound reasons for entertaining the prospect of an early spiritual awakening?"

Yea, brother. That which you have greatly hoped for has come upon you. The world is lousy with spirituality. Look around you, glance at the newspapers, read our competitors in polite journalism. Deep in the Kyffhäuser Redbeard has yawned and shrugged awake. His beard shatters the stone it has grown through, the old gods wake too, and a shriven and exalted people rejoice in their salvation and go forth crying holy names. They have been washed clean, brother, and their faith has made them whole, and a white robe has been given unto every one of them. They shall wait for a little season until their fellow servants also and their brethren that shall be killed shall be fulfilled. (Rev., 7:11.) Rise and sing, brother, for this is the clear stuff; the spiritual awakening is here.

Bind on your phylacteries, brother, and go forth and sing. Let the sea roar and all the trees of the wood rejoice, as men rejoice when they divide the spoil. (Isa., 9:3.) For the foster children of the she-wolf have seen the aloe blossoming in the waste places. Every one has a harp and a golden vial full of odors which are the prayers of saints, and in Africa and Spain they are spoiling the unbelievers till the land is full of blood and the third part of the sea is blood. Plenty of awakened spirituality where Rome sitteth upon the waters, brother.

And what of Enoch, brother, and all the spirits of just men made perfect? Play on your harp, for the spirit has waked there, too, where it is used to waking, and the doors are shut in the streets, and they rise up at the sound of a bird (Ecc., 12:4), and nearly any other sound. Lots of spirituality in New Jerusalem, brother: they are stoning the prophets in the streets and the fig tree is casting its untimely figs. The first heaven and the first earth have passed away, in New Jerusalem, and there is a new heaven and a new earth. They need no candle there, brother, neither light of the sun, for all the people cry out with one voice. Or if any doesn't it is just too bad.

The heathen in the Far East have got pretty spiritual too, brother.

So far our spirituality hasn't waked much, Amen. We don't know how you feel about it in Arkansas but as for us, that's just fine. Watch and pray, brother. Go cut yourself a gad, and beat hell out of anyone who starts any spirit-awakening in your neighborhood. Let's use up our finger rings for golden calves, brother, not war loans. Let's hold fast to covetousness and gluttony and the other sins that hold the spirit down. Let's not allow the American eye to wander away from vile, material things. We've got pretty far that way and, compared to the spiritual nations, we don't look so bad. If you see anybody fingering a seal, brother, or looking very long at a pale horse or a black horse, don't waste time. Take him and slay him at the passages of Jordan.

SIR: Letters to the editor are a problem as well as a pleasure. If we undertook to publish all we get these days we should be forced to borrow an idea from a distinguished competitor and issue a supplement devoted exclusively to them. The amount of such mail frankly delights the editors, who find it very valuable as well as gratifying, and who know, further, that our letter page is one of the departments of the magazine that interest our readers most. Nevertheless space is space and, being space, is not extensible. (This will produce some letters from readers of Eddington.) We can publish only one page of letters per issue and the reservoir of those we cannot publish therefore grows larger every day. Now that complaints begin to come in because we have not published earlier letters which complained because we had not published letters earlier still, it is time to state some principles of selection.

But first it should be pointed out that the freedom of the press is in no way involved, though several indignant writers of unpublished letters assert that it is. Freedom of the press is a principle that protects a magazine, not one that insures a writer publication. Freedom of the press does not mean that the editors of this or any other magazine have to publish your letter: it means that, subject to criminal prosecution under the statutes and civil suit for damages from libel, they will be protected if they do publish it. It means that if they do not want to publish it, you can start your own magazine, publish it there, and be protected. They are under no compulsion or obligation of any kind whatever to publish it, if for any reason, good, bad, whimsical, arbitrary, or preposterous, they do not care to.

The basic principle by which we ordinarily select letters for publication is that of potential interest to our readers, but there is another principle that takes precedence over that one. We realize that a magazine which reviews over a thousand books a year must occasionally do injustice to some of them. We therefore mark "must" letters which make a plausible claim that injustice has been done by one of our reviews. Brevity being the greatest virtue that the letter page knows, we run the short ones first. If several letters making the same protest come in, we publish those which seem to cover the question, and cover it in the smallest compass. While the world remains imperfect we cannot often recognize protests two thousand words long, though justice weep and the angels of righteousness avert their eyes.

Apart from protest and reparation, the page should be devoted to information and comments on the literary scene — unofficial reportorial and editorial work by our readers. Such letters are our closest contact with our readers and of the readers with one another. Many subscribers turn to the letter page first of all — because they have learned to expect there novel points of view, unorthodox opinions, and unusual items of information and amusement. That is the kind of letter nearest to our own taste and therefore most likely to be published. It is personal journalism of the best kind. Here also brevity counts most. The person who can be novel, unorthodox, or informative in two hundred words rather than two thousand is a child of light and will be welcomed as one.

Disagreement with the opinions expressed on this page comes next. So long as we get enough letters disagreeing with us violently enough, we shall be confident that the editorial page is healthy. We will publish as many of them as we can, but the other considerations come first. And we must judge them quite arbitrarily. If a disagreement is merely a misunderstanding or seems trivial, if someone else has expressed it better, if we have devoted as much space to the question as we think it worth, then we cannot publish it. And, once more, brevity is more precious than rubies. Mr. H. W. L. Dana writes us in regard to "Minority Report," "Sir: I have a great respect for your opinion — on novels. Very sincerely yours." Mr. Dana's letter is herewith granted first papers as a classic.

We will not publish anything that is merely abusive. Our own manners are of the finest — we are scrupulous to cut off heads so delicately that even the owners of them do not realize what has happened until they sneeze. We are soft-spoken, gentle, and conciliatory, and a more than Southern chivalry informs our style; and although such benignity may be inimitable, letter writers have got to imitate it if we are to publish them. Every mail brings letters which hurl bloodcurdling epithets at us, our contributors, or sometimes our opponents and victims. Mostly they are dull, but even when they make good reading we will not run them. We are not altogether averse to literary controversy, but controversialists should have a low blood pressure and a normal temperature. Let the blood boil if it will, but keep the brain air-conditioned. And do not suppose that you have demolished an idea when you have called the man who expresses it a name. And better read over what he wrote before you write in, for an astonishing number of complaints are received here about statements never made in this magazine.

If we will not publish bad-tempered letters, neither will we publish letters that support the palpably absurd. Every editor in America receives such letters every day, and we get our share of them, or perhaps a little more than our share. We preserve them, lovingly, but we will not run them. Literature's geoplanarians, salesmen of the mind's Perunas, the embattled hosts of moonshine and idiocy, will get no hearing here; other presses may be free to them but ours is not. As for writers of anonymous letters to the editor, they know what they can do. If they do not, let them supply name and address and the editor will be happy to tell them.

THE LOGIC OF   Flash. Good life takes bad beating.
SENTIMENT   Economy of abundance trips over abstraction. Words are not things, says nemesis of American
business. Famous conservationist seeks operational definition
of integrity.[1]

In the current *Harper's* Mr. Stuart Chase publishes the first
of three articles on his discovery (midway in a career that
has not been altogether inhospitable to rhetoric) of the dangers latent in words, personifications, abstractions, and verbal
proofs. Beginning with the observation that the word "idealism" has no meaning, he went on to test for meaning a good
many more words, phrases, and concepts which he had used
in developing his favorite theories. The test led him to read
widely among writers who had undertaken a similar search,
notably Ogden and Richards, Bridgman, F.C.S. Schiller, and
"parts of Pareto." As a result he has abandoned some of his
former conclusions and determined to rely on a new method
of thinking. There have also been some interesting by-products
of the research. "A brief grounding in semantics [the science
of meanings] besides making philosophy unreadable, makes
unreadable most political speeches, classical economic theory,
after-dinner oratory, diplomatic notes, newspaper editorials,
treatises on pedagogics and education, expert financial comment, dissertations on money and credit, accounts of debates,
and Great Thoughts from Great Thinkers in general."

It would be interesting to know whether Mr. Chase still finds
The New Economics readable, but one is compensated for
that omission by the slur on pedagogics and the realization
that it appears in Mr. Chase's part of *Harper's*, not the Easy
Chair, which is frequently in hot water for remarking that
what pedagogical theorists say has no meaning. But there are
some striking gaps in Mr. Chase's list of the geysers of verbalism. If newspaper editorials have no meaning, what about
liberal journalism? Liberal journalism (referent: the *Nation*

[1] See "Good and Wicked Words."

and the *New Republic*) is vocational verbalism. It consists of arguing for people who agree with you before you begin, finding logical arguments to rationalize nonlogical sentiments, building structures of verbal proof out of abstractions and personifications, and asserting for your comfort and the encouragement of those who agree with you that those structures correspond to verifiable entities in the objective world. That sort of thing, one understands, is what Mr. Chase is currently objecting to.

It is news, of course, when any writer, especially an intellectual, resolves to use words in strict reference to things and to controllable and consciously used abstractions. The customary rejoicing in heaven has been arranged for, and the editor of this journal welcomes all volunteer allies to the task of policing beautiful thinking. But they mustn't bring any unconscious metaphysics with them, and the editor is not sure that Mr. Chase has crossed over into camp ground washed wholly clean of original sin. (Metaphor, not abstraction: see Mr. Chase's footnote in the back of *Harper's*.) The problem is not simply to give words exact and verifiable meanings, but there are horrid intimations that Mr. Chase thinks it is. "People [he says] are not 'dumb' because they lack mental equipment; they are dumb because they lack an adequate method for the use of that equipment." The good life has just moved one step farther away: behind that assertion crouches the theorem that when people have got an adequate method everything is going to be pretty lovely. Isn't that a metaphysical theorem? Isn't it just a subtler symptom of the disease that makes the class struggle out to be a combat between a hero and a villain and thinks that justice and truth and capital are things you can go out and bark your shins on? And what about the people who are perfectly capable of mastering the already existing methods for the use of the equipment Mr. Chase has in mind, but don't master them? Why don't they? What are we going to make of the fact that they don't? What does Mr. Chase propose to do about the fact, and how does it work in with his discoveries and resolutions?

Maybe he had better read some more "parts of Pareto." It was Mr. Chase, not the editor, who hauled Pareto into this discussion, but it was the editor who hauled liberal journalism in. Well, in last week's *New Republic* a writer used Pareto's name as a curse, precisely as in his evangelical youth he used to use Satan's. Now Pareto was an actual man who wrote, among other things, a book called *Traité de sociologie générale*, which examines the mechanisms Mr. Chase is discussing, and which, by personification, has come to have an animate existence of its own and has been christened with its author's name. All right, we can give the term "Pareto" a precise meaning, an operational definition: people can read the book and agree on what it says. The *New Republic* writer is capable of performing that operation; if he performed it, he would mean by "Pareto" exactly what Mr. Chase means by it. By reputation he is an intelligent man (operation: Binet-Simon test, Alpha, Stanford Revision), but he would righteously and angrily repudiate the suggestion that he use the term "Pareto" in an operational sense. As he uses the term it has no meaning — no meaning as Mr. Chase, Mr. Bridgman, and the rest of us define meaning. In fact, it would be a rare issue of any liberal journal (referent as above) in which Mr. Chase could find ten statements all told that had meaning.

But though the epithet "Pareto" as the *New Republic* writer uses it has no objective, verifiable, or operational meaning, it is heavily charged with private meaning, and that meaning is both clear and useful to the writer and to the people he writes for, the people who share his sentiments. It means, ho, such bugs and goblins. It means "fascist" — another word which, Mr. Chase says, has no meaning as it is commonly used. It means any dislike, any apprehension or any phantasy, any consoling swear-word, any emotion conformable to the emotional pattern that employs it. It corresponds to nothing in the objective world and to nothing that people have experienced who do not have the same sentiments. But it does correspond to some lively emotions in the *New Republic* writer. And when he uses it, he evokes similar emotions in the people he is writing for.

This phenomenon may be observed in practically all departments of human behavior except those under experimental or empirical control. Pareto (referent: the *Sociologie générale*) classifies the phenomenon as the logic of sentiment. The phrase itself doesn't matter — the label might as well be x — but the phenomenon is a matter of experience. The abstractions, personifications, and verbal proofs which Mr. Chase objects to are only a part of the logic of sentiment. He had better go on and see what Pareto (same referent) has to say about the other parts and, more crucially, what he has to say about the sentiments that produce the behavior which the logic attempts to justify, explain, and defend. If he does, he will extend his list of unreadables and change his mind about some of the deplorable occupations. He may even find that his unconscious theorem is not so simple or his program so hopeful as he now appears to believe. It would also be an improving exercise to enumerate and analyze the individual items out of which he builds up his picture of abstractions careening through modern thought. The exercise might reveal that his choice of them had some tangential relation to the logic of sentiment.

THE
SPECIALIST   ORGANIZATIONS which devote themselves to the extralegal protection of public morals by means of censorship and terrorism are usually not heavily endowed. They have invested funds as the result of bequests from people who believe in their disgusting activity, but these are dishearteningly small and the societies are forced to depend for their existence on contributions. The people who make contri-

butions are worthy but incline to be negligent; it is easy to forget one's duty to the uplift unless frequently reminded of it. So
our censors remind their supporters by making spectacular
drives on pumped-up waves of pornography and on conspicuous books against which a momentarily plausible allegation of
obscenity can be made. The more spectacular the better, and
the more conspicuous the better. The publicity thus produced
reaches the contributors and notifies them that their organization is on the job. It is by no means necessary to win the case;
success in such a prosecution is so much velvet, the real desidera-
tum being the publicity, which brings in contributions. Whenever you read that an anti-vice society is taking action against
some book, play, or picture you may be pretty sure that its
managers are worried about the budget. This is the economic
determination of public purity.

Twenty-four years of altruistic devotion to dirty postcards
and the kind of books boys of thirteen read in back alleys
have trained Mr. John S. Sumner to detect pornography where
decent people cannot find it. As a specialist in pornography he
has all the authority that a lifelong habituation to it can give
him: such an authority as can be achieved only by spending
hundreds of sleepless nights judicially studying photographs
produced for the tourist trade, turning them over and over till
dawn comes, repeatedly consulting trained responses to determine which fall short and which get over the line. The routine
material of the Society for the Suppression of Vice, whose
secretary Mr. Sumner is, is the back-alley and rear-room trade,
but one judges that this does not produce a satisfactory income, for every so often the Society takes up literature in a
big way. It always gets slapped down: you can step into any
bookstore and buy *The Genius, Jurgen, God's Little Acre*,
and many other books it has conspicuously proceeded against.
But it keeps coming back so often as to suggest that mere
purity may not be its principal objective. Let us remember the

chance of contributions when we consider the prosecution newly brought against one of the best American novels of 1936.

You and I and all normal people fail to detect pornography in Mr. James Farrell's *A World I Never Made*. By a striking coincidence the Book-of-the-Month Club has just awarded the author of that novel a prize of twenty-five hundred dollars five days before Mr. Sumner's contemptible proceedings are due to bring him into court. What blinds our guilty eyes is Mr. Farrell's intellectual integrity, his high artistic achievement, his book's memorable representation of human pain and human tragedy. But Mr. Sumner has trained himself to disregard such things in his professional pursuit of other values. His guess is that he can make out a plausible case against the book. He will feel good if he does; and, of course, even if he doesn't, his efforts will produce a lot of publicity.

One more skirmish in the endless battle for the right of the public to read literature and of authors to write it. The battle must go on so long as there is bigotry in the world, so long as there are minds which have to disguise their abnormal pleasure in eroticism as a — detailed — horror of eroticism, and so long as money can be raised by alleging pornography in places where it does not exist. The fact that it is getting easy to defeat the Society for the Suppression of Vice must not make us lax. It's time to turn out the guard again. Men of goodwill, decent people, normal people, people who believe that literature must be defended against diseased minds, people who believe in liberty, people who believe that bigoted minorities must be prevented from working their purposes on society, people who have the probity of the law and of American culture at heart, must take up the fight again and see it through.

Fortunately Mr. Sumner has made our job easier by attacking a book whose validity as a work of art cannot be impugned. Mr. Sumner has to prove that *A World I Never Made* is lewd and pornographic, whereas it is neither under any construction that anyone, even a psychopath, can put on those terms. He has to prove that it tends to corrupt a normal person, whereas it could not possibly corrupt even Mr. Sumner. It is, of course, frequently unpleasant and sometimes revolting, but those qualities have nothing to do with Mr. Sumner's allegations. It is a bitter book, a violent book, but neither bitterness nor violence comes under the statute. It is an austere book with much nobility of thought and feeling, a book of dignity and exalted moral purpose, but our laws are not so favorable to disease that Mr. Sumner can penalize austerity, nobility, dignity, and morality. The likelihood is that, no matter how insulting to Mr. Farrell and the public the present prosecution is, it will end in another decision that will make success even more difficult for Mr. Sumner in the future. The hearing in a magistrate's court will occur while this issue of the *Saturday Review* is on the press. The editor expects that the complaint will be dismissed there and is confident that, if it isn't, Mr. Farrell and his publishers will win on trial, adding one more precedent to the legal distinction between pornography and the presence of obscene expressions.

But Mr. Sumner and his Society, always a bore, are getting to be an intolerable nuisance. And this fighting a defensive battle is getting to be a bore too, and has always been a mistake in tactics. Surely it is time for decent people to begin a counterattack. There must be ways of carrying the war into the enemy's terrain, ways of making common decency militant. The editor does not know what they are but volunteers to serve on any committee that will find out what they are and will put them into effect. Certain literary lawyers have valuably served our cause: let them be conscripted to determine the most effective legal procedures. Writers, publishers, booksellers, libraries, and the general public should all be represented on a permanent board which should harass the Society for the Suppression of Vice and all similar organizations. It should attack them with every permissible legal device, with every form of publicity that will convey ridicule and contempt, and with every other weapon that can be made effective against such enemies of decency, literature, and democratic institutions.

The law of injunctions is attractively flexible: can we not enjoin the Society's activity? Is there not reason to believe that a private enterprise which interferes with the rights and liberties of citizens can be prosecuted as a public nuisance? These are important questions, and they should be explored in the public interest. We know that the censorship exercised by threat and terrorism over booksellers is extralegal, and actual tests have proved that the law will not sanction the prosecution of literary masterpieces. All right, let's see what resources the law has for offensive warfare. It must have some, and if we use them persistently we may get somewhere. . . . And meanwhile it is always possible to alter the kind of publicity that smut-hounds receive in such a way as to reduce their desire for publicity.

GREAT   THE nation would be wise to make the most of its
CIRCLE   1937 Christmas. It has no war on hand this year: it
may have one when Santa heads southward in 1938. Something more than half of its citizens have jobs and wages and there is food for the rest: our expectations have now dropped so low that that seems bountiful, and by a year from now rather fewer of us may have jobs, though if food fails doubtless the ever-normal statistics will be nourishing. Let nothing you dismay: what has gone from American life is hope, and it appears to have gone for as long as the eye can peer ahead, but this Christmas a good many of us can have a pleasant time, and there have been more savage and despairing Christmases in the national past. We may know better, by a year from now, what they were like.

You'd like some reading for Christmas? You might try a piece in a recent *New Republic* by a man who knows more about us as we are and have been than anyone else now practising in the magazines, William Allen White's "A Yip from the Doghouse." He offers it, he says, as some nails for our masters of the moment to chew on. The nails are hard enough and pointed enough but Bill White knows as well as anyone that the people they are intended for will spew them out. He just wanted to have his say. Read it and then, if like Henry Adams you enjoy measuring movement from place to place, you can see the distance we have traveled during one man's lifetime by reading Bill White's *Court of Boyville*. The distance, not the direction. That early book of his has delighted its thousands, and the country it describes belongs in geological time now, and when you hold it against "A Yip from the Doghouse" you realize we have moved quite a way. No one can tell you where we're headed but you can see where we've got to.

Henry Adams concluded that we were moving toward the abyss; he assumed that we were traveling in a straight line. In Bill White's "Yip" there is a hint of a different idea, that the line is really curved and tends to turn back on itself. Spengler thought so too and the idea of cycles has other respectable supporters, from Professor Sorokin on back to Vico, who was the master of curved lines. And the other day Vico got independent confirmation when a drowsy boozer with a long beard wandered down from the Kaatskill Mountains. He found that the old winding paths had been surfaced with concrete but they followed the same course. And that was as it should be, for when you are lost, Rip Van Winkle remembered, you travel in a circle.

Dame Van Winkle was going barelegged except for ankle-length socks and these were made of cotton; she had organized a group of public-spirited consumers in the village, and you couldn't have sold a yard of silk anywhere along the Hudson. Her husband blinked and wondered if his long sleep had been only an after-dinner nap. He had seen this high-minded boycott help to draw the United States into two formal wars and into another one which, in a quaint modern way, we fought in 1798 but didn't bother to declare. War thus getting into his thoughts, he listened with particular interest to the gaffers at the ordinary when they got to debating the current struggle over the centralization of governmental authority. If no one else remembered, Rip remembered that we had fought our two biggest wars, in great part, over that question. We fought one of them to prevent centralization and another one to effect it. The going here seemed to be even more than circular: it was vertiginous.

On the very day when he came down from the mountains a dream much older than his sleep was broken when the House voted to recommit a bill that was intended to fix wages and hours. What that dream broke against was the sections, and Rip Van Winkle felt no surprise. Even a slumberer must know that there were sections before there was a nation; even the dream-bound must know that the nation, when sometimes there is one, always fades out whenever the sections are endangered, always breaks up along the section lines whenever the precarious equilibrium among them is disturbed. Rip Van Winkle knew that parties, classes, interests, ideologies, creeds, and visions always shatter on the hard edge of the sections; since those who have heard the thunder of dwarfs at bowls among the peaks have something of the seer in them, he dared say that they always will, as far into the future as thought can reach. But Rip had learned that no one ever learns anything from history, the thoughtful and the visionary least of all. For the thoughtful there are no sections. There never will be until sometime, with something more tangible than a bill for fixing hours, and it may be more painful, they bark their shins against that unmoving edge.

Rip, and Bill White too, and you and I (once, when we were calmer) knew a good many things it is now held intelligent or radical to ignore. One of them which Bill mentions is the thin film that holds a native talent for violence in check, a film pierced so often and so easily that perhaps it is more comfortably ignored once more at Christmas. Especially this Christmas of 1937, which, if not planned quite the way it comes out, was at least planned.

The resource of humility, and of the sleeper returning, is to remember that, cycle or straight line, the nation has always been made up of people. If we have nothing else, we have their symbols — of Christmas and other things. Mr. Branch was reminding us of some of them in these pages, three weeks ago. Literature is not the opium of the masses but it may be the barbital of the bewildered, and there is no weakness in employing it when your nerves are jumpy or your sleep bad. It is an irrational reassurance you derive from being reminded that there was suffering and desperation at Plymouth beach, at Valley Forge, along the Yadkin and beyond the Gap, where the trees first fell in the Western Reserve and prairie soil was first turned in Illinois, but that something nevertheless survived and the line was somehow traced. Irrational because your comfort comes from forgetting what did not survive, from omitting to number the graves beside the road, from convincing yourself that hunger was not an agony in the bowels if only it occurred a hundred years ago.

Nevertheless, Rip said, reason has not served us too handsomely this Christmas and you may honorably recline on the irrational for comfort, while any remains. You might read some of the things Mr. Branch was talking about: "Christmas Night in the Quarters," say, and the chapter in *Little Women* that has kept its serene, unclouded sweetness through the decades. They will give life to symbols for a while, voices singing in darkness, the sound of sleigh bells in still air, torches carried among live oaks, lights shining across snow. That will do you no harm, and you might go on, then, to read whatever strikes your fancy in Mr. Beston's *American Memory*, which makes a better Christmas gift than most books do. Reading it, you may think for a moment that you perceive something like a pattern, you may believe for a moment that the pattern is likely to prove stronger than everything that now endangers it. That too is irrational. But, Rip said, though we do not know what is to come, we do know that here, written in this book, are the things that will shape it.

He turned back to the Kaatskills, convinced that he could find no better twenty years to sleep through than those just ahead. But as he passed into the purple shadows, he had one more remark to make. When the Constitutional Convention met, he said, John Dickinson advised it, "Experience must be our only guide. Reason may mislead us." If truly we move in a cycle, Rip Van Winkle said, some day we shall get back to John Dickinson.

PERILS OF PAULINE THE Western Writers' Congress favors us with a specimen of a new art, an art which owes something to "The Perils of Pauline" but more to astrology. It sends us a copy of a telegram which it recently dispatched to Harcourt, Brace & Company.

EXECUTIVE COMMITTEE WESTERN WRITERS CONGRESS NOTES AN-NOUNCEMENT I COVER THE WORLD EDITED BY EUGENE LYONS CHAPTER ON RUSSIA BY WILLIAM HENRY CHAMBERLIN BOTH NOTORIOUS FOR ANTI SOVIET BIAS STOP WE PROTEST WHAT MUST INEVITABLY BE DISTORTION OF TRUE FACTS AND WILL REGISTER PROTEST PUBLICLY

Why stop there, with the buzzsaw half an inch from Pauline's soft throat? The Western Writers' Congress is unfair to the reading class. Fair practice and a minimum living honesty would require it to announce what statements in this book which it has not seen distort what facts.

Back Eddies

~~~~~~

THE MODERN
KEYHOLE

IMPROVEMENT in photography moves at a rapid rate. The ordinary snapshot film of commerce is eight times as fast as it was when you were a boy, and the highest speed plates are about twenty-four times as fast.[1] Emulsions sensitive to the whole visible spectrum and beyond can be bought at any drugstore. Large-aperture anastigmat lenses are produced by quantity methods cheaply enough for any purse. The cumbersome flash-gun is ancient history, the camera has shrunk from an armful to watch-fob size. Anyone can be a photographer; practically everyone is. . . . But practices older than dry plates have not lost their usefulness. A public convinced that pictures do not lie is an excellent medium for them to exercise creative imagination on. The retouching pencil that restores a blurred outline may go on to evoke anything that wasn't there when the picture was taken but would have added interest if it had been, composite printing can join together anything at all that bad luck has kept asunder, and

[1] This speed has been tripled since the editorial was written.

"montage" is by no means confined to the modernist's salon.

The methods of transmitting and reproducing photographs have also steadily improved. Transmission by wire or wireless is now commonplace. Fundamental improvements in halftone and gravure are developed about once in six months, and presses that were up to the minute five years ago are now well on the way to obsolescence. Whatever masterpiece the photographer may achieve by skill, luck, or cunning this morning, the printers are equipped to share it with millions of people this afternoon.

They are happy to share it. The public is insatiably interested in photographs, and neither newspapers nor magazines need ultraviolet light to bring out the handwriting on the wall. If in bilious moments the editor of this periodical wonders whether he is not really editing a puzzle page with occasional literary comment, he is aware that the editor of, say, *Scribner's* must sometimes pause waist-deep in candid shots and over-corrected telephotos of the Empire State Building to regret the golden days when he could think of fiction. The *Saturday Evening Post* runs a photographic cover, and the *Ladies' Home Journal* has a page of close-ups of chorus girls. And so on. Art magazines that give the vice crusaders insomnia snow the news-stands under, and this week a new periodical appeared with what must be a mathematically calculated combination of formulas. It is a technical magazine designed to help and instruct the new hordes of amateur photographers; it contains pictures of a raped and murdered girl and of a number of other girls in the shower bath, in their underclothes and doing strip acts; and it tells the amateur how these photographs were taken and how he may go and do likewise.

A well-turned blonde with some or all of her clothes off has always been news, of course, and has been advertising as well for just about twenty-five years. You remember the daring ad that began it all—showing mother, father, and Junior as jovial as could be in knitted union suits. Junior and father rapidly dropped out of that picture and pretty soon burial vaults and Portland cement were customarily advertised by means of a debutante in scanties. Now the scanties are gone; soaps, cosmetics, towels, and nearly everything else that can or can't be associated with a bathtub are advertised by the debutante clad only in an occasional patch of shadow. From the advertising to the editorial pages was just a step, barefooted, and there was a poignant moment when *Time* was scandalized by the discovery of some photographs of naked women in *Look*. It was negligent of *Life* to omit *Time's* editors from its free list.

Female nakedness and deshabille, however, though a fixed part of the formula of the newest journalism, are only a part of it. Another constant is the candid-camera shot, defined as any picture of anyone whose name is familiar to the customers, taken at a moment when he would resent, or would pretend to resent, its being taken. Less publicized people have to be freakish, maimed, monstrous, or grotesque to be worthy of candid treatment. Add a department in which more or less public figures may gratify their exhibitionistic impulses and which is designed to satisfy the *voyeur* in all of us. And finally a specialization, the most important part of the formula: photographs of the horrible, the terrifying, the cruel, and the disgusting. Shrewd editing tricks these out with captions which assure the reader that his interest in them is educational, that the death rate from cancer and reckless driving is thus cut down, and that journalism serves truth, science, freedom, and the future of democracy by showing how the corpse looked when the lynchers were through with it. This is yellow journalism, 1937 model, on crusade. Its old-fashioned, inane, Hearstian predecessor, which was sometimes thought to be debauching the public, lacked the modern keyhole that can be set at f:1.5.

Horror, cruelty, sensationalism, the undressed blonde, and the invasion of privacy mark the advance of the new picture journalism. The two new magazines which are rumored to be imminent must adopt the formula established by the two already on the market. *Life* differs from *Look* in that it has infinitely better paper and presswork, pays gifted literary people to write its captions, and has an annoying air of being at once smart, leering, censorious, and institutional. Both papers also serve, and serve splendidly, the far from novel function of photographing the news, but the big money is in the public's curiosity and nerves. Magazines which merely photograph the news can't get much beyond the fifty thousand mark, whereas a wounded gangster, a snake swallowing a giraffe, a dressmaker's model taking off her clothes, and a row of dismembered corpses bring us over a million. Beyond that is the delirious vision of the millions who can't read even the simplest words without needing aspirin but can read pictures, however sophisticated the process of producing them.

At a guess, the new journalism is a self-limited disease. The supply of people eager to be photograhed in any posture or costume is probably inexhaustible. But the other necessary subjects are not, and monotony, repetition, and the law of diminishing returns are bound to be a heavy drag. The body has only so many organs and only so many operations on them can be pictured; the animal creation is also limited and large parts of it cannot swallow other parts; after the beckoning vistas of vivisection, flogging, flaying, lynching, and mob panic have been traversed, further excursions even at cut rates will prove tiresome; it is the nature of nudity that it can be no farther undressed and has only a few bizarre aspects, leaving ingenuity with nothing to work on but the same old stuff. A paper that sets out to feed the public appetite for sensationalism must feed it ever increasing doses, which must end by building up an effective immunity. What provides a spinal shudder to-day will end by failing even to provoke a yawn. Blood, guts, rape, and the peephole will lose their voltage, and there will be only the news to fall back on.

Meanwhile no harm is being done. Except possibly to children. The fears and phantasies of childhood can be horribly snarled by such pictures as the new magazines publish, and you had better send your copies of them to the soldiers' home if you have children. But the public at large is not being damaged. Its taste for novelty is being gratified, which makes for order. Probably also its stomach muscles are being strengthened; a clear gain, for it will need strong ones before this novelty is exhausted.

AT THE CANNON'S MOUTH In the current *Harper's*, Mr. Dumas Malone climbs out on a long limb and names the forty most important Americans. Such lists are about as safe as fulminate caps but Mr. Malone is nonchalant about his for he has an answer to all howls: his criterion is the amount of space allotted to his forty immortals in *The Dictionary of American Biography*, which he edited. He has made some adjustments, presumably because the contributors did not always observe the space limits assigned to them, but he does not go beyond the original editorial calculus. Inside that original decision, his criterion is objective and makes an interesting yardstick for reputations in our era.

Mr. Malone's list contains eight men of letters, and their names show at once how relatively unstable literary reputation is. His twenty-three names from public life are all fixtures in history; at most only two of them are open to objection, and though our successors may rearrange the order in which they are listed they are not likely to amend the list. But the critical opinion that determined the space allotted to the eight authors has already become unacceptable. To-day's criticism would change both the names on the list and the order in which they are ranked. Mr. Malone lists them thus:

Emerson	Poe
Hawthorne	Thoreau
Mark Twain	Henry James
Whitman	Cooper

That is about where criticism stood when *The Cambridge History of American Literature* was written, except that Mark Twain has too high a place and Melville does not appear. Even at that time two of the judgments represented pure academic scholarship; they probably would not be accepted by such scholarship to-day and certainly would not be by the generality of educated opinion. To-day Cooper is hardly more than a textbook figure. The Leatherstocking books continue to be classics of boyhood, his other novels and his polemical works have a small but devoted following, and European scholarship is much engaged with him — but few critics or readers would name him among the first eight. Poe is important chiefly as a vested interest of professional scholars; he has been more widely and more exhaustively studied than any other American writer. But his importance ends with scholarship. Outside the vested interest hardly anyone would put him on such a list; hardly anyone would call him, except as a historical figure, a first-rater.

Fifteen years ago Whitman might well have been first on the list, except that the *Cambridge History* was a professorial undertaking, and that he may still be ranked fourth shows how great his reputation was at its crest. The crest came in the decade following 1910; through the Muckraking era and down to midafternoon of Greenwich Village he was at least three-fourths of American literature. For a number of reasons — his untraditional verse forms, his Bohemian mannerisms, his over-celebrated sexuality, and his offensiveness to the Philistines — he became a sacred symbol of revolt at a time when literature was rebelling on all fronts. The elegist of an America that was already dead when he wrote, he was strangely accepted as the prophet of an America then supposed to be at dawning. Most of those who quoted him in that glorious dayspring invariably quoted the same passages, and stopped quoting where the anthologies stopped; it is unlikely that anyone but Christopher Morley, Carl Van Doren, Louis Untermeyer,

and a few other *aficionados* had read all of his poetry or much
of his prose. Mr. Malone says that his reputation is increasing
but the evidence all points the other way.

Hawthorne is probably ranked too high on the list for to-
day's opinion, and Henry James and Thoreau are certainly
ranked too low. Thoreau's reputation is unique in American
literary opinion, in that it has grown steadily ever since his
death and continues to grow. A poll of intelligent opinion
to-day would probably advance him to third on such a list,
and it is a reasonable prophecy that he will rise still higher
in the future.

The first three places are the ones most interesting to play
with in this admittedly idle game of opinion. Mr. Malone is
right in naming Emerson first. He has not only held that place
in the past but he holds it now. Some years ago Mr. James
Truslow Adams asserted that Emerson's appeal was primarily
to adolescence, and that opinion is widespread, but it holds
only for the literary and ethical essays, and as they decline in
reputation other sides of his genius receive increased respect.
The Emerson of *Nature* and "Compensation" has faded somewhat; the Emerson of the poems and the Emerson of "Experience," "The Young American," and the *Journals* cast a longer
shadow than he ever did before. The Transcendentalist may
sink still farther, but the student of behavior and the analyst of
events may just be coming into his proper fame.

Emerson, Mark Twain, Thoreau; Thoreau, Emerson, Mark
Twain; Mark Twain, Thoreau, Emerson — one or another of
those groupings probably represents the average informed
opinion of this generation. Probably more qualified critics
would agree that these three are our top flight than could be
brought to agree on any other three. Is there not a marked gap
between this group and whichever names you care to list after
them?

Agreement about the next three would be much harder to
secure. Probably Hawthorne would get the most votes and

probably Poe would not get any. Many would place Henry James here, and some would protest his exclusion from the first three. The Melville boom, a product of his centennial and his usefulness as one more scourge for Philistine America, has apparently subsided; now that they can look at him dispassionately, most critics would probably put him in this group. Lowell does not appear on Mr. Malone's list at all, but a strong case can be made out for the first American critic of importance and the author of *The Biglow Papers*. Part of Emily Dickinson's earlier reputation was due to the fact that she too could be explained as an artist whom the brutish America had somehow impaired, but she has survived the enthusiasm of the rebellious decade much better than most. Howells is also a good bet for the long pull. He is more widely read to-day than Cooper (probably more than Poe also), and he has a historical importance at least as great. And Mr. Brooks may succeed in rehabilitating Dr. Holmes.

So much as a guess about reputations to-day. A personal opinion is something else. If asked to rank in order the eight most important American men of letters, the editor would decline on the ground that such ratings are meaningless. If forced to make one, he would confess that his preference for the first three is Mark Twain, Emerson, Thoreau, and would hastily add that he doesn't expect anyone to agree with him. Still protesting, he would list the others in this order:

Hawthorne
Henry James
Melville
Whitman
Lowell

The list is for to-day only and has no necessary relation to opinions its compiler held last year or may hold next year. Public notice: he will not debate it on this page or by letter.

OUR DRIED VOICES [1]   THE EDITOR is slow to disagree with a contributor so learned in her specialty as Mrs. Lutes, but he believes that Hostetter's Bitters had a bourbon rather than a rye base. The point is important for history, and the opinion of antiquarians is solicited. It may even be possible to appeal to fact. Dr. Miles's Indian Snake Root Remedy still works its healing, and perhaps the dark, fluted Hostetter bottle, with its label printed in 5-point, can still be bought by those who suffer from spots before the eyes, backache, dizziness, or sinking spells. Great as Hostetter's was in therapy, however, it was greater still as a preventive, and through a long life the editor's grandfather seldom went to bed without three fingers of it inside him to immunize him against the possible miasmas of the morrow. He, too, was a lifelong teetotaler. He knew how miserable rum makes human life and no misery afflicted him when, the evening jolt of Hostetter's glowing in him, he tipped back in his chair beside the sitting-room stove and hummed "The brewer's big horses" or recited:

Not for myself do I come here now; *I* could suffer on, alone — I come for my fatherless children, helpless and starving at home; Starving because their father for liquor sold his life. Thank God for the Adair Liquor Law! the friend of the drunkard's wife.

Children, how many of you know what the Adair Liquor Law was? Just about as many, at a guess, as have worn the Daisy White Bronze Braided Bustle, which Mrs. Lutes mentions, or the Pompadour Porte-Joupe or Dress Elevator, which she doesn't mention. This was a belt from which hung eight cords that ended in loops. The loops went over buttons sewn inside the hems of various skirts, and there was a master cord which came out over the belt and which could be hauled in by the wearer when she reached a muddy crossing. Modesty

[1] See also "Friday Afternoon at Country Day."

is all very well but nobody wants to bring mud into the house on six petticoats at once.

Well, how many of you, on Friday afternoons, have stood up before the seventh grade and recited "The Psalm of Life" or "The Rainy Day"?

> Be still, sad heart, and cease repining;
> Behind the clouds is the sun still shining.
> Thy fate is the common fate of all;
>   Into each life some rain must fall,
> Some days must be dark and dreary.

Poor simple sentimentalists, equally absurd in their easy tears and their silly courage. We have got past all that. Yellow flows as readily as blue used to, and the seventh grade is probably full to the bung with the brave modern spirit, telling one another:

> Our dried voices, when
> We whisper together
> Are quiet and meaningless
> As wind in dry grass
> Or rats' feet over broken glass
> In our dry cellar.

Our ancestors were pretty funny.

Mrs. Lutes could have mentioned a lot more literature. The editor did not grow up on the Southern Peninsula (*si quaeris peninsulam amoenam circumspice*) but he did grow up amidst that poetry. The young Della must have thumbed through annuals and gift books left over from her mother's day, and probably owned such paper-backs of her own day as *One Hundred Choice Selections*, which was arranged by one Phineas Garrett, sold for fifteen cents, and began a series of the same name which ran to heaven knows how many numbers. Mr. Mark Sullivan has decided that William McGuffey formed the tastes and shaped the minds of millions of nineteenth-century Americans, and the docile spirits who tell us about

American literature take Mr. Sullivan on faith. But if you look
for the literature that those Americans quoted, deliberately or
unconsciously, you will find that the greater part of it was
barred from McGuffey. The McGuffey influence on our culture, in fact, is mostly a boom phenomenon of collectors' enthusiasm and the sectional pride of the Middle West. The millions knew much more literature than McGuffey ever taught
them. You could learn to love honesty and thrift in the Fifth
Reader but you couldn't learn to love much else. The passion
for pure art, the noble lust for literature, was best fed by the
annuals and the anthologies.

There was a lot of tears and mourning, drunken fiends,
tubercular maidens, noble farmers, and dying warriors in that
literature, but the important thing is, as Mrs. Lutes says, that
it was declaimed. . . . "At midnight in his guarded tent, The
Turk lay dreaming of the hour" — if you don't think that can
be resounding, close the windows and try it. By the time you
get to "Strike for your altars and their fires! Strike for the
green graves of your sires! God and your native land!" someone will be pounding on the floor above you. (A lesser generation may need to be notified that "Strike" has nothing to do
with picketing.) A biography of this autumn has shown us
one of the most cultivated of Americans, John Jay Chapman,
quoting on his deathbed from "Bingen on the Rhine." Such a
sanction may set some of the literary to researching in their
origins. Let us hope that they do not miss Fontenoy ("Thrice,
at the huts of Fontenoy, the English column failed"), or the
upper Tennessee ("Move my arm chair, faithful Pompey, In
the sunshine bright and strong"), or the name which the Muse
of History, dipping her pen in the sunlight, will write in the
clear blue above Washington's. But perhaps this is jingoism.
Well, oppressed, "if we must fight, let us fight for ourselves!
If we must slaughter, let us slaughter our oppressors! If we
must die, let it be under the clear sky, by the bright waters, in
noble, honorable battle!"

Lots of class struggle in that literature. And our forbears shed tears over "Give me three grains of corn, Mother, Only three grains of corn." Two generations before a recent genius wept to see a Vermont child eating roast woodchuck (but ask Elliot Paul, cook and gourmet, who knows that woodchucks are garden-fed game) their tears rose to,

> I could get no more employment;
>   The weather was bitter cold,
> The young ones cried and shivered —
>   (Little Johnny's but four years old) —
> So what was I to do, sir?
>   I am guilty, but do not condemn,
> I *took* — oh, was it *stealing?* —
>   The bread to give to them.

They were anti-fascists too. Try Bob Ingersoll's vision at Napoleon's tomb. Bob decided that he would rather have lived in a hut with a vine growing over the door and the grapes growing purple in the kisses of the autumn sun, and gone down to the tongueless silence of the dreamless dust than to have been that imperial impersonation of force and murder. On Friday afternoon our fathers agreed with him.

We had a serious point to make, before this nostalgia attacked us: that the whole course of American literature before our own time was affected by this declamation. We will come back to that, for we promise you that it is important and has been too little taken into account. At the moment, however, we can't get past the text to the moral. Mrs. Lutes has made us think of the Blue and the Gray, little brown hands ("They drive home the cows from the pasture"), the Leak in the Dike (which is always misquoted), and Belzoni's mummy ("Then say what secret melody was hidden, In Memnon's statue, which at sunrise played").

They were a vain and tawdry folk, our ancestors. They didn't put the Oedipus Complex into their poetry. How does "My son's wife, Elizabeth" go?

THE TEST FROM last week's Bowling Green: "Joe Miller,
OF TIME for whom the Jest Book was named, died 200
years ago this year. Has anyone ever seen the book itself? It's
probably terrible." Also from last week's Bowling Green:
"Gesso, we learned from our favorite pangnostic, Old Bill
Benét, is the artist's word for gypsum: a sort of scholar-
gypsum."

Why, yes, we've seen *Joe Miller's Jests: or The Wit's Vade-
Mecum*, and, in spite of the evidence, are willing to accept the
Bowling Green's assurance that Mr. Morley has not. The title
page describes it as "A Collection of the most Brilliant JESTS;
the Politest REPARTEES; the most Elegant BON MOTS,
and most pleasant short Stories in the *English* Language." The
two editor's vade-mecums on our desk disagree about its authorship. One fathers it on John Mottley, a lugubrious dramatist. The other ascribes it to Joe Miller himself, a minor actor
at Drury Lane, who is traditionally supposed to have been
illiterate and to have learned his sides by having them read to
him. But what the title page says is "First carefully collected
in the Company, and many of them transcribed from the
Mouth of the Facetious GENTLEMAN, whose Name they
bear; and now set forth and published by his lamentable friend
and former Companion, *Elijah Jenkins*, Esq."

The book is inscribed "*To those* CHOICE SPIRITS *of the*
AGE, Captain BODENS, Mr. ALEXANDER POPE, Mr.
Professor LACY, Mr. Orator HENLEY, and JOB BARKER,
the Kettle-Drummer." It was "Printed and Sold by T. READ,
in *Dogwell-Court, White-Fryars, Fleet-Street*." It was published in 1739, the year after Joe Miller's death, and at once
secured his immortality. How many times it was reprinted
during the next hundred years, pirated, counterfeited, no one,
probably, has ever counted. A collection at Widener Library
which makes no pretense of being complete must number
scores. There are Joe Millers of every age and kind, even
American ones — with Daniel Boone uttering quips in balanced

St. James's prose which Joe attributed to Congreve but which had reached the Phoenicians at second hand. Witty *ripostes* which Miller put in Dryden's mouth, ignorant that Aristophanes had once had Aeschylus say them, are mentioned as originating among the wits who gathered at Pfaff's, our first Village Café — Fitz-James O'Brien, George Morris, a dozen other mad wags when there was another new day in American literature.

It is too bad that "Joe Miller" has come to mean such a pun as we quote from Mr. Morley. For the point about the immortal Jest Book is not that it collected some bad jokes but that it dipped into the common pool of the world's humor and proved that it exists outside of time altogether. Nothing is older than a joke and there are neither new jokes nor invented ones. "Old Maeonides the blind said it three thousand years ago," not Mr. Kaufman or Miss Parker this morning, and he was innocently quoting his ancestors when he said it. It was good then and it's good now. When we have worn it to shreds it will lapse to the comedians who fill in between the strip-tease acts at the burlesque show (where all jokes are good and demonstrate the survival of the fittest), and when the Apollo Theater is done with it, it will turn up in the works of Robert Forsythe, where it will still be good.

It was Doctor Johnson who, being asked to make a pun extempore, inquired "Pun what subject?" and, when the King suggested, said, "The King, Sir, is no subject." Was it? The first edition of Joe Miller ascribes the latter half to "Daniel Purcel, the famous Punster." Oldsters among you will remember Bert Leston Taylor's long pursuit of the Valve-Handle Wheeze, the letter of complaint to which a postscript is appended noting that the valve-handle has been found. B. L. T. knew that the wheeze had originated with the dawn-man and classified its variations by genera and species. Joe Miller's number 47 reads: "An *Irish* Lawyer of the *Temple*, having occasion to go to Dinner, left these Directions written, and put in the Key-Hole of his Chamber-Door, *I am gone to the* Elephant *and* Castle, *where you shall find me;* and if *you can't read this Note, carry it down to the Stationer's, and he will read it for you.*" That is a mutation of the Valve-Handle Wheeze, and it was scratched on clay and brushed on papyrus before the time of Meonides. It is also, if you prefer a different taxonomy, a species of Irish bull, but who made the bulls before they were Irish?

Why yes, the Jest Book is "terrible." But one has a recurrent notion that the most terrible jokes are the best ones — like the common people whom Lincoln (and who else?) said God must love, since He had made so many of them. If a terrible joke isn't a good one why do people like it so much, why does it outlast the diuturnity of our reliques, why does it carry an April freshness from Noah's time to ours? Stop us if you've heard Joe Miller's number 82: "Two gentlemen disputing about Religion, in *Button's Coffee-House,* said one of them, I wonder, Sir, you should talk of Religion, when I'll hold you five Guineas you can't say the *Lord's Prayer,* done, said the other, and Sir *Richard Steele* shall hold stakes. The Money being deposited, the Gentleman began with *I believe in God,* and so went cleverly thro' the *Creed;* well, said the other, I own I have lost; *I did not think he could have done it.*" This item furnishes the revues with half-a-dozen blackouts a year, always wowing the audience, and the editors had a fine time with it recently when Mr. Roosevelt remarked that the Constitution guaranteed everyone the right to the pursuit of happiness.

Number 22: "A Gentleman eating some Mutton that was very tough, said, it put him in Mind of an old *English* Poet; Being asked who that was; *Chau — cer,* replied he." That is a gesso story for the Bowling Green, which should cheerfully abide the violence to its favorite poet. Number 103: "The Emperor *Augustus,* being shewn a young *Grecian,* who very much resembled him, asked the young Man if his *Mother* had not been in *Rome;* No, Sir, answered the *Grecian* but my *Father* has." That one has rippled through history since the first tribes stormed the Caucasus and they whisper it in Rome to-day about a ten-cent emperor. Probably the Bowling Green has found it in Troy, and you may test your upbringing by spotting it in the Old Testament. Number 232 has floated just as freely through literature, with its dying squire telling his coachman that he was setting out on the longest journey he had ever taken and the coachman reassuring him that it was all downhill. Joe Miller's mild bawdry, too, is but something he accepted from the ages with one hand and passed on to us with the other. If the burleycues and the revues dramatize dozens of his anecdotes every year, Mr. Peter Arno can recognize his own handiwork in number 164, and *Esquire* would have to run at least four blank pages a month if number 108 should be forbidden the mails.

There are no property rights in jokes. They are literature's communism, as free to all of us as the weather, as much a part of the common wealth. Just once in Joe Miller's book one wishes that this were not so, and that it were truly Rabelais who, after receiving Extreme Unction, said that he was ready for his journey now, since "they have just greased my boots." Joe Miller, number 26: one more wheeze, one more immortal bad joke. There are a lot of them like that, in Joe Miller and in other repositories of legend, nonchalant but not too original defiances flung at the dark from deathbeds. This one unquestionably originated when the darkness gathered outside a Dordogne cave, but it should have been Rabelais's, who loved equally bad jokes and the eternal, as if he found them — and the darkness — a little difficult to distinguish.

ABOUT-FACE OF MR. STEARNS It would be easy to allude to the joy in heaven, and possibly also in Rotary, as the compiler of *Civilization in the United States* goes on developing his conviction that civilization is now practically synonymous with the United States. It would even be enough to allude to that repentance if Mr. Harold Stearns, while reversing his opinions, continued to have them in sets. Mr. Stearns was he who christened the Young Intellectual and it was the Young Intellectual who, for the most part, established the points of view and findings of American literature during the 1920's. A type-characteristic of the Young Intellectual was that he had his ideas in sets, and another one was that he acquired them by deduction from General Ideas and the Good Life and by a process of mystical illumination which was set in motion by prolonged navel-gazing. The same process may lead just as easily to equally absurd ideas which fit each other with the same neatness and economy but are colored with pearl and rose. But as Mr. Stearns's *America, a Re-Appraisal* carries his escape from the Left Bank into a third volume, it becomes evident he is repudiating the methods as well as the findings of his critical generation.

But not altogether. Having spun much of his denunciation out of sheer theory, he spins much of his hope and praise from the same gossamer, and time after time he rushes happily, as before, into the fallacy of insufficient example, creating a triumph of universal benevolence out of what most of us would call only a pleasing incident, just as he once found the collapse of moral values in what was obviously just a bit of police-court news. This is not a happy moment, what with the General Motors Strike and the La Follette Committee, to announce that corporate hostility to labor is on its way out. In deciding that the depression extended the social reach and realism of medicine, it might have been well to inquire first how far it also extended the scope of chiropractic and mail-order therapy. While rejoicing over the disappearance of certain mass fads and hysterias, it is unwise to ignore the appearance of as many new ones. And so on.

Also, much that delights Mr. Stearns and his fellow convertites is far from news. The fact that he is now willing to see what is squarely before his eyes, however, is important as marking a realistic advance in criticism. It is pleasant to have the intellectuals concede the existence of the American family, though its existence is hardly a stop-press flash to anyone who reads the life-insurance statistics. It is also pleasant to be informed by a person of Mr. Stearns's intellectual history, hardly a century and a half after the mold for books by visiting foreigners was set, that a great many Americans have good nerves and good dispositions, that on the whole we are an exuberant, music-loving, sport-loving, joke-loving people devoted to arts and crafts and games, that we are energetic and hopeful and confident, that we are addicted to neighborliness and co-operative self-help, that you can find much tolerance and self-criticism among the Americans, that our democratic modes remain flexible, responsive, and sensitively adaptable to change. But such a recognition, though it repeals much that the intellectuals have said, does not matter of itself. An important question is suggested: having accepted a lot of plain facts, are they willing to accept the implications also? All right, the American family is not breaking up, it is instead a social mechanism of enormous power — so what? All right, we have a vigorous native culture which works according to its own interior organization, not according to principles deduced from radically different organizations — where do we go from here? Are the intellectuals willing to adjust their ideas to such facts?

Mr. Stearns seems willing to. If parts of his book are just self-generated optimism and other parts merely a belated acceptance of the obvious, there are still other parts which begin a new analysis of American institutions and mechanisms based on the incorporation of such important facts. What Mr. Stearns has to say about politics and especially about business shows that he is now engaged with energies of fundamental importance. Nothing could be more favorable for a description of how America actually works. We cannot expect useful description from critics who are committed to their findings in advance — whose dogmas promise us that profits are evil and therefore doomed, that the business system is headed toward communism by way of war and fascism, that businessmen are just fools, bunglers, and crooks, and that the rest is doomsday. But if liberals truly are people whose minds are open to evidence and who are willing to pursue an inquiry regardless of where the facts may lead, then the present tendency of Mr. Stearns's thinking is a favorable omen. It is an astonishing fact that the actual social liaisons of business have been completely ignored by literary people and almost as completely by everyone else. Just how much first-hand help the literary can give such pioneers as Elton Mayo and T. N. Whitehead is not clear. But they may be able to give them some help, and they can act valuably as interpreters of them to the troubled radicals and to the general public. There, if you please, is a promising avenue to the much-desired rewriting of American sociology. Mr. Stearns's book more than occasionally suggests that he is prepared to venture down this new path unchaperoned by metaphysics or eschatology.

Overlooking the Campus

"STERCORACEOUS PERHAPS you do not understand the
COMMENT" phrase. It is a scholarly euphemism
which is intended humorously and enables a learned writer
in *PMLA* to convey a four-letter meaning without commit-
ting vulgarity. Perhaps you do not know what *PMLA* is.
Well, in bilious moments it has been referred to as the trade
journal of the literary embalming business, but apt as that
description may sometimes be, it is not always just. *PMLA*
is a quarterly publication of the Modern Language Association, to which most American professors of language and
literature belong. The ideal it sets itself is the publication
of studies too learned or too profound to find print in the
journals of commerce which must nevertheless be permanently
added to our culture and made available to generations of students yet unborn. Unhappily it gets too few chances to act
upon its ideal. Permanent additions to our culture are uncom-
mon, and when one occurs commercial editors and publishers
are prone to snap it up. The result is that *PMLA* tends to be

filled with articles of pure scholarship by people who have acquired a technique of research and must use it, articles which seldom have any relation to literature and which are read only by scholars on a busman's holiday. Publication in it counts ten, twenty-five, fifty, or a hundred when a young instructor has been told to publish something for the head of the department to show the dean, or when the dean is looking for someone to fill a vacant assistant professorship. Such efforts may be pious but they do not add to life's benignancy.

The phrase quoted as the title of this sermon occurs in the September number of *PMLA*, in an article called "The Analysis of Literary Situation" by Mr. Carl E. W. L. Dahlström. Mr. Dahlström uses it to describe the verdict of criticism on *The Thirty-Six Dramatic Situations* of Georges Polti, a work intended as erudite analysis of literature but long since forgotten except as one more item which correspondence schools in the writing of the short story may sell to their suckers. Polti's destiny seems harsh and pitiful to Mr. Dahlström, and with a fine impatience he sets out to carry the work in which Polti pioneered toward a happier, more comprehensive, and more scientific conclusion. His object is to determine the total number of esthetic situations available to writers. What is an esthetic situation? One "is born of a conflict between two principal directions of endeavor." A conflict must have something to do with force and Mr. Dahlström finds that there are five kinds, or as he prefers to say, categories, of forces. They are the physical, the organic, the social, the egoic, and the divine, which he will designate P, O, S, E, D. If you are going to write a poem, a story, or a play, you must necessarily deal with a situation in which these forces are arrayed against themselves or against one another in various combinations. Mark this profundity, however, "The isolation of forces is achieved in the laboratory of the mind rather than in literature. We do not find literature pertaining to man solely as molecular structure; but, on the contrary, things of molecular structure may be personified. So, too, with the other forces; and when we have a character in literature he is frequently an agglomeration of molecules, protoplasm, socius, ego, and soul. Each man is an hypostasis of all, and the differences among men rest in the dominance or weakness of particular forces."

Well, the simple formula $P \longleftrightarrow O$ gives contention between physical and organic, which might be a doe swimming in a river, or $P \longleftrightarrow P'$, contention between physical and physical, as the raindrop wearing away the stone. Let the doe be wounded by a hunter and we have $PS \longleftrightarrow O$, for "an aggregate of forces may be on one side of the line of opposition with a unit or a similar (or different) aggregate of forces on the other side." Again, "instead of arranging forces in positions indicating successively weaker governance by each, we may devise means of indicating parallel strength," as $P(OS)E \longleftrightarrow D(OS)P$, which gives Ixion's wheel or a delayed buck behind a running guard.

After a series of complicated mathematical distributions, including correction of the basic formula to allow for duplicated oppositions, Mr. Dahlström arrives at this equation:

$$N_2 \ (nPr) \ (mP'q) - \frac{(mP'q) \ (mP'q) - (mP'q)}{2}$$

A number of subsidiary equations which cannot be reproduced here are required before he comes to his grand climax, the triumphant issue of his research. Only five categories exist and when n is equal to 5, there are exactly 52,975 different "arrangements of situational forces," which "will represent fundamentally different situations if the n factors are basically different, and if position in aggregates of forces indicates primary, secondary, or weaker stress in a given opposition. If, on the contrary, the n factors are fundamentally similar, the 52,-975 arrangements will in great part represent situations which are not basically different."

That is algebra's latest contribution to our knowledge of literature. Mr. Dahlström indicates its usefulness, saying that his calculation "has one important role to play in the discussion of literary esthetics: it points to the infinite variety that is available for the artist." You may have needed that pointer, and surely the artist will be reassured.

This is what happens when the *Minderwertigkeit* of literary scholarship seeks to assuage itself with science. Some honest minds are betrayed into it by logic: the "best" knowledge is exact knowledge, only the sciences are exact, therefore the study of literature had better be scientific. Others retreat into it because of incompetence: unable to deal with literature as an art, they console themselves with a parade of spurious scientific method and terminology. And everyone who does makes the future of literary scholarship more precarious, for he turns a few more intelligent candidates for the doctorate from the English Department to the Department of History.

Neither Mr. Dahlström's results nor even his effort has any meaning. No one who ever wrote a poem began by wondering if all the permutations had been used up. No one ever read, enjoyed, or criticized a poem with the algebra of permutations in mind. No one would get anywhere if he did, as Mr. Dahlström makes clear. His grand conclusion, that a writer has a lot of things to write about, hardly needed algebra and hardly gains from it. His further notes, applying his study to *As You Like It* and other works, are elementary truisms within the capacity of any freshman and have no relation whatever to the square root of minus one.

The writer of these lines is a member of the Modern Language Association and his dues are paid up. By reason of many years' enlistment in the cause it serves, he feels a fraternal affection even for its aberrations. But he wishes that it would sometimes stop considering literary scholarship an end in itself — that it would sometimes move on to the synthesis and criticism toward which all such scholarship is at best only a preliminary step. That may be too much to ask. Scholars capable of more than the preliminary step may be too hard to find, and *PMLA* may have to devote itself chiefly to an endless exhibition of scholarly technique forever detached from the objectives that are supposed to justify it. But surely it need not print and circulate absurdity for absurdity's sake alone. . . . Mr. Dahlstrôm, however, gives us leave to hope. He complains that not many scholars can be interested in mathematical esthetics. Thanks; and no wonder.

THE FACULTY A FEW weeks ago an article by a college teacher of literature came to this office on a morning when we were sending to the printer an article on the same subject by a professional writer. The sharp contrast between them was everywhere in favor of the professional but was most marked in the writing itself. The professor's article was fifty per cent longer than its content justified. It was ponderous, torpid, opaque, rambling, diluted. There were no incorrect case forms and no verbs at variance with their subjects, but fully half of the sentences were inept enough to rouse an English A instructor's passions. They strayed away from their original objectives, or they bogged down in vague and abstract polysyllables, or they frayed out in that maddening indefiniteness which permits the writer to believe that he has said something, perhaps something pretty acute, when he has actually said nothing at all. It was a villainous bit of writing. Our reviewers are never permitted to write so badly and, sending it back, we wanted to inclose with it a copy of the theme manual used at its author's university.

It started us thinking: as its author would say, it gave us furiously to think. Many English teachers write well or even brilliantly; we use some two dozen of that species as reviewers in this magazine. But for every one who writes well, and for every two who write acceptably, there must be from ten to fifty who write abominably. We turned to the latest issue of *PMLA*, the house organ of the Modern Language Association, which chance had confided to the same mail. For years that quarterly has served us as a restorative whenever we have felt that our mental powers might be waning, but we have never before read it with an eye to style. So from now on we are going to attribute at least twenty per cent of the anesthesia of *PMLA* to sheer bad writing. Look at it yourself: it is the most hopeless kind of prose, flabby but resistant, without grain or crystalline structure, amorphous, gelatinous, verbose, tautological, inert. If worse writing regularly gets published in the United States, the periodicals that contain it do not exchange with the *Saturday Review*.

Yet the people who write that gruel are the people who give college courses in writing. Whenever we visit a college, we find the English Department in a mood of soul-searching and dismay because the undergraduates aren't ambitious to write great novels or five-act dramas in blank verse. The profs are always asking one another why their students don't write better, why more novelists and poets don't sprout under the local elms, what can be done to create a "climate" favorable to the excitements and enthusiasms of literature, how alma mater can best fan such sparks of literary talent as from time to time blow in with the freshman class. Their concern is genuine — and it is pathetic. But it almost never gets intense and intelligent enough to do the most obvious and hopeful thing, which is to scrutinize the local courses in composition.

Here and there, in isolated instances, in this college or that one, the teaching of composition is strikingly better than it was a generation ago. But it remains pretty bad on the average. Bad? Dreadful, scandalous, sometimes unspeakable. If there are a dozen colleges in the United States which do not assume that anyone can teach composition and that the feeblest members of the department can be most usefully occupied in teaching it, if there are six colleges where the teacher of composition is not looked down on by his colleagues and kept permanently in the junior ranks, we have somehow missed them in our travels, which have been pretty extensive. The boys mourn because they don't seem to be producing a decent quota of the nation's novelists, but they continue to staff their courses in writing with the people who write the stuff that *PMLA* prints.

Not all this frustration is due to the contempt of predestinate genitive-counters, which is a thinly masked suspicion and envy. Some educators have held that training in writing must be regarded as "professional" and must therefore be confided to the graduate schools. That is theoretically profound but the slightest experience of writing, or of undergraduate illiteracy, destroys the theory. Other presidents, deans, and department chairmen sincerely believe that writing cannot be taught; and, if it can't be, there is no sense in spending money, care, or thought on the courses that perfunctorily try to teach it. But that idea is simple nonsense. Or academic nonsense.

No one can make a novelist or a poet out of a college student whom an all-wise providence has designed to be a professor of education; no composition teacher can add the twentieth part of a cubit to any literary talent. But any intelligent student can be taught to say clearly and decently what he wants to say, which is more than the average English professor, if *PMLA* represents him, has ever learned. And any student who has literary talent can be helped on his way — can be taught many things that will implement his talent, draw it out, mature it, and help it to work free of its earliest contradictions and impediments.

A period of apprenticeship is an excellent thing for any artist. If a writer can get it in college, so much the better. But you have to apprentice a writer to a writer. The particular skill he is trying to learn can be learned only from someone who has that skill. Only one kind of person can teach a college student how to be a writer: a person who is himself a writer. Writers have been there; they have learned how to do the job. Looking at a student's manuscript, they know in their nerves and by the patterns of professional experience what is wrong with it, what must be done to make it better, how the next job can best take off from where this one leaves off. They can communicate their knowledge because it consists of experience — and that is how writing can be taught. The occasional exception, a Copey or a Dean Briggs, is an inspired teacher — and there are no rules about inspiration.

The simple first step, then, in any program to improve the teaching of composition at a college, is to hire writers to do it. Every time a poet or a novelist is taken into an English faculty the situation improves by just that much, but there are still far too few of them. The next step is to realize and acknowledge that such teaching is just as valuable as any other in the department of English, that it is probably more difficult to do and certainly harder to get. This will require teachers of literature and scholarly method to abate their contempt, whether of their own impulse or with outside help. Literary talent, of itself alone, does not necessarily make a man inferior to scholars whose business is to lecture about it.

The literary climate so much desired will prove to be a function of literary people. It consists only of like-minded people, undergraduates and their elders, who are interested in literature from within rather than from without, and who like to get together and talk shop, discussing their common problems. The colleges will have more of it when they make room for people who are not only interested in the arts but actually practise them as well. If you want to produce writers at alma mater, you have got to have some writers there for the undergraduates to make friends with. Judging by the products that the trade journal prints, alma mater hasn't many of them on hand just now.

EPPUR SI
MOVE!
How easily it might have got lost in the flood of beautifully printed pamphlets that reach this desk! It might have been mistaken for one more announcement of one more unneeded subscription edition of one more third-

rate author's collected works, or of one more collection of Persian erotica sold only to physicians, lawyers, serious students, and those who have the price. But it wasn't, for the great tidings got home. "For the first time," the prospectus says, "the fundamental principles of writing obeyed by ALL successful authors of the past or present, have been arranged logically in a code of universal laws." That, then, was why the earth swerved a little and the planets strained their bonds, what time the Perseids fell. Tidings of desolation ran on the wires from all over Europe and beyond, but in America a loftier Argo cleft the main. Copernicus was born, or this was Newton, this was Galileo in 12-point Bodoni, young talent might hope at last, critics might lay away their bludgeons, and the world's great age begin anew.

"The fundamental principles of writing obeyed by ALL successful authors of the past or present have been arranged logically in a code of universal laws." Something a little ominous in that "code" perhaps, some suggestion of a legal assembly, or some faint echo of the phrase "crack down" — but no matter. It is, of course, "for the first time," but one is moved to envious emulation. It may be a fundamental principle of writing that all successful authors must make marks on paper with pen or pencil or typewriter, or on parchment or papyrus with a brush, or on clay or wax with a stylus, or on stone with a chisel, or on metal with a graving tool. But no, there was Henry James, who just talked to an amanuensis; and there is Mr. Oppenheim who talks to four of them, and the geniuses of the improbable Hollywood who talk directly through a vacuum tube to celluloid.

Well, can it be a fundamental principle that what you write must carry some meaning? The hypothesis so eagerly advanced must be at once abandoned before the brigade of specimens that leap to mind. Then that the words you put together must make sentences? No, Miss Stein is a successful author both past and present. Then that what you put in sentences must be words? No, chromatic steams swirl in *Transition's* laboratory and Edward Lear is born again in eerie syllables that speak for the unconscious to the unconscious and display a curious fondness for the letter *o*, suggestive of wind on the vowels. Then surely it is a fundamental principle that the art of writing is so repulsive that all writers thank God for any noise in the street or any telephone call which will reprieve them from the desk. It is a universal law that all writers will count the spots on the wall paper rather than begin to write. But no: this leaves altogether out of account the poetess and the man who has found a misprint on this page. They love to write.

Clearly, that effort to follow Galileo's plow gets us nowhere and we must try another tack. Well, all authors of the past and present are uninterested in what reviewers say about their work and merely paste their clippings in scrapbooks to appease the antiquarian interests of their children. Surely that is as fixed as $\frac{gt^2}{2}$ and we may press on to another principle: it is a universal law that writers write not selfishly or for themselves alone, but only that their thought may find its way to print and so to the elevation of other minds. But even one exception will destroy a universal, and comes now the Macmillan Company with this season's fairest rose of all publicity releases. Here is an author who writes solely for her private amusement, sends her book out only because she envies a friend's quaint privilege of boasting that *his* book has been rejected by every publisher in America, and has to be pursued by half the office force, lassoed and hobbled, forcibly subdued, and blackjacked into a contract. In the presence of that honey, that twenty-four carat, twenty-one jewel nifty, the search for universals must be abandoned to Galileo. He has avenues to truth which our earth-bound feet can never travel.

His lot may be difficult, though, for the septic world distrusts genius and may put him to the torture chamber, from which one sees him emerging to raise his bloody head again and mutter, "They are STILL universal laws." Or now that we move toward national planning, will the threat of a new monopoly pass unchallenged? Galileo is the head of a school for writers and there are thousands of people in his trade. Technological unemployment stares them in the face for, like the Rust cotton picker, this discovery will make them obsolete, victims of the advance of science that no hand can stay. Riots break out in the street, the constabulary charge throwing tear bombs, and a march on Washington is halted only when a flash comes that Rex Tugwell will head a resettlement commission to provide subsistence teaching till the new literature of abundance is established.

But we are assured that the advance of technology does not decrease employment permanently. Presently, after a short time-lag, the displaced vendors of fiction formulae will become vendors of fiction, literary agents for the greatly increased production of authors. The discovery of the fundamental principles of writing obeyed by ALL writers and their arrangement in a code of universal laws — you cannot keep the news of that mousetrap from spreading. Already millions of aspirants must be beating a path by telegram to Galileo's door. The hesitant and the unconfident need delay no longer. Writing ceases to be a hazardous occupation; the laws are universal and have been codified. How do you know you can't write? This is the neotechnic age: you learned how to drive an automobile, didn't you? Lights burn past midnight in a million studies, fiction is on a rising curve, smoke pours from the nation's chimneys, the dinner pail is full, and the American renaissance begins at last. Market tip: play Mergenthaler for a rise.

But observe how precarious is the equilibrium of this complex world, how a new industry may be paralyzed, how a renaissance may be sandbagged by reactionary holdovers from the horse-and-buggy days. Some skeptic, some literary royalist, some vestigial individualist with silk hat rushes to the protection of privilege and the old order. The way is cleared before his suit, which rises rapidly through the hierarchy of our legal system, and the code of universal laws reaches the Supreme Court. What, in that hour of decision, what will the nine old men do?

THE AMERICAN SCHOLAR   THIS is the season when associations of learned men hold their trade conventions. The editor is off to Providence to instruct his betters in the writing of history but wishes he could also be at Richmond, where the Modern Language Association will convene shortly after this issue comes from the press. Some twelve or fourteen hundred professors of literature, a formidable cultural bloc, will assemble there to consider their professional problems, exhibit their skills, and take counsel for the future.

The happiest of them will be the phoneticians. They will have their movie films of the vocal cords in action, their X-ray plates which catch the teeth and palate in the very act of forming *z*, their timers and metronomes and pendulums and spark gaps and fluoroscopes which stalk the heartbeat and the breath, their graphs, maps, tables of statistics, slide rules, phonograph records, and tuning forks. Spontaneous ecstasies will arise and spread among them, as among the saved at camp meetings, and in the anterooms off the convention hall you will see them dashing up to one another, thrusting flashlights down their throats, and murmuring round them, "Watch me say *vtk*." Much of their contentment will spring from the honest fascination of their toys, and from the knowledge that if their job isn't scientific, at least it is nearer science than you can get anywhere else in the *M.L.A.* But part of it, one suspects, comes from a realization that, thank God, they aren't forced to waste any time on literature.

But the most vigorous group will be the American Literature section. In the last twenty years, and especially in the last ten years, this once humble stepchild of literary scholarship has had an amazing development. It has not only reached a parity with the other departments but, in the opinioɩ of the editor at leas:, is now doing the most humane and most valuable research that the *M.L.A.* can show, is dealing with literature in the most consistently intelligent way, and has the most promising future ahead of it. Its publication, *American Literature*, is more interesting and more steadily concerned with literary values than *PMLA*, the dissertations it supervises are on the average more important than those devoted to English literature, and the whole climate it works in is vigorous and stimulating. The scholar in American literature has a new confidence as well as enthusiasm and he is free of an emotional conflict which, as it appears in the English scholar, the editor asks leave to diagnose as a sense of guilt.

A number of causes unite to produce this eupepsia. For one thing the insurgents have succeeded in somewhat relaxing the philological requirements for the doctor's degree in American literature, and so are able to attract more candidates who are interested in literature as an art and have a natural feeling for it. For another the body of American literature resists the pursuit of sources, influences, and parallels which has enfeebled research in English literature and made it too often a merely mechanical exhibition of scholarly technique in which even the lowliest minds can engage.

More important is the fact that there is still room in American literature for a scholar to find a subject that interests him, whereas English literature has been sifted and resifted so often that the whole problem comes down to finding a subject that no one else has worked with. The only subjects left are tenth-rate authors or worthless aspects of more important ones and even these subjects are being rapidly exhausted, so that the dissertation of the future is likely to be a mere gloss on earlier dissertations. But in American literature there are still some first-rate literary figures quite unquarried by scholarship and whole battalions of second-rate and third-rate figures who can be studied with interest and profit. The scholar can work directly with literature, with literature of importance, and with literature as an organic integration rather than as a detached or vestigial fragment.

Again, in American literature the opportunities for archeology and philology are limited, and the scholar is encouraged, even forced, to deal at first hand with esthetics and history. This forced alliance with history not only invigorates the scholar but is producing a new, fruitful, and very promising kind of literary scholarship — a development which at last brings the academic study of literature back into touch with the study of it in the world outside. The American scholar to-day is a social historian, and taps the vitality of his own social inheritance. The "influences" which he studies are not the alleged, inconceivable borrowings of one literary person from another that make so much literary research absurd, but the social and intellectual linkages that once made a living man part of the culture of his time. The literary man who is the subject of such a research ceases to be an animated phonograph record and memorandum pad, which he tends to be in the typical academic study in English unless the researcher happens also to be John Lowes — a mere sentient recording device for the purely literary ideas of his predecessors, insulated from the world and society, capable of no more worldly or complex consciousness than a "relation to the main current of romanticism" or an "attitude toward nature." He is instead a living man whose thought and emotions are played upon by many forces of the age in which he lived, whose life is intricately affected by the social and economic and intellectual experiences of his time, whose books record something of the process by which the mind acts on the substance of history, whose literary significance cannot be isolated from his social significance. Obviously these matters are beyond the reach of the methods used by the source hunter and parallel detector; obviously they require the scholar to equip himself with different and more difficult weapons than the traditional literary scholar has used. A kind of analysis that has been only occasional in the academic study of English literature, and then has been rebelliously written and reluctantly received, is getting to be the accepted thing in American literature. That fact has an immense significance. It is the best portent for the art of literature discernible in the universities, for it might end by bringing the English departments as a whole back into effective relationship with life.